DEMOCRACY IN CAPITALIST TIMES

DEMOCRACY IN CAPITALIST TIMES

Ideals, Limits, and Struggles

John S. Dryzek

New York   Oxford
OXFORD UNIVERSITY PRESS
1996

Oxford University Press

Oxford   New York
Athens   Auckland   Bangkok   Bombay
Calcutta   Cape Town   Dar es Salaam   Delhi
Florence   Hong Kong   Istanbul   Karachi
Kuala Lumpur   Madras   Madrid   Melbourne
Mexico City   Nairobi   Paris   Singapore
Taipei   Tokyo   Toronto

and associated companies in
Berlin   Ibadan

Copyright © 1996 by Oxford University Press, Inc.

Published by Oxford University Press, Inc.
198 Madison Avenue, New York, New York 10016

Oxford is a registered trademark of Oxford University Press

Library of Congress Cataloging-in-Publication Data NBF
Dryzek, John S., 1953–
Democracy in capitalist times : ideals, limits, and struggles /
John S. Dryzek,
p. cm.   Includes bibliographical references and index.
ISBN 0-19-510599-0   ISBN 0-19-510600-8 (pbk.)
1. Democracy.   2. Capitalism.   I. Title.
JC423.D726   1996   321.8′09′049—dc20
95–42341

1 3 5 7 9 8 6 4 2

Printed in the United States of America
on acid-free paper

To

ROSE CATHERINE DRYZEK

born in the middle of everything

Preface

My earliest political memory consists of tearing down Conservative Party election posters during the 1959 British general election campaign, when I was six years old. This book represents a continuation of that project. The means are now a bit different, but the interest is similar, concerning as it does the prospects for political change in a world that seems to have reached a point of foreclosure at which little in the way of political experimentation is possible. The global demise of socialism seems to have left us with just one basic political–economic model, consisting of liberal democracy plus capitalism, or, for short, capitalist democracy. Despite appearances, I shall argue that this combination is not easy, happy, or perhaps even sustainable. Democracy in capitalist times is subject to erosion by a variety of structural and ideological forces that I shall detail. My intent is to explore the prospects for democracy in the face of these forces, all of which originate in the capitalist political economy. My purpose is not just to demonstrate the power of these forces but also to identify the limits to their reach and the points at which they might be opposed. The resulting assessment of democratic prospects and possibilities should avoid the utopianism of much prescriptive democratic theory, on the one hand, and the conservative apology for the status quo that appears in many descriptive accounts of capitalist democracy, on the other. Democratic ideals and models cannot emerge unscathed from their encounter with real-world political–economic constraints. But such encounters should be strengthening as well as chastening and so sharpen the focus for efforts both to defend existing democratic accomplishments and to deepen democracy in key areas of political life.

Chapter 5 is a heavily revised and extended version of "How Far Is It from Virginia and Rochester to Frankfurt? Public Choice as Critical Theory," which appeared in the *British Journal of Political Science* in 1992.

Chapter 6 incorporates much of "Reconstructive Democratic Theory," which appeared in the *American Political Science Review* in 1993. This article was written with Jeffrey Berejikian. The additional text in Chapter 6 is mine alone, which is why, about a third of the way through Chapter 6, I shift from *I* to *we*. In earlier chapters, I also incorporated some passages from "The Good Society Versus the State: Freedom and Necessity in Political Innovation" (*Journal of Politics* 54, 1992, pp. 518–40, by permission of the University of Texas Press).

I began this book in England, wrote most of it in Australia, rewrote it in the United States, and gave it a final polish back in Australia. I am grateful to the University of Oregon and its political science department for providing a congenial home when I really needed one, although it eventually became time to move on. A summer research grant from Oregon helped get the project under way. Most of the writing was done while I was a visitor in the Research School of Social Sciences and Graduate Programme in Public Policy at Australian National University, and for their hospitality I thank the directors of these two parts of ANU, Geoffrey Brennan and Francis Castles (whose good humor did not waver even when I got his car stolen). The research reported in Chapter 6 was supported by National Science Foundation Grant number SES-9009743. I have benefited from discussions with and comments on draft chapters and related papers from Terence Ball, Deborah Baumgold, Jeffrey Berejikian, John Braithwaite, Valerie Braithwaite, Steven Brown, David Carruthers, Terrell Carver, William Case, Margaret Clark, Rom Coles, Patrick Dunleavy, Robyn Eckersley, Stephen Elkin, Erik Engstrom, James Farr, Pam Ferrara, Robert Goodin, Patricia Harris, Hans-Kristian Hernes, Barry Hindess, David Jacobs, Martin Janicke, Chandran Kukathas, Stephen Leonard, Gerald Mackie, Jane Mansbridge, William Mitchell, Richard Mulgan, Claus Offe, John Orbell, Philip Pettit, David Schlosberg, Douglas Torgerson, and Oran Young. Some of my most productive disagreements have been with Iris Young, who also read and commented on the entire manuscript. As readers for Oxford University Press, Charles Lindblom and Ian Shapiro provided a number of useful criticisms. The usual disclaimer about responsibility applies, although I'm inclined to blame Robert Goodin for the fact that this is appearing a year later than it might have (on the other hand, it is a bit better as a result).

Northcote, Victoria
January 1996

J.S.D.

Contents

DEMOCRACY IN CAPITALIST TIMES

1

Is More Democracy Possible?

We live in capitalist times, in that the range of plausible economic models now seems to extend only from naked unregulated capitalism to uneasily mixed capitalism. We also live in democratic times, in that hardly a political leader or activist anywhere would claim to be anything other than a democrat. So democracy is what we all want, and capitalism is what we all have got; yet capitalist democracy is not an easy, happy, or perhaps even sustainable combination. My intent in this book thus is to explore and assess the prospects for democracy in the face of major hazards generated by the capitalist political economy and, in light of these hazards, to identify the kinds of democratic endeavors that are plausible, worthwhile, and attractive.

Historically, capitalism has often been good for democracy, for a number of reasons that I will discuss. But capitalism has now mostly outlived its democratic usefulness. States in capitalist economies are becoming less democratic to the extent that public policy becomes dictated by the need to compete and flourish in the transnational political economy. Free trade's culmination in capital mobility across national boundaries means that public policy is constrained by fear of upsetting actual or potential investors. Popular sovereignty cannot be allowed to stand in the way. Free trade, market liberal ideology, economic rationalism, and aggressive individualism combine to obstruct any deeper democratization and to erode existing democratic achievements. The democratic response, I argue, needs to be multidimensional and often unconventional. The prospects for democracy in capitalist times are better, however, in civil society than in the formal institutions of government, across rather than within national boundaries, and in realms of life not always recognized as political. Thus, democratization is more readily sought against the state, apart from the state, and across states, rather than by or in the state.

Some Basics

The obvious way to begin a book on democracy is with a definition of democracy, but I will not do so, for democracy is an essentially contested concept: Different democratic theorists necessarily define democracy in different ways designed to be conducive to their preferred model, and only the blandest of definitions would satisfy all the contestants. Because I approach democracy as an open-ended project that does not head for a single destination, I do not present a single model on which this project might or should converge, or a single definition of democracy to fit any such model. And as the democratic quest proceeds, the meanings of democracy can be expected to change—in the future, just as in the past.[1]

What I will do, however, is define a democratic "concourse" within which the explorations of this study will proceed. A *concourse* represents a place where ideas, positions, opinions, arguments, criticisms, models, and theories run together; it is the sum of communication on any topic (Stephenson, 1978). The democratic concourse may be defined as pertaining to the collective construction, distribution, application, and limitation of political authority. Within this concourse, there is plenty of room for variety in terms of how, where, when, and by whom democracy might be pursued. It is important to remain open to the possibility of democratic innovation in novel and surprising places.

There is, then, little reason to expect, any time soon, consensus on the meaning or essence of democracy. A cynic, or minimalist, might see in democracy "only a system for processing conflicts without killing one another" (Przeworski, 1991, p. 95).[2] Yet such cynicism itself may help spoil the prospects for democracy as an open-ended project. If there is no debate about what its future direction should be and about how further democratization might be possible, then democracy itself will be impoverished. There is an important sense in which one of the goals of democracy always has to be more democracy. In the same sense that the good life might often consist of striving for the good life, the democratic life consists in large part of searching for democracy.

In a way, a democratic political system is like the capitalist economy with which democracy has such an uneasy and complex relationship, for neither can stand still. A capitalist economy must either grow or decay into economic slump. And a democratic polity that ceases its search for further democratization is likely to witness the gradual entrenchment of "new classes" of various sorts that profit from their stable occupancy of key points in the system, and an impoverishment of political life through its focus on relatively mundane issues of public administration (see Arendt, 1958). As Anthony Downs put it (in a substantial departure from some of his earlier thoughts on the matter), "Democracy is a dynamic process of governance and even of living in general, not a static institutional construct. Supporters of democracy must continue to change its specific meaning and forms" (1987, p. 146). Similarly, William Connolly contends that the essence of democracy is that identities and relationships are always subject to challenge, disturbance, and reconstitution (1991, pp. 476–78). According to this view, democracy can never be a settled political order.

In his 1990 address to a joint session of the U.S. Congress, President Vaclav Havel of the former Czechoslovakia suggested that democracy is best conceptualized as an ideal for which we should continually strive, even though we can never attain it. Approving of Havel's position, Michael Lienesch concluded that "it may well be dangerous to try to make democracy perfect. But it is even more dangerous, and ultimately more destructive of democratic government, not to try to make it at least a little more perfect than it is" (1992, p. 1012).

Thus my basic justification for attending to the possibilities for further democratization is democracy itself. Democracy can move forward or backward, but it cannot stand still. This study is based on the premise that any worthwhile political future involves progressive democratization, not just in terms of the geographical spread of existing institutions widely thought to merit description as democratic, but also through a deepening of the democratic qualities of key arenas of life.

What does it mean to say that democracy is deepened? I will use the following three criteria to identify democratization:

1. *Franchise* refers to the number of participants in any political setting. An example of increase in franchise would be the removal of property, racial, or sexual qualifications for voting. A less obvious example would be an extension of workers' participation in the management of a firm.
2. *Scope* concerns the domains of life under democratic control. So, for example, the feminist insistence that "the personal is political" might increase the scope of democracy by extending it to areas of life traditionally considered private, such as the division of labor within the family.
3. *Authenticity* is the degree to which democratic control is substantive rather than symbolic, informed rather than ignorant, and competently engaged. In practice, nominally participatory processes can, as Lindblom (1990) stressed, feature severely impaired probing. Agents of impairment include misinformation, indoctrination, conformism, public relations exercises, corporate philanthropy, "groupthink," and preemptive claims of consensus. Democratic authenticity benefits from the removal or attenuation of these impairments. For example, a public hearing conducted in a language intelligible to a broad range of participants offering comprehensive and clear information on the issue at hand is more authentically democratic than one arranged according to restrictive legal rules

governing the admissibility of evidence in which information is presented in highly technical fashion to nonexperts.[3]

Some Guidelines

Positive movement on any one of these three criteria constitutes democratization. Two additional guidelines should be borne in mind when applying the criteria. The first guideline is that no dimension should ever be sacrificed for the sake of another. One reason for respecting this first guideline is to eliminate ambiguity in the assessment of democratization, for there is no easy way to weight the relative importance of each dimension and so judge any sacrifice worthwhile.[4]

A more important reason for specifying that no dimension of democratization ever be sacrificed for the sake of another is the danger entailed in any such sacrifice. Given the uncertain condition of our knowledge on these matters, especially concerning the calibration of sacrifices, it is hard to determine whether a sacrifice is indeed a small one or whether we stand at the top of a slippery slope. Consider what can happen when any one of the three dimensions of democratization is pursued with zeal and disregard for the other two.

The unconstrained pursuit of democratic authenticity leads at an extreme to democracy for the privileged few on a narrow range of issues. Among recent democratic theorists, Hannah Arendt is especially attracted by this possibility. She believes that authentic democracy requires time, commitment, and virtue that can be found only in a self-selected minority. Not only franchise is restricted: Arendt believes that truly political affairs involve only matters of high principle concerning the identity and basic direction of individuals and their polity.[5] Thus the scope of democracy should be narrowed to exclude what she refers to as "social" questions pertaining to the economy, inequality, poverty, or just about the whole range of policy issues that have a tangible impact on the lives of ordinary people. Even this democracy is a fragile accomplishment, likely to lapse into elitism and oligarchy when it avoids irrelevance to much of the real stuff of public affairs. Leaving policy issues to administrators leaves the latter free to perfect their own threats to democracy. Think, for example, of recent experiences with institutions designed to be off-limits to democratic control, such as central banks, intelligence services, military organizations, and transnational economic authorities like the World Trade Organization and the International Monetary Fund.

Reckless enlargement of the scope of democratic control is equally dangerous. Without safeguards, it points at an extreme to a situation in which no areas of life are immune to political scrutiny but in which those under scrutiny have no recourse or protection and find themselves unable to participate effectively in or against the mechanisms of social control. Herein lies the liberal's fear of democratic excess leading to totalitarianism. The standard liberal solution is to specify rights that secure a private realm immune from public scrutiny and political control. The democrat's contribution here can be to insist that the democratic franchise and, especially, democratic authenticity never be sacrificed for the sake of expanded scope. To illustrate the effects of such sacrifice, consider the expanding scope of political control in North American universities in recent years, into areas such as appropriate speech, appropriate sexual relationships, and appropriate course content. Combined with the identification and privileging of ever more kinds of politically relevant victimhood, the result is the institutionalization of new kinds of euphemism, orthodoxy, repression, and self-censorship, all policed by an expanded university bureaucracy.

A somewhat different hazard arising from the reckless enlargement of democratic scope is what Shapiro (1994, p. 143), crediting Sirianni (1993), calls the "paradox of participatory pluralism." The essence of this paradox is that scarce time means that expanding participation into a new realm may lower participation in other areas. Sirianni's concern is with feminist attempts to politicize more areas of life in declaring that "the personal is political." The problem is that expanding scope can eventually reduce authenticity and/or franchise in both new and old issue domains. Authenticity may suffer because individuals become less informed, less patient, and more easily deterred from probing issues deeply. Franchise may suffer as a result of the burnout of overstretched activists and the wariness of potential activists. The solution to the paradox of participatory pluralism is, in principle, straightforward: An expansion of the scope of democracy should be sought only when no loss of democratic authenticity or franchise is anticipated.

In regard to the reckless extension of the democratic franchise, the obvious danger is manipulation of the newly enfranchised by skilled elites, be they corporate advertisers or populist demagogues, leading to the wholesale loss of democratic authenticity. The experience of referenda in a number of U.S. states is sobering. Every two years, my former state of Oregon presents around twenty statewide ballot initiatives. The results rarely contribute to a flourishing democracy and instead often undermine constitutive democratic values of equality and tolerance. In 1990 a measure was passed purportedly to reduce the property taxes of ordinary citizens, but in reality to shift the burden of taxation away from corporations and onto individuals. Every two years a new attempt is made to brand homosexuality abnormal and force the state to repress gay rights, each time coming very close to passing. The use of referenda to repress unpopular minorities is equally apparent in California, where in 1994 immigrants were the target. On the other side of the coin, initiatives that would protect the environment or consumers are normally defeated after massive "no" campaigns financed by corporate wealth.

An unconstrained extension of franchise pays no attention to the quality of public opinion sought. The registering of misinformed, uninformed, unstable, and unreflective preferences contributes nothing to democracy, as a glance at the history of opinion survey research should make clear.

My account of the problems entailed by the unconstrained pursuit of any one of the three dimensions of democratization does not imply that the sacrifice of one dimension for another is always and inevitably bad. But it does imply that such sacrifices are always and inevitably dangerous. This danger follows directly from our limited political knowledge, which is always uncertain, dispersed, and incomplete. Thus we rarely know enough to be able to make even seemingly small democratic sacrifices with the confidence that they really are small.

These warnings about the reckless pursuit of any single dimension of democratization should not be adduced as support of those hostile to deeper democratization of any sort, or to democracy itself. We live in a world where democratic franchise, scope, and authenticity all are generally restricted and, as I will argue in the following chapters, under siege from a variety of forces. Democrats should not add to these problems the dangers caused by the blinkered and single-minded pursuit of any one dimension of democracy. The others are too important. I will return to this issue in Chapter 3 with a discussion of the history of feminist democratic experimentation, which contains pertinent lessons, both positive and negative.

The second guideline that should be borne in mind when applying the three criteria of franchise, scope, and authenticity is that none of the dimensions should be sacrificed in the short term for the sake of any or all of them in the long term. Short-term democratic sacrifice for the sake of long-term democratic benefit is the strategy of Leninists and the excuse of military dictators who seize power in the name of stabilization. This association with Leninists and military dictators does not necessarily rule out the use of such a strategy in a more benign fashion and to better effect. For example, some contemporary advocates of marketization in former communist systems claim that economic reform can proceed effectively only under authoritarian political control and that these societies should wait for the democratic benefits that market-based prosperity will eventually yield.

Such arguments remain unconvincing. The real problem with any strategy of short-term democratic sacrifice is that the uncertain state of political and economic knowledge means that we cannot be sure that the democratic benefits will indeed arrive in some longer term. What we do know is that authoritarian attempts to impose any political–economic blueprint (democratic or not) violate the social conditions of human intelligence. The relevant knowledge is, as I have already noted, always uncertain, dispersed, and incomplete, and so the authoritarian elite can have only a partial perspective that will produce all kinds of unanticipated and unwanted results. One of the classic arguments here is that of Karl Popper (1966), directed against communist political engineering. But Popper's critique is equally applicable to authoritarian attempts to engineer free-market utopias (see Pickel, 1993). Political rationality is never, then, to be found in the calculations of any governing elite. Rather, as John Dewey argued at length (for example, Dewey, 1927), political rationality is a matter of experimentation carried out by democratic publics conceived of as communities of inquirers, each one of whom initially brings only a partial perspective to bear. In this light, to sacrifice democracy in the short term for the sake of purported long-term democratic benefits is the height of political irrationality.

Antidemocratic Constraints

The present condition of democratic innovation is paradoxical. In one respect, there is a lot of it about. As I have already noted, everyone today is a democrat (at least symbolically). Authoritarian regimes flounder and fall around the world. But their successors rarely adopt anything new; liberal democracy plus market capitalism seems to be the universal model of choice, and variation comes only in falling short of that model. Meanwhile, the older liberal democratic societies seem to be suffering a decline in their own self-confidence and develop little in the way of institutional innovation. Peremptory foreclosure seems to be the order of the day when it comes to any possibility of deeper democratization. It seems that all we can have is a minimally authentic liberal democracy, which may be defined in terms of competitive parties, limited opportunities for public participation through voting and organized groups, constitutional constraints on government activity, the insulation of the economic sphere from democratic control, and a politics that mostly involves the pursuit and reconciliation of interests defined in private life.

Capitalist democracies also are home to gathering forces either skeptical of or hostile to any deeper democratization. Some even suggest that perhaps we have gone too far already. Today, these enemies of democratization—and, if my earlier assumption is correct, of democracy—are not fascists, monarchists, scientific socialists, and assorted other would-be guardians of the common good. The twentieth century has witnessed (among other things) a decisive refutation of such doctrines, and democratic theorists such as Karl Popper and Robert Dahl have driven effective stakes through the hearts of their corpses. I have nothing to add to what Popper, Dahl, and others have done in this regard.

Instead, my purpose is to identify, highlight, and confront some more subtle and insidious political–economic forces and their associated doctrines hostile to democratization—and thus democracy. These doctrines tell us to be happy with what we have in the way of democracy and to seek no more, and in a few cases they are prepared to erode existing democratic accomplishments. In highlighting these forces and doctrines, I do not intend simply to pour cold water over aspiring democrats and democratic possibilities. My intent is quite the opposite. When democratic theory meets the real world, it should emerge strengthened as well as chastened. The basic purpose in identifying constraints is therefore also to identify opportunities. So my "realist" focus is intended to be creative and enabling, not just chastening and constraining. At a minimum, it might tell friends of democracy when they are wasting their time, so that their energies might be better spent in other places. More important, it might show what kinds of democratic innovation are possible and fruitful in particular kinds of times and places. The efforts of democratic theorists and advocates are likely to be productive to the extent they are directed toward the real opportunities for freedom in democratic innovation that exist amid a host of necessitarian constraints.

The antidemocratic constraints I will consider are structural, ideological, and intellectual; often they combine ideas and more impersonal structural forces. Some have been friends of democracy inasmuch as they once facilitated the growth of liberal democracy, even though they now impede further democratic development. Others are more overtly antidemocratic. Throughout, I will do my best to show that developments seemingly hostile to democracy can often, on closer scrutiny, be turned to good democratic use.

All these antidemocratic constraints are associated with the idea that liberal democracy in a capitalist economic context is the pinnacle of feasible democratic achievement. This idea has gained considerable support in the wake of the collapse of Soviet-style communism and the crisis of confidence among socialists of all sorts in the West.

Liberal democratic capitalism may have triumphed for three reasons. First, this kind of system might be essentially consistent with some key aspects of human nature. Second, market capitalism as a form of economic organization might impose all kinds of constraints on what can be done politically as well as economically and effectively block movement toward any alternative structures. Third, there may no longer be any ideas that seriously challenge liberal democratic capitalism. In Chapter 2 I shall take up these three possibilities and argue that the truth of the matter lies not in human nature but, rather, in political–economic structure and ideology. The political foreclosure associated with the seemingly global triumph of liberal democratic capitalism may then be unpacked into four aspects, to each of which I will devote a chapter. These aspects are as follows.

The Capitalist State

The state, irrespective of the degree to which it is liberal or democratic, is the dominant kind of political form in the contemporary world. When democratic theorists contemplate actual and desirable political orders, they generally target the state. Yet states in capitalist societies cannot be designed just as one pleases, and once in place there are many things they simply must do. In today's world, all states must keep civil order, curb the vicissitudes of economic life by operating as welfare states (at least in economies in which this is at all affordable), and ensure that a healthy capitalist market system delivers the goods in terms of both revenues and public support for government. Thus states are highly constrained in both what they can do and how they can be structured. To the degree that both operations and structure are conditioned by welfare and economic imperatives, there is often little possibility for democratic innovation.

The International System

States face outward, toward the international system, as well as inward, toward their own societies. And they must keep afloat in that system. In the past, this meant military security, but increasingly, economic survival is at issue. The emerging transnational economic order features a freer movement of goods, services, finance, capital, and people across national boundaries. This order and its institutions such as the International Monetary Fund, World Bank, and multinational corporations and banks impose massive constraints on what all states (and not only debtors) can do. Democratic initiatives can easily run up against the dictates of the international political economy. These dictates are not necessarily applied consciously by any international actor; they can also be embedded as structural constraints in international trade regimes. Countries in the disadvantaged periphery of the international system are particularly restricted, but even the more prosperous core countries are by no means free.

Economic Rationality

Capitalism has historically been a friend of democracy in that liberal constitutional regimes have arisen only in the context of capitalist economies. U.S. social scientists have traditionally attributed this concurrence to middle-class virtues produced by the growth of capitalism. Rueschemeyer, Stephens, and Stephens (1992) argue convincingly that the real reason that "formal democracy" flourishes with capitalism is that the latter produces a *working* class which has the most to gain from democracy and so pushes for democratization. However, this kind of development may have reached its limit in advanced capitalist countries whose industrial working class is now shrinking. The universalization of the capitalist market as the principal form of economic organization is now accompanied by a decline in collectivism and a rise in individualism, which in turn involves a transformation of human beings and so of their politics. Contemporary market persons are rational in the sense of their capacity to calculate in pursuit of their self-interest narrowly defined, and their politics becomes one of the pursuit of private desires. Contemporary social science in the form of increasingly popular rational choice or public choice analyses provides backing for market liberal policies that reproduce this kind of economically rational individualism. (This is an example of the interrelation of ideas and structural forces that I mentioned earlier.) But as public choice analyses of politics have themselves inadvertently shown, this kind of behavior—however functional for capitalist economic activity—is deadly for democratic politics. Thus the penetration of the market and economic rationality into all realms of life threatens not just to impede further democratization but also to undermine existing democratic accomplishments.

Ideology

Capitalist democracy describes an ideology as well as a political–economic system, and the two, though interrelated, are not necessarily identical. The ideology helps underpin the system, and its liberal aspect in particular has, over time, proved extraordinarily effective in assimilating and disarming potential critics of the system, including democrats. The ideology of liberal democratic capitalism has not yet achieved global hegemony, as nationalism, Islam, and more authoritarian capitalist ideologies still compete. But if there are no serious competitors among democratic ideologies, ideas for democratic alternatives will be in short supply, and the prospects for democratic innovation will be correspondingly impoverished.

These, then, are the four challenges to democracy presented by the contemporary capitalist political economy. A radical pessimist regarding them might conclude that the pursuit of democratization under capitalism is ultimately futile. So should we look forward instead to a deeper democracy in some postcapitalist future?

Required here would be some agent for the demise of capitalism. Ecological crisis is a good candidate, as capitalism's addiction to growth cannot be sustained in a finite ecosphere (see Dryzek, 1987). But the time scale is uncertain, and waiting for and pinning hopes on capitalism's demise would violate the second constraint on the pursuit of democracy that I introduced earlier. Moreover, even if an ecological denouement or any other sort of terminal crisis of capitalism does eventually arrive, any democratic outcome will depend on society's ability to negotiate the transition in a democratic fashion. This ability in turn depends on the degree to which democracy can be nurtured and protected against fallout from the capitalism–state nexus that is the central political fact of our time. Construction and maintenance of fallout shelters here would, should the terminal crisis arrive, offer the "old regime legacies" in political structure which, as Skocpol (1979) argued, even revolutionaries must utilize in their construction of a new society. (Skocpol developed her argument in the context of the French, Russian, and Chinese revolutions, and the legacies she emphasized were economic as well as political.)

Recent East European experience indicates that these legacies need not be confined to the state structures that Skocpol stressed. The character and form of the democratic opposition in Poland and Czechoslovakia in the 1970s and 1980s enabled these societies to negotiate the transition smoothly and democratically when, much to their own surprise, former dissidents found themselves in power in 1989. For all these reasons, I emphasize the democratic possibilities that exist in the shadow of capitalism and its state, rather than the postcapitalist alternatives.

Resources for Democrats

This quest for democracy in the shadow of the capitalist political economy is not a futile one. My intent in the chapters devoted to each of the four constraints is not merely to describe the challenge in question and demonstrate its power but, more important, to expose its limits and vulnerabilities. In so doing, I will try to draw some more positive conclusions concerning possibilities for democracy and democratization. Throughout, the idea is to see how democracy might be reconceptualized and strengthened in the face of some powerful antidemocratic forces.

Contemporary liberal democratic capitalism is not without its contradictions (though, of course, Marxist theories of inherent contradiction in capitalism producing its eventual downfall are now out of fashion). I shall explore the possibilities that have resulted from conflicting pressures on contemporary states. I have already noted that these pressures—notably those to promote economic growth and correct for the instability generated by capitalism, the economic and welfare imperatives—appear as antidemocratic constraints. But when these imperatives point states in different directions, matters look somewhat different. Writers influenced by Marxism refer here to the contradiction between accumulation and legitimation (for example, Offe, 1984). I shall argue that additional imperatives originating in the international system and in environmental crisis now confront all states, making for complex combinations of cross pressures. What one may make of all these is less certain. States may be able to muddle through without fundamentally changing their internal structure and relationship to their societies (though I believe this is ultimately unlikely in the context of the ecological imperative). Alternatively, contradiction and confusion may be exploited by those whose interest is in more fundamental political innovation and different kinds of political–economic arrangements.

A somewhat different kind of political–economic contradiction is created as a result of the kind of people that liberal democratic capitalism increasingly produces. I noted earlier that the penetration of economic rationality into the political behavior of individuals devastates democratic politics, which makes that rationality an enemy of democratization. However, this dynamic does not make life easy for existing liberal democracy either. Liberal democracy requires public-spirited *homo civicus* as well as narrowly selfish *homo economicus*, and to the extent the former is displaced by the latter, politics in liberal democratic societies becomes increasingly problematic. Because there is no reason for *homo economicus* to be committed to liberal democratic norms, the result is that the institutional status quo may run out of defenders while its politics becomes more confused and incoherent as self-interest runs wild.

The antidemocratic forces originating in the capitalist political economy sometimes have a limited reach. The imperatives facing states do indeed act as structural constraints. But attention to what is determined by these constraints also enables one to identify what is not determined. In a sea of structural necessity, there remain islands of structural possibility, although it may take some imagination to locate and expand them. Here, I will focus on spaces for political innovation in the structural possibilities associated with war, depression, local politics, revolution, the anarchic politics of the international system, feminist redefinitions of the boundaries of the political, collapsed peripheries of states, community politics, workplace decision making, and—perhaps most significant—public spheres constituted by democratic opposition to the state and its imperatives. In all these cases the economic, welfare, and international constraints facing states are inoperative, substantially relaxed, or themselves the impetus for democratic opposition.

Such contradictions and possibilities do not automatically produce anything in the way of democracy. Instead, to take advantage of them, one needs to apply ideas in the form of analyses and proposals, political theories and political activism. But ideas are resources in another sense, for the ideas that are "out there" in the public realm may support democratic possibilities that go beyond the institutional status quo. On the other hand, they may not, if indeed they all have been subsumed by the ideological hegemony of capitalist democracy. Whether such alternative ideas, ideologies, or even political theories exist within the public is therefore an empirical question. In Chapter 6 I shall offer some evidence to suggest that there really are alternative conceptions of democracy held by the public that depart from the status quo. This evidence will show that these alternatives exist even where that system is more entrenched than anywhere else in the world—the United States. The alternative discourses of democracy to which citizens subscribe merit the attention of democratic theorists and advocates, who would do well to relate their own ideas to these discourses. Ideas matter, and the way we talk and think about politics really can change the way politics proceeds. Chapter 6 also points to the existence of stocks of motivation for political action beyond rational egoism, stocks that are themselves significant resources for democrats.

This brief survey of the forces frustrating democracy in today's world and the resources that might be deployed against them is now complete. The following chapters will explore the interplay of these forces and resources with the intent of showing how, why, where, and when democracy can be advanced.

Democracy in Different Places

I have already pointed out that the product of these inquiries is not a single model of democracy (on a par, say, with the classical, protective, developmental, direct, competitive elitist, pluralist, legal, and participatory models surveyed by Held, 1987). There are many sites in which democracy can be pursued, and different kinds of democracy may turn out to be appropriate to different sites. Still, I shall make arguments about the kinds of democracy worth pursuing, on behalf of a democracy that is deliberative rather than aggregative, republican rather than liberal, communicative rather than strategic, disrespectful of the boundaries of political units, pursued in civil society rather than the state, and consistent with broad rather than narrow definitions of politics. This point, that our definitions of politics need to be broadened, has been made most insistently by feminists, which is one reason for the attention devoted to feminism in Chapter 3. It turns out, though, that feminism's main contribution to democracy in capitalist times is not a model of democracy. Rather, this contribution is in the form of lessons about democratization as a process, in terms of how to pursue and how not to pursue democracy.

In contemplating the forms of political organization conducive to democratization in capitalist times, it is necessary to do more than enumerate sites for democratic development and specify what is possible in each of them. Interactions across the boundaries of these sites are important, too. Counterintuitive results are possible here in that undemocratic organization in one place may be conducive to democracy in another.

Consider, in this context, the four main sites or arenas in which democracy and democratization might be pursued: the state, the economy, civil society, and the international system. (Civil society can be a contested and elusive concept; I will devote more attention to its definition in Chapter 3.) Most political theorists have focused mainly on the state. Over the last hundred years or so, the economy has received some attention, principally by advocates of workplace democracy and market socialism. Until recently, civil society (as an arena of social interaction distinct from both the state and the economy) and the international system have received little attention. For the most part, however, these four realms have been treated in isolation from one another, save for the occasional hope that democratization in one realm (for example, the workplace, or civil society) might somehow spill over into another (the state), and the more recent recognition that one realm may act as a source of constraints for another.

I will try to enumerate enabling as well as constraining interactions across these four domains. The state may hold little promise for its own democratization (despite some possibilities at the margins which I will address). Yet it still turns out to matter enormously how the state is organized, even if the limits of state democratization may have been reached. What kind of state, then, is most conducive to democratic development? The obvious way to answer this question would be to examine the intrinsic democratic merits of different forms of state organization: bureaucracy, representation, legal system, parties, interest intermediation, and so forth. But if, as I have suggested, the prospects for deepening state democracy are minimal, a different approach is in order. Crucial here, I argue, is the pattern of exclusions arranged by the state. To put it crudely, an exclusive state can be good for democracy, provided that the exclusions are suitably arranged.

To anticipate the conclusion of an argument I develop in Chapter 3, observe that liberal democratic states that adopt inclusive forms of interest representation can undermine the vitality of civil society by co-opting, compromising, devaluing, and inducing strategic behavior on behalf of interests and actors. Actively exclusive states can destroy civil society directly by attacking autonomous forms of public association and indirectly by promoting aggressive individualism. With these alternatives in mind, the passively exclusive pattern of interest representation adopted under social democratic corporatism is attractive. Such states are exclusive because they limit effective representation to encompassing business and labor associations, and passive because they do not try to disrupt or repress other kinds of political association. Thus they inadvertently create the conditions for effective oppositional public spheres in which radical democracy can flourish.

Before turning to these issues in more depth, a fuller examination of just why liberal democratic capitalism seems to have triumphed is in order. The reasons for this triumph matter a great deal. If it were a question of consistency with human nature, there would be little point in trying to push democracy any further. On the other hand, if the triumph were due to the capacity of capitalist democracy to undermine attempts to change its basic structure or due to a paucity of ideas about what might work as well or better, the situation would appear more hopeful. I will argue that the truth here lies in structures and ideas (or ideology) rather than human nature, thus opening the door to a contemplation of how democracy in capitalist times might be redeemed.

2

Why Capitalist Democracy Emerges Victorious

Historicists and Whigs

The idea that history has a meaning, a trajectory, and a destination used to be advanced most confidently by Marxists who thought the destination lay in some imminent or discernable future. Among non-Marxists, such a view has been held by those for whom the past is to be understood as precursor to a happy present, which can only expect to be perfected still further in any likely or conceivable future. This view of history as ineluctable progress toward the present has been characterized (and criticized) by Butterfield (1950) as the Whiggish interpretation of history.

Both Marxist historicism and Whiggish optimism fared badly through much of the twentieth century. Marxist laws of history started to look decidedly un-law-like in the face of the persistence of capitalism and its transmutation into the mixed capitalism of the Keynesian welfare state. Marxists themselves now stress the nondeterministic aspects of their approach (for example, Wright, Levine, and Sober, 1992, pp. 13–46). Karl Popper declared, quite correctly, that one could never know what some future epoch might hold; for if that future is constituted in large part by human knowledge, then we in the present simply do not have access to that knowledge or that future (Popper, 1972). Whiggish renditions of history were shaken as societies turned to Stalinism, fascism, and other kinds of authoritarianism.

Matters have changed rather dramatically in the last few years. Liberals who once spoke hesitantly about where the world might move now dust off their Whiggish inclinations. Although there might have been a few unexpected detours along the way, progress has produced a happy liberal, democratic, and capitalist present after all. Marxism is in defeat and disarray, but its historicist clothes can now be borrowed by liberalism. But Popper's liberal argument against historicism loses its force if we have already arrived at history's destination. That is, there is nothing mysterious about the human knowledge that exists here and now, as opposed to in some projected future, even though it might be a bit arrogant of this generation to suggest that any human knowledge generated in the future will not upset the order of things. Despite any minor reservations along these lines, however, liberalism triumphant has little need to be modest, for it has won the global struggle of our times.

The most confident and most overtly historicist (if ultimately regretful) celebration of the triumph of liberalism appears in Francis Fukuyama's article "The End of History?" (1989) and his subsequent book *The End of History and the Last Man* (1992). The latter is very much the book of its historical moment, defined by the demise of Soviet socialism and the seeming global victory of capitalist democracy. The end of history thesis interprets this moment with "two simple claims: Marxism offers nothing to the underdeveloped world, and, to the extent that countries manage to make social, political, and economic progress, they discover that liberal democracy is what they had better settle for" (Ryan, 1992, p. 4).

Fukuyama gets his theory of history directly from Hegel. At the beginning of the nineteenth century, Hegel believed he was observing the conclusive victory of rational modernity with the defeat of the reactionary Prussian aristocracy by Napoleon at the Battle of Jena in 1806. Fukuyama's Jena is played many times over, in London and Paris no less than in Warsaw, Prague, Moscow, and Berlin. The victor (aside from local setbacks such as Beijing in 1989) is more clearly defined than in Hegel's time and consists of liberal democratic politics and capitalist economics, or, for short, capitalist democracy. With the effective discrediting and disappearance of fascism and communism, there no longer are any alternative models. Fukuyama's critics point to continuing conflict connected to nationalisms and religious fundamentalism, especially in the Islamic world. But if one believes with Fukuyama that (1) ideas move history and that (2) only ideologies with global ambitions matter, then his argument is immune to attack on such grounds, for nationalism and fundamentalism take effect only in particular corners of the world.[1]

Fukuyama's view of the destination of history bears a striking resemblance to the development paradigm formulated by U.S. social scientists in the 1950s and early 1960s and subsequently enshrined in the policy of the U.S. government and multilateral aid agencies.[2] This modernization paradigm avers that the stages of economic growth (Rostow, 1960) culminate in a liberal capitalist economic system with the political characteristics of the Western democracies. But such views went out of fashion in the late 1960s, 1970s, and early 1980s in favor of dependency, world systems, and other models that saw development as far more problematic. With the dramatic global realignment of the late 1980s, however, these views have resurfaced, and—an apt symbol—Rostow's avowed "noncommunist manifesto" was republished.

Fukuyama's kind of grand historical vision does set him aside from most observers of the fortunes of capitalist democracy. In particular, many U.S. social scientists distrust such schemes as suspiciously French or German and probably tainted with Marxism. But a belief that capitalist democracy is the only future worth talking about is remarkably pervasive, as a booming academic industry with substantial philanthropic and government support attests. The burgeoning literature on democratization (for example, Di Palma 1990; Huntington, 1991; Rueschemeyer, Stephens, and Stephens, 1992) generally treats capitalist democracy as the only option. As Sartori noted with glee, "In today's modern world, there is but one 'rightful government': freely elected government. But remember, the winner is an entirely liberal democracy, not only popularly elected government, but also, and indivisibly, constitutional government; that is, the hitherto much belittled 'formal democracy' that controls and restrains the exercise of power" (1991, p. 437).

Brief talk of a "third way" that attended the 1989 East European spring is now rarely heard. In 1991 the American Political Science Association Conference featured a symposium entitled "America as a Model for the World." There is bold talk of exporting democracy (Muravchik, 1991) but no talk at all of the core countries of the industrial world importing any kind of democracy. Such views have fewer doubters and critics than they once did, and even many of those who believe that institutional innovation merits serious attention accept the inevitable. Accordingly, Karol Soltan, in the newsletter of one of the most creative such groups, declared "Let us not waste time with alternatives to capitalist democracy" (Soltan, 1992, p. 4). Announcing his own abandonment of socialism, Robert Heilbroner proclaimed that "the contest between capitalism and socialism is over: capitalism has won" (1989, p. 98). No other contenders are in sight, for "one residual effect of the collapse of communism is apt to be an inhibition of the social imagination. In larger part, however, my skepticism stems from an absence of plausible social blueprints whose realization seems worth the risk of venturing beyond the known terrain of capitalism" (Heilbroner, 1990, p. 99).

Despite widespread agreement that there are currently few alternatives to it, the question remains as to exactly why capitalist democracy should constitute not just a temporary resting place but a more permanent halt. I can think of three possible answers to this question. The first is that there is something fundamental about what it means to be a human being that is satisfied by, or is somehow consistent with, the basic tenets of capitalist democracy. The second is that there is something about the structure of capitalist democracy that automatically undermines any attempt to change it. The third is that proponents of capitalist democracy have a monopoly on ideas, that nobody else has any notion about how to change it or any intimation of what might work better. I shall now deal with each of these answers, to show that the truth lies in the second and third, not the first. This determination in turn provides a sharper focus for efforts to push democracy further.

Human Nature

There are many ways to describe human nature. Perhaps the most basic would take note that human beings are, among other things, the product of biological evolution. Are there implications for how politics is or can be organized here? Practitioners of the burgeoning biopolitics subfield of political science answer in the affirmative. According to Roger Masters (1989), the circumstances of human evolution suggest that some kinds of political regimes—notably autocratic and totalitarian ones—are unnatural and unjust. Conversely, regimes featuring constitutional government, liberal freedoms, and democratic participation are naturally just. According to Darwinian biology, humans, no less than other creatures, are engaged in struggles for survival and reproductive success. However, Masters argues, we have tended to create more elaborate social institutions than other creatures have, one such institution being the state. There are individual advantages to be gained from social cooperation, and the state is one way of securing these. It provides for the convenience and protection of individuals and promises a secure environment for their descendants. Its coercive powers are necessary to prevent free riding by self-interested individuals trying to gain the benefits of the state without contributing to its costs. Any state must be strengthened further as it comes into contact with potential enemies.

Moving beyond this explanation of the origins of the state, Masters takes pains to argue that not all kinds of states are equal in terms of either evolutionary adaptation or moral defensibility, factors he wishes to conjoin. To begin, states must adapt in response to changes in their natural and social environment. The kind of flexibility one finds in liberal constitutional regimes is, according to Masters, a distinct advantage here. If so, one might wonder why human history since the rise of the state has been dominated by unnatural forms of political organization. Perhaps Masters is on firmer ground when he claims liberal constitutionalist regimes also are "naturally right" in that, just like the face-to-face discussions of hunter-gatherers, they can take advantage of the adaptive human trait of variety in perspectives about an uncertain and dangerous environment (p. 245). Moreover, they are to be preferred to "modern autocratic and totalitarian regimes" because the latter "subject large portions of the community to behavioral constraints that are not part of our primate heritage or of the patterns of hominid behavior that have evolved over the last five million years" (p. 225). And respect for others' right to life and liberty is naturally right because it is in the collective human interest that genetic and cultural variation persist, for genetic variation is essential to the survival of any species in a potentially hazardous world (pp. 228–29).

The difficulty with Masters's argument here is a simple collective-action problem. Genetic variation may benefit the species, but it does not favor any individual as he or she pursues a personal genetic maximization project. So tolerance may be naturally right for the species but naturally wrong for the individual.

Darwinian biology has been used to justify the marketplace as well as the kind of constitutional liberalism favored by Masters. Most notoriously, nineteenth-century social Darwinists such as William Graham Sumner believed that Darwinism justified the unregulated struggle of capitalism and extreme social inequality. More recently, this disposition toward the marketplace, shorn of the mean spirit and elitism of social Darwinism, is attractive to market-oriented economists who see in Darwinian biology a reflection of their science. If one substitutes individual maximization of genetic success for individual maximization of utility, there will be essentially no difference between the reasoning of microeconomics and that of Darwinian biology. And if microeconomics concludes that the market is the optimal form of social organization, that conclusion will have a biological warrant, too (Hirshleifer, 1977). If we add this justification of market capitalism to Masters's arguments for liberal democracy, we would seem to have a biological grounding for capitalist democracy in its entirety.

Should we accept such a justification? Caution is suggested by the number of different kinds of political and economic regimes that Darwinism has been used to justify (see Dryzek and Schlosberg, 1995). Murray Bookchin (1982), picking up on an argument advanced by Peter Kropotkin long ago, believes that nature is essentially nonhierarchical and cooperative and that until about the last five thousand years, so was human society. To Bookchin, this means that a decentralized, anarchist polity is both natural and desirable. A diametrically opposed conclusion was drawn by Somit and Peterson (1991), who see in human prehistory social constraints very different from those stressed by Masters or Bookchin. To Somit and Peterson, until very recently our evolutionary history occurred in hierarchical societies. And they noted that the behavior of our closest relatives, the primates, shows that hierarchy and domination pervade their societies, too. Somit and Peterson thus concluded that autocracy, not liberal democracy, is the kind of polity best suited to human nature. Historically, Darwinian biology has also been used to justify political ideologies and systems ranging from fascism and Naziism to Marxism.

Although Darwinian biology can generate insights into human social behavior and perhaps even the broad contours of social and political structure, it cannot and should not be used to explain and justify the particular form taken by complex social arrangements. In the mid-1970s, sociobiologists tried to account for a whole range of human institutions. But as Kitcher observed in his critique of sociobiology, even if we accept that individual behavior is biologically conditioned and simple, an enormous range of macrolevel consequences neither sought nor wanted by individuals still remains possible (1985, pp 29–30). A biological explanation of political institutions requires too many large inductive leaps. So even if one accepts Masters's argument that the blend of coercive capability and flexibility available to liberal constitutional regimes has some biologically defensible aspects, one should not conclude that liberalism is natural or that it cannot be improved on in such terms.

Darwinian explanations of the absence of alternatives to capitalist democracy are, therefore, unconvincing. Do arguments based on psychology or philosophical anthropology fare any better? Drawing on ideas about politically relevant human nature from Plato and Hegel, Fukuyama (1992) believes that the human attribute of *thymos* makes capitalist democracy a particularly satisfactory arrangement. Fukayama's *thymos* (which is not necessarily the same as Plato's) is the desire for recognition by others. A healthy society accommodates both *isothymia*, an individual's desire to be recognized as an equal, and *megalothymia*, the desire of individuals (be they politicians, entrepreneurs, artists, or media stars) for special recognition and respect. To Fukuyama (1992, p. 185), *megalothymia* is essentially an aristocratic quality, although *thymos* itself is a universal and timeless human attribute (p. 138). In capitalist democracy (but nowhere else?) *megalothymia* can coexist with the bourgeois impulse toward material self-enrichment. And only under capitalism can *megalothymia* find a productive outlet in entrepreneurship.[3] The problem here is that a world in which the only competition is for market shares may prove to be so dull that the thoroughly bourgeois "last man" ultimately lamented by Fukuyama may decide to rebel just to overcome boredom.

To Fukuyama, *thymos* and material self-interest characterize capitalist democracy in its entirety; both operate in politics as well as economics. Mark Sagoff (1988) offered a related account of politically relevant human nature that separates politics from economics but that can be used to justify the same capitalist democracy. Sagoff points out that anyone can be motivated as both a consumer and a citizen. Thus, to use one of Sagoff's own examples, the same persons who would, as consumers, enjoy using a ski resort proposed for a wilderness area will, as citizens, oppose its construction because it would despoil the wilderness they have no intention of visiting but whose value they recognize. Sagoff's own purpose in making this distinction is to warn against the efforts of economic policy analysts who reduce everything to consumer preferences and to justify a liberal, political venue for policy determination. But it is easy to interpret the argument as a justification for capitalism as well as liberal democracy (however much this interpretation might be resisted by Sagoff himself). That is, an individual's consumer preferences are properly expressed in, and constitutive of, the marketplace, just as that same individual's citizen preferences are properly expressed through, and constitutive of, liberal politics.[4]

Fukuyama and Sagoff improve on biological and microeconomic theorists who reduce psychology to human nature in that they postulate no single, simple human self; rather, the self has two dimensions. However, this recognition is also the undoing of any attempt to explain and justify political–economic institutions through reference to any simple and constant model of human nature or human selfhood.

The human self is not simple, and there is no reason that it can be encapsulated in just one or two dimensions. The fact that selfhood and subjectivity are multidimensional has been well established empirically and analytically. Thus Elster criticizes economists for believing that there exists a single self with a single utility function and celebrates instead the multiple self (1986b). This multiple self deliberately engages in self-deception, often exhibits a weakness of will in choosing not to pursue goals it knows are right, invokes different programmed subroutines at different times, lets a parallel self daydream, and possesses contradictory beliefs and contradictory sets of preferences that can come into play at different times. There is no reason to suppose that this list is exhaustive.

The best-developed empirical approach to the study of human subjectivity is Q methodology, which I will explain in more detail in Chapter 6. Q methodologists have found that the same person can react in very different ways to a particular domain of life, depending on the context in which the reaction is made and sought. Moreover, the list of aspects of subjectivity that can be so revealed is essentially open-ended. In politics, egoism, trust, sympathy, impartiality, civic-mindedness, sociability, and resentment all might come into play. In other realms of life, different aspects of the self might come to the fore. This recognition of the multiple dimensions of selfhood and subjectivity does not imply that there is no such thing as human nature (which in turn can constrain politics) but merely that appealing to a fixed and one-dimensional human nature is a mistake.

In this light, to speak of a single model of the human self—whether grounded in biology, psychology, anthropology, or philosophy—is to engage in an unwarranted and probably misleading simplification of a complex entity. And different dimensions of selfhood can underwrite different kinds of social arrangements such as political and economic systems.

Any effort to use a model of human nature to explain and justify particular systems is undermined by the fact that the prevailing social context can have a massive influence on the dimensions of subjectivity that are highlighted. Even according to Fukuyama's own account, the aspects of human subjectivity he recognizes are associated with two particular historical eras. *Megalothymia* characterizes the aristocratic age, and material self-interest typifies the bourgeois. Thus different kinds of societies may bring different aspects of subjectivity to the fore, perhaps even constituting these subjectivities (Halliday, 1992, p. 93). Anthropological studies, as the psychologist E. L. Thorndike wrote, "have the great merit of being almost a sure cure for the acceptance of the customs of Europe from 500 B.C. to 1900 A.D. as laws of nature or of God" (1940, p. 727). Even if we stick to the customs of Europe, we find considerable variation over time. Before the rise of bourgeois society, it would have been hard for anyone to construct an account of society based on the universal rational pursuit of self-interest. One need not go so far as to agree with Marx in his sixth thesis on Feuerbach that "the human essence is no abstraction inherent in each single individual. In its reality it is the ensemble of the social relations" (Marx, 1968, p. 29). There may indeed be some constants in human nature, but different aspects appear in different contexts.

Fukuyama's explorations of human nature and psychology are undermined by his own historical sensibility. Partial and contextually specific accounts of human nature and motivation should not be mistaken for timeless truths. It is Fukuyama's historicism that gets him into trouble here. He successfully avoids one of the problems of Marxist historicism (as criticized by Popper) in that he does not try to predict a future different from the present. But in relating *thymos* and material self-interest to particular eras of human history, he implicitly accepts one of the defining features of historicism: that what is true of one era is not necessarily true of another, and this applies to the future as well as the past. In other words, the argument for capitalist democracy based on human nature fails, for the future may hold different subjectivities, different identities, and thus different political and economic institutions. Human biology and psychology do not rule out dramatic political change. So let me now turn to the two less easily dismissed aspects of the triumph of capitalist democracy: the structural and the ideological.

Political–Economic Structure

In a structural account, capitalist democracy signals the end of the road in political innovation because its structure guarantees punishing or preventing deviations. At work here are some powerful forces originating in market capitalism that also have direct implications for what can be attained in terms of political structure.

To begin, market capitalism does not determine a particular kind of political structure beyond a state to carry out the essential functions of enforcing contracts, securing private property rights, and issuing and controlling money, without which markets cannot easily function. Authoritarian political systems, therefore, can and do exist in a capitalist economic context. In the last four decades or so, this combination of political authoritarianism and capitalism has flourished in southern Europe, East Asia, and Latin America. Equally clearly, there is a strong positive association at the aggregate level between the degree of capitalist development and the extent of liberal democracy obtaining in a country.

Why this association should exist is not entirely obvious. Celebrators of unbridled capitalism such as Milton and Rose Friedman (1962) assert that economic freedom (to engage in market transactions) is a necessary but not sufficient condition for political freedom, without explaining exactly why economic rights should carry over into political rights. Charles Lindblom (1977) suggests that the correlation between capitalism and

liberal democracy is a result of their common historical origins in constitutional liberalism; as such, his explanation is idealist rather than structural.
Phillips Cutright (1963) argues that capitalism produces a complex and
differentiated economy, which in turn produces a complex and differentiated political system with multiple centers of power. Seymour Martin
Lipset (1959) believes that capitalist prosperity increases the size of the
middle class, which among all social groups is the one most committed to
the liberal virtues of tolerance and moderation. All these generalizations
are simple and sweeping. In-depth comparative historical studies of the
development of capitalism and liberal democracy invariably tell more complex stories (see, for example, Moore, 1966). One thorough study concludes that capitalism produces "formal" democracy not because capital-
ists themselves want it (they do not) but, rather, because capitalism
produces a working class with a vested interest in democratization, in the
hope that the result will be more in the way of substantive political and
economic equality (Rueschemeyer et al., 1992). It follows that authoritarian political systems in capitalist economies are inherently unstable because the economy produces a class that opposes authoritarian politics.

Whatever the precise mechanism at work, capitalism has historically
been a friend of democracy inasmuch as it has been instrumental in the
establishment of liberal democracy. However, capitalism's blessings for
democracy are now at best mixed and at worst negative. Any states that
exist in a capitalist market context are restricted both in terms of what they
can *do* in the way of public policies and what they can *be* in terms of political
organization. The implication is that democratic popular control cannot
go much further than the level already achieved in the world's existing
liberal democracies. Indeed, that level of democracy may be subject to
erosion with time. Let me explore this constraint in more detail.

Whether the market exists by the choice of governments or as a legacy
from the past, once in place the market is a constraining mechanism of
remarkable power and persistence. Governments in market systems are
constrained by the need to induce enterprises to invest. If firms do not
invest, the resultant downturn in economic activity will punish governments in two ways. The falling tax revenue reduces the resources available
for government schemes, and a perceived inability to (literally) deliver the
goods in terms of employment and income jeopardizes the popularity and
ultimately the legitimacy of the government (Block, 1977; Cohen and
Rogers, 1983, pp. 51–53; Lindblom, 1982). Thus governments typically
do not dare pursue policies with a significant negative impact on business
profitability, let alone explicitly antibusiness policies, for fear of precipitat-
ing a "capital strike." The operative mechanisms are purely automatic, and
business need have no intention, still less undertake any intentional action,
to constrain government. These mechanisms can be avoided only by re-
lying on extranational sources of finance, such as foreign aid, but the conditions of such assistance almost always point in the same direction as
market constraints, as I shall show in Chapter 4. The presence of all these

constraints means that it is not parliament or public opinion that constitutes the most important sounding board for government policy but, rather, markets, and especially financial ones. Astute government officials will therefore anticipate and attend to the reactions of markets, and not to those of legislators, interest groups, or the public.

These automatic mechanisms are generally discussed in terms of their constraints on the content of public policies (especially concerning taxation and regulation). But the argument may be extended to the existence and operation of institutions that threaten business profitability or confidence. Referring to institution building in new liberal democracies, Di Palma observed that "the economic bourgeoisie, whose interest [is] that the new democracy will not harm the reproduction of capital, requires accommodation" (1990, p. 77). Di Palma's observation obviously requires that there be a bourgeoisie to accommodate. That may be the case in democratizing societies in the capitalist world, particularly those of Latin America and East Asia. But even where there is no indigenous bourgeoisie to accommodate, as in the former Soviet bloc, the constraint of the capitalist market is still felt, albeit in a somewhat different form. The issue in such countries involves the hope of investment rather than the fear of disinvestment, so policies and institutional designs are constrained even when the market's presence is more virtual than real.

Institutions in more established liberal democracies are no less constrained and no less subject to punishment when they damage market confidence. Consider, for example, the experience of the welfare state in the Western world in the 1980s. To be sure, the new right's program to roll back the welfare state never was enacted. Nevertheless, the 1980s saw the curbing of the inertial growth of the welfare state and the enactment of selective cutbacks. This tentative retrenchment occurred precisely because the welfare state seemed to threaten the incentive structure that makes the capitalist market work. The new right in the Anglo-American world advanced this argument most enthusiastically, but governments in other Western countries, even in Scandinavia, eventually accepted a need to reduce their commitments to welfare. The reasons that these cutbacks could not be more extensive will be discussed shortly.

The fate of some U.S. regulatory agencies in recent years also is instructive in this context. Of course, such agencies can sometimes be controlled directly by the business interests that the agency is supposed to be regulating. The automatic punishment of the market can be expected only when an agency escapes such capture; among U.S. federal agencies, perhaps the Environmental Protection Agency (EPA) and the Occupational Safety and Health Administration (OSHA) fall most clearly into this latter category. Both had their wings clipped in the 1980s as a result of their perceived damage to business profitability, despite substantial public support for their mission (at least in the case of the EPA). The EPA in particular suffered both budget cuts and purges of staff committed to its mission (see Vig and Kraft, 1984).

One general lesson here is that any conscious subversion of institutions and innovations by corporate elites is a less insidious constraint than the market's automatic recoil, because deliberate subversion can, at least in principle, be recognized and counteracted. In practice, of course, it may be hard to counter the influence of corporate elites, especially when the distribution of political power is highly skewed in their direction (see Lindblom, 1977). But market necessity involves more subtle constraints, so corporate elites need not even bother to influence government consciously and deliberately in order to obtain probusiness policies; automatic processes do it for them.

In short, if more democracy is bad for business profitability, then major structural forces stand in democracy's way. According to Bowles and Gintis, "The presumed sovereignty of the democratic citizenry fails in the presence of capital strike," which "also thwarts those forms of learning-through-choosing by means of which democratic societies may come to deepen their fundamental commitments and capacities" (1986, p. 90). Democracy is bad for business if it threatens the ability of the state to carry out its functions as determined by market necessity. And this will be the case should more political democracy mean more regulation of business, income redistribution, a more extensive welfare state, higher business taxes, attacks on the privileged position of business in governmental policymaking, or pressure for more in the way of economic democracy (worker participation in management).

To illustrate, consider the widespread perception that took hold in the late 1970s throughout the industrial world, that government was increasingly overloaded and society ungovernable (see, for example, Brittan, 1975; Crozier, Huntington, and Watanuki, 1975). Overload meant, in effect, the proliferation of interest-group demands resulting from post-1945 economic prosperity and stability—for the most part, a simple expansion of the amount of conventional liberal democratic participation.[5] Brittan described it as a matter of "excessive expectations" generated in part by democracy itself (1975, p. 141) and a "disruptive pursuit of group self-interest" (pp. 129–30). Such demands came from workers, women, ethnic and regional minorities, the poor, the old, the young, environmentalists, businesses, and so forth.

The governmental response was a proliferation of agencies, laws, regulations, and programs, all sought by particular interests, but all of which had to be financed through taxes. Business was hurt not only by the growing number of laws by which it had to abide and the ever-increasing time and money it had to expend on dealing with government, but also by the increased taxation necessary to finance expanded government activity. So corporate profitability declined (Bowles, Gordon, and Weisskopf, 1983, pp. 91–97). Moreover, governments found it easier to print money rather than turn down interest-group demands, thereby leading to inflation. Thus political overload helped cause the progressive slowdown in economic growth that became apparent in many countries in the 1970s.[6] Mancur

Olson tried to put these kinds of developments in broader historical perspective in *The Rise and Decline of Nations* (1983). According to him, nations decline—or, more precisely, their rate of economic growth declines—when an increasingly dense web of complex understandings among proliferating organized interests (often ratified by government) stifles competition.[7]

In the wake of the 1970s slowdown in economic growth, the political constraint imposed by market capitalism came into play, and not just in the Reagan administration in the United States and the Thatcher government in the United Kingdom. The full force of governmental restriction on the ability to organize and exercise political influence was felt by the trade unions, especially in the United States and Britain. But a wider range of groups such as local governments, environmentalists, ethnic minorities, and poor peoples' organizations also had their access to government restricted—and their politics repressed. Too much (liberal) democracy had proved to be bad for the economy and the state's economic prerogatives, and so it had to be cut back.

A still clearer-cut example of the capitalist market's automatic recoil against an excess of democracy may be found in that least capitalist of Western societies, Sweden. In 1975 its Social Democratic government was presented with a proposal from the party's left wing and the national Labor Organization. The proposal envisaged wage-earner funds financed by a 20 percent tax on business profits, the proceeds to go to trade unions so that they could gradually buy out private corporations in the interests of democratizing the economy. From the outset the Social Democratic Party leadership did its best to contain and undermine the proposed funds on the grounds that they "frightened investors" (Steinmo, 1988, p. 437) and were an electoral liability. While in opposition in the 1976–82 period the party elite succeeded in diluting the scheme, so that when they returned to government in 1982 the party could legislate a modified proposal financed by a tax on *workers* and hedged with all kinds of limits on the amount of stock that could be owned. The modified proposal was justified in part as a new source of risk capital, not a step toward economic democracy (Steinmo, 1988, p. 433). In this Swedish case, unlike the overload issue I just discussed, the market's recoil and its impact on voters were anticipated by political leadership, so that the proposed extension of (economic) democracy never took place.

To find the most profound and severe constraints imposed on democracy by the capitalist market system, we should look not at the established capitalist democracies (such as the United States, United Kingdom, and Sweden) but, rather, at aspiring members of the capitalist democratic club in Latin America and Eastern Europe. In both areas, transitions away from authoritarian rule have been accompanied by market-oriented reforms. In Latin America, the intent has been to liberalize markets, in Eastern Europe to create markets. But irrespective of the details here, market-oriented economic reform has had a distinct and peremptory political logic. The reforms themselves are generally inspired by detailed blueprints (often developed in U.S. universities and think tanks), which are not easily comprehended by any broad public and which generally have painful short-term consequences (not to mention uncertain long-term benefits). These reforms usually require an element of surprise if they are not to be preempted by defensive reactions by the population who might, for example, rush to stockpile a commodity if they think its price is about to be deregulated (Przeworski, 1991, p. 183). For all these reasons, "market-oriented reforms are introduced by decree or are rammed through legislatures" (Przeworski, 1991, p. 184). This kind of process is hardly democracy in action: "The political process is reduced to elections, executive decrees, and sporadic outbursts of protest. . . . All the power in the state is concentrated in the executive" (Przeworski, 1991, pp. 186–87).

Przeworski's pessimism (shared by Elster, 1990, and Offe, 1991) rests on ordinary people in these societies acting politically with their own short-term material gain in mind, that is, in economically rational fashion. However, the democratic negotiation of political transition can be saved if people leave behind their economic rationality when they vote or otherwise enter politics (a possibility that Przeworski must ignore, given his methodological commitment to rational choice). Andrew Arato (1993) interprets in these terms the recent development of East European civil society. Yet the problem remains that economic rationality and its attendant political hazards are themselves promoted by marketization, which therefore undermines the political conditions for its own success. So in the immediate postrevolutionary period, even if people are willing to make personal material sacrifices for the social good (and there is survey evidence to this effect), they will nonetheless become progressively less willing as the marketization proceeds.

Przeworski seems to think that the dynamic he outlines is confined to the new or aspiring capitalist democracies. But his description precisely captures the experience of New Zealand in the 1980s, which was administered heavy doses of market-oriented reform by governments of both major parties, which had promised the opposite at election time. Furthermore, these changes were forced on a reluctant parliament and citizenry with a minimum of consultation (see Mulgan, 1992).

In the face of all the constraints that the capitalist market imposes on the state and its politics, how can we explain the existence of the welfare state, the most profound and consciously designed alteration to the liberal capitalist political economy? The answer is that the welfare state emerges not so much as a product of voluntary choices in pursuit of social justice but more as a necessary accompaniment to the capitalist economy. Indeed, it is arguable that the very survival of the capitalist economic order is due to the alleviation of some of its negative symptoms (unemployment, poverty, income insecurity, alienation, etc.) by the Keynesian welfare state. And welfare state spending can help maintain the level of demand during recessions. Aside from maintaining the structure of capitalism and curbing its anarchy, the welfare state also helps legitimate the prevailing economic and political order in the eyes of those who would otherwise suffer even more from its vicissitudes (Fisk, 1989, pp. 184–85; Offe, 1984). As national borders become less significant, the welfare state may become increasingly necessary, for the more open an economy is, the more it will be subject to external shocks. In this regard, Cameron (1978) found that welfare spending as a proportion of national income varied directly with the openness of a country's economy.

The welfare state is, then, a structural necessity in the national and international political economy. But the fact that the Keynesian welfare state entered the political landscape because it was necessary does not mean that this entry was neutral from the point of view of democratization. The Keynesian welfare state facilitates the effective extension of the democratic franchise to the organized working class. The legitimation of the liberal capitalist political economy via the welfare state is an imperative to which the defining interest of the organized working class can be assimilated. Thus socialist parties and politicians and union leaders could now participate in meaningful fashion in policy development. Although the mere fact of the welfare state may be a structural necessity, many of the details of its organization can be matters for democratic choice. These details, such as universalistic versus means-tested programs and social insurance versus social assistance, matter a great deal from the viewpoints of both social justice and democracy.

The necessity of the welfare state helps explain why the the new right's program in the 1980s was more successful in restricting access to political power (as I have already noted) than in reducing the size of the welfare state. Contemporary market advocates (for example, Friedman and Friedman, 1984) fail to appreciate what the welfare state does for capitalism. In a capitalist system, the only stabilizing alternative to the welfare state may be dictatorship, of the sort found in Pinochet's Chile (Przeworski, 1985, pp. 220–21). The Chilean experience may be an extreme case, but my point is more general. Indeed, it may be possible to compute a marginal rate of transformation between repression and welfare, and Pion-Berlin (1989) demonstrated a positive correlation between free-market monetarist economic policies and political repression in Latin America. In Britain, the Thatcher government's assault on the welfare state was accompanied by restrictions on press freedom, on the ability of civil servants to divulge information to Parliament (let alone the public), on the rights of criminal suspects and defendants, and on the ability of trade unions to organize (Kavanagh and Seldon, 1989). In this light, it is not surprising that "every democratic country has rejected the practice, if not the ideology, of unregulated competitive markets" (Dahl, 1993, p. 278). Any country that accepts unregulated markets must, therefore, cease to be democratic.

There are, of course, countervailing pressures to limit the welfare state. I stated earlier that the threat of an investment strike and capital flight severely restricts the scope of state intervention in market systems. Furthermore, this threat hinders the ability of the welfare state to maintain a size and scope sufficient to secure and legitimate capitalism. Accordingly, far from making welfare state expenditures more necessary, an open economy may make it harder to maintain them.

Offe conducted an analysis along these lines to reveal one of the core contradictions of the welfare state (1984, pp. 130–54). Offe himself believes the welfare state may be capable of muddling through in the face of such cross pressures. But there is also a possibility, which Offe also seems to recognize, that cross pressure and contradiction may create a space for freedom in political innovation. I shall return to this point in Chapter 3.

Beyond frustrating the schemes of new-right reformers, the simple presence of the welfare state can also impede more democratic institutional innovation (although as I explained earlier, the development of the welfare state was accompanied by state democratization in the form of an effective enfranchisement of the organized working class). The fact that the welfare state is always present as an alternative for the satisfaction of basic needs inhibits any attempted shift of control away from the state and toward self-governing communities. Karl Hess (1979) provided a good account in these terms of the disintegration of a social experiment in community self-control. Hess chronicled the life and times of a project in self-sufficiency, community development, and participatory democracy in the Adams-Morgan neighborhood of Washington, D.C. The project eventually collapsed largely because some of its most able members discovered easy pickings in government aid such as community development grants, which came with bureaucratic strings attached.

Structural necessities in the political economy of market capitalism and the welfare state are, then, powerful constraints on democratic innovation. Certainly, they have more to do with the current entrenchment of capitalist democracy than do any of the ideas about human nature that I discussed earlier. Let me now turn from the realm of structure to the realm of ideas.

Human Ideas

Those content with the global victory of capitalist democracy typically have little time for the kind of structural arguments dealt with in the previous section. Instead, they prefer to believe that this victory is a result of thoughtful comparison of the relative merits of different kinds of political–economic systems. Thus it is what people think that is ultimately decisive, and nobody has any better ideas, or at least any ideas that stand much chance of widespread adoption. Although human ideas do not, of course, float free from social contexts, the implicit assumption is that it is ideas that underwrite institutions and practices.

Before Fukuyama attached the psychology of *thymos* to the 1992 book-length version of his argument, his own explanation (1989) of the end of history relied on just such an idealistic account. The ideas in question are not isolated creative acts by philosophers, statesmen, or generals. Instead, as for Hegel, they constitute a flow and a pattern through time in which meaning can be discerned.

To Fukuyama (1992), the "mechanism" that now dominates history consists of scientific reason developed and put in the service of human desire under capitalism. In these terms, capitalism is a highly functional economic system, and liberal democratic politics complements it nicely. But it is not just the intrinsic qualities of capitalist democracy or its consistency with human nature that eliminate alternatives; rather, we simply have no ideas about what might work as well or better (see also Heilbroner, 1990). At first glance this looks like the victory of one ideology over others, although if capitalist democracy is without plausible competitors, it is rational and not just ideological for people to accept that fact.

Rational judgment across ideological alternatives does not, however, exhaust the possibilities here. When an ideology vanquishes its opposition and secures political dominance one should suspect that there are forces at work other than simple rational judgment by individual persons. Such forces would include the extrarational dissemination and enforcement of ideas and the exercise of political power, not just the deployment of reason.

There may, then, be more to the triumph of capitalist democracy in the realm of human ideas than a provisional rational judgment by large numbers of people that capitalist democracy is for the moment the best system available. Liberal democratic ideas are more deeply and profoundly ingrained than that. To use the language popularized by Michel Foucault (for example, 1980), capitalist democracy is a discourse that conditions not just the way people think but also their very identity.

To Foucault, a discourse is a system of possibility for apprehending the world; it is what enables people to make sense of the world around them. Foucault himself analyzed in great detail the history of discourses about crime, mental health, sex, and so forth. Indeed, to Foucault, history *is* the succession of discourses (or, in his later work, the succession of institutional practices that produce discourses). Discourses are never neutral; they always embody power and secure individuals in their grip, so history is also the succession of repressions. Repression is accomplished in that a discourse makes matters that are in reality thoroughly conventional and socially constituted, such as sexual or social behavior, appear natural. Moreover, discourses are very hard to escape, for they also possess their own standards of truth and rationality. To Foucault, there can never be any separation between truth and power; truth always helps constitute power.

In these terms, capitalist democracy is not a system that has been fairly compared with its competitors and universally chosen as the best option. Instead, it constitutes individuals in such a way that they are unlikely to choose anything else. Desires to acquire material possessions, to pursue the interest of the self above other concerns, to secure a private realm of life against political control, to expect certain civil rights and the ability to participate in choosing governments, to recognize the authority of the state, and so forth, are not matters of any invariant human nature; they are established by the dominant discourse.

Thus if capitalist democracy has won the global struggle at the level of ideas, it is because it has been extraordinarily successful in providing people with the criteria by which they can choose alternative systems. Based on these criteria, liberal capitalism always wins. These criteria include material prosperity, social peace, negative liberty (freedom *from* constraint), equality of opportunity, and political competition. Alternative criteria such as the conservation of social traditions, ecological harmony, spiritual satisfaction, solidarity, and positive liberty (freedom *to* develop one's capabilities in political association) are found only at the margins of politics.

Yet the very fact that such criteria are found anywhere—even if only in the scribblings of obscure academics and agitators—suggests that the kind of all-encompassing power attributed to discourses by Foucault and his followers is an exaggeration. Moreover, Foucault himself demonstrates a well-developed capability to get outside discourses (at least as far as some metadiscourse) by identifying, describing, and criticizing them—thus contradicting his argument that no vantage point from outside particular discourses is possible. Why should not others follow his lead?

Such problems notwithstanding, it remains the case that a Foucauldian analysis of the ideational underpinnings of the victory of capitalist democracy has much to be said for it. Foucault and his followers err only in exaggerating the degree of dominance achieved by particular discourses, which should be welcome news to anyone interested in alternatives to the prevailing political–economic order.

Conclusion

If one were to try to devise a political–economic system with the maximum possible staying power, it would combine rigidity in its essential structure with flexibility in its ideological justification. Capitalist democracy possesses just such a combination. Its basic structure resists change, as institutional innovations that threaten market confidence are automatically punished.[8] Its ideology is peculiarly flexible in that liberalism can often look like a synonym for what is good, right, and just. This flexibility becomes understandable once liberal capitalist democracy is understood as the discourse of our times, which has been effective in producing standards for its own judgment.

Liberalism has also been quite good at producing its own critics. Liberal philosophers and ideologists do not always engage in uncritical celebration of the status quo. They also advance universalistic principles from which existing societies often fall short. These principles are quite varied, ranging from the quasi-scientific "open society" of free debate and policy experimentation of Karl Popper (1966) to the egalitarian principles of justice advanced by John Rawls (1971) to the aggressively libertarian set of individual rights endorsed by Robert Nozick (1974).

Liberalism is also very good at assimilating critics who start from outside its camp. Accordingly, social democratic parties that once wanted to transform capitalism are now content with managing it and smoothing some of its rougher edges; their commitment to democracy has been translated into support for (limited) liberal democracy, to the exclusion of economic democracy. Seemingly radical democrats such as Barber (1984) claim that all they want to do is raise the quality and amount of liberal political debate. Those who assert the ideal of community and constrast it with liberal individualism are told that liberalism can accommodate the idea of community quite well, thank you (Caney, 1992). One of the most trenchant critics of industrial society, Jürgen Habermas, who comes from a line of critique that begins with Marx, now finds his ideas assimilated by liberals. Spragens (1990) uses the standards of communicative rationality advanced by Habermas to justify not radical alternatives to liberalism but a liberalism of participatory dialogue, civic virtue, and public responsibility. Habermas himself eventually found it hard to resist the liberal embrace. Postmodernists who begin by calling into question everything about Western society can end up being told by Rorty (1989) to celebrate the pluralist expression of differences allowed by liberal democracy. Other postmodernists celebrate the involvement of capitalism in creating a formless, rootless parade of media images as a substitute for "reality." This openness on the part of liberal ideology at first sight appears very decent. But its net effect is to assimilate potential critics of capitalist democracy without changing anything in the way of political–economic structure—which, as I have noted, is peculiarly resistant to change.

The global victory of capitalist democracy is, then, a matter of self-perpetuating structure combined with a discourse that constitutes individuals in certain ways and is flexible enough to accommodate and disarm critics. It would be wrong to conclude at this point that capitalist democracy is unassailable, for the system is surely less immutable than if its victory were a matter of its consistency with what it means to be human. The task that remains is to locate possibilities for democratic innovation in the face of these structural and ideological constraints. I shall begin in the next chapter by looking in a bit more detail at the structural constraints surrounding the liberal democratic state, with a view to how they might be overcome.

3

Democracy Versus the State

It is often assumed that if we care about democracy, the proper—perhaps the exclusive—focus for our concerns and efforts should be the state. As Dahl puts it in a seemingly unremarkable aside, "Advocates of the democratic process have always meant it to be applied to the state" (1989, p. 37). Irrespective of the precise kind of democracy they favor, most such advocates simply take it for granted that it is the state that is the target of their concerns (see, among many others, Barber, 1984; Popper, 1966; Rueschemeyer, Stephens, and Stephens, 1992; Sartori, 1987; Spragens, 1990). Unlike Dahl, they regard this focus as so unremarkable that it is hardly even worth a mention.

The small minority of democratic theorists that has taken Marxism seriously recognizes that democratization of the capitalist state is necessarily problematic. Yet this recognition does not prevent them from identifying the state—inasmuch as it is unlikely ever to wither away as Marxists once hoped—as a major locus for democratization (see Held, 1987, p. 257). Marxist participatory democrats such as Poulantzas (1980) and MacPherson (1973) are concerned with the democratization of society beyond the state, but the state remains their main concern, at least insofar as they can regard the state as anything more than an instrument of class rule.

This eventual embrace of the state is shared by another group of participatory democrats who, one might expect, to be profoundly suspicious of it. Green parties generally begin with an awareness of the social and ecological ravages wrought by contemporary states, but their "realo" wing nevertheless concludes that a centralized—if somewhat weakened and democratized—state remains necessary. Such a state is needed to match the scale of ecological problems, equalize across communities with different ecological and cultural endowments, counter corporate power, and chart the path to a greener future (see Eckersley, 1992, pp. 182–85).[1]

In this chapter I shall suggest—contrary to the hopes of many democratic theorists—that any deeper democratization of the liberal capitalist state is often a remote prospect. That is, once the basic parameters of capitalist democracy have been achieved, the state is peculiarly resistant to further democratization. Only in some special and unusual circumstances is this resistance likely to falter. What this means is that advocates of democracy might better concern themselves with the possibility of democratization *against* the state and democratization-*apart from* the state, rather than democratization *of* the state. Certainly, they should not seek or expect much in the way of democratization *by* the state. Democratization *of* the state is not necessarily inconceivable, but it should not be the exclusive, or even primary, focus of democratic theory and action.

Profound democratization *of* the liberal capitalist state occurred in the past with the emergence of its basic economic and legitimation functions, as described in the previous chapter. I shall try to show that democratization of the state may still be conceivable in unusual circumstances, especially those surrounding economic depression and war but that even then the process is highly problematic. More ordinary circumstances generally allow only a marginal deepening of state democracy. Such a deepening can occur in connection with any indeterminacy in fulfilling state functions, in cases in which these imperatives conflict with one another, in local governments to the extent they can distance themselves from these essential maintaining functions, and in any collapsed peripheries possessed by otherwise flourishing states. Democratization *against* the state is possible not only in the very rare (and often implausible) circumstances surrounding revolution, but also in public spheres and social movements that can more persistently confront the state. Democratization *apart from* the state can occur in connection with community politics, control of economic enterprises by employees (workplace democracy), and feminist rethinking of what areas of life count as political. By definition, the last opens up new sites for democratization, although feminism also calls into question what democracy means in established political venues, such as the state. In this chapter, I will address all these possibilities for democratization of, against, and apart from the state. I shall conclude that the state's adoption of exclusionary forms of representation can actually facilitate democratization against and apart from the state, provided that the exclusions are properly arranged.

Democratization of the State

The state may be defined as the set of individuals and organizations legally authorized to make binding decisions for a society.[2] As I noted in the previous chapter, states in contemporary capitalist societies are subject to all kinds of constraints. All such states must keep order in their societies, compete internationally, induce business to invest, maintain the political–economic order through either the welfare state or more coercive means, and secure finance for these other activities. If an excess of democracy threatens any of these activities, it is normally democracy that will give way. As Elkin puts it, "a citizenry that is in full democratic cry [cannot] be accommodated for very long in a liberal democratic state" (1985b, p. 193). Fear of such excess is well represented in the arguments of Crozier, Huntington, and Watanuki (1975) on the need to protect governmental functions from too much democracy.

There is, in fact, a temptation for states to assign their essential maintaining functions to institutions immune to liberal democratic political control, let alone any more direct involvement by the citizenry. Perhaps the best example here is afforded by central banks. Most notably, the Bundesbank follows its own economic policy to protect the value of the deutsche Mark and German economic stability. The rest of Europe can suffer mightily as a result of this policy, and the elected German government may plead for policy changes, but the Bundesbank remains unmoved in its mission. The U.S. Federal Reserve is less notorious than the Bundesbank, and foreign victims are less obvious and less noisy, but it too is largely insulated from liberal democratic control.

Central banks may be an extreme example of state structures that pursue essential maintaining functions beyond the reach of democratic control, but the point is a more general one. Contemporary capitalist states resist democratization that might impinge on any of these functions. In this light, what scope remains for a guided democratization of the state?

Some social scientists who have studied the state and the structural constraints on it would answer, none at all. These structural social scientists often write in deterministic terms (see, for example, Evans, Rueschemeyer, and Skocpol, 1985). History unfolds with an iron necessity, and there is nothing that political leaders or anyone else can do about it. Institutional change can occur, but it is caused, not chosen; and state officials simply must behave in certain ways, given that the goals they pursue and the resources available to them are determined by their structural location (Krasner, 1984, p. 225). In their less guarded moments, structuralists may allow intentions and ideologies into their explanatory schemes. But no *intended* consequences enter, for such ideas take effect only as they are combined, enabled, and constrained by social structures (Skocpol, 1985, pp. 87, 94). Thus structuralists "should not make the mistake of assuming that the talkers and the legislators could ever straightforwardly shape outcomes" (Skocpol, 1985, p. 93), and their explanations remain "nonintentionalist at the macroscopic level" (Skocpol, 1985, p. 86). In criticizing this school of thought, Sewell notes that it treats "structures . . . as impervious to human agency, to exist apart from, but nevertheless to determine the essential shape of, the strivings and motivated transactions that constitute the experienced surface of social life." Thus individuals and other actors become "cleverly programmed automatons" (Sewell, 1992, p. 2).

Students of democratization are less prone to such extreme determinism, although their probabilistic analyses can still effectively deny that human creativity can shape outcomes. In this context, Di Palma (1990) criticizes development theorists who claim that a high level of economic development is a necessary condition for stable liberal democracy for denying that the odds can ever be beaten. He believes that liberal democracies can be crafted, even when economic conditions seem inauspicious.

I have already drawn on structural arguments to identify some of the major constraints on states and their officials and consequently on the efforts of anyone who would seek to reform (or even overthrow) them. However, in this chapter I intend turning the structuralists' determinism on its head. For in outlining what is determined, structuralists also inadvertently enable the identification of what is not determined, although it may require some imagination to locate such possibilities.[3] As I shall try to demonstrate, even if the structuralists are substantially correct in the constraints they identify (and I believe they are), considerable room for democratic political innovation remains.

What about the room that remains for further democratization within the capitalist democratic state? Clearly there is some room. Even such a necessitarian as Block (1977) admits to times when policies that threaten business profitability fail to be punished. The kinds of policies Block has in mind involve extension of the scope of the state's intervention in the economic system rather than democratization as such, but his analysis can be applied to democracy as well.

Block's exceptional times are depression, war (with which I shall deal in the next chapter), and postwar reconstruction. During depressions, business confidence has already collapsed, investment is at a low level, and so disinvestment is an empty threat. Nonmilitary economic activity is at a similarly low level at the onset of postwar reconstruction. A concern with the possibilities for democratization suggests that these exceptional times should be examined in two ways. First, can we point to any degree of democratic innovation that has actually occurred during such times? Second, irrespective of the record, could democratic innovation be pursued effectively during these occasions?

Depression

The core capitalist countries have experienced only one full depression in the twentieth century. The Great Depression saw several countries turn away from liberal democracy and toward fascism and other kinds of authoritarianism. The United States and Sweden were exceptional in that they developed moderately effective responses to the Great Depression while retaining their liberal democratic political systems. But in both cases the response involved substantial extension of the state's control of the economy and executive power and little in the way of expansion of popular control in government. In the United States, the typical New Deal agency (such as the National Recovery Administration or the Soil Conservation Service) was deliberately insulated from congressional control so that the experts controlling the agency could operate free from liberal democratic interference.

Irrespective of the actual record, could democratic innovation ever prosper during an economic depression? The capitalist market's economic constraint may be suspended in depressions, to be replaced by structural necessity related to the welfare state. However, the welfare state as such is not an antidemocratic institution, and inasmuch as it secures the basic needs of life for greater numbers of people, it can release them from the struggle for survival to engage in other pursuits, such as politics. In terms of the three criteria established in Chapter 1, this release can help increase franchise. Moreover, an extension of the welfare state may have widespread popular support. And even if the welfare state does enter as an imperative felt by state officials, they nevertheless feel it in part because of their fear of public unrest. So expansion of the welfare state under such circumstances means conceding to popular demands—and as such, a positive move on the "scope" criterion established in Chapter 1. The concession itself may be administered in authoritarian fashion; think, for example, of Bismarck's founding of the German welfare state in the nineteenth century. Authoritarian administration is attractive to officials because any democratization of the state under such dire circumstances would introduce an element of uncertainty as to whether the constraint might be effectively met and the depression effectively remedied. Still, the news for democracy is not all bad.

The Western world has not experienced a real depression since the 1930s precisely because of the presence of the Keynesian welfare state. Instead, today's depressions are felt elsewhere. A severe constraint arises in these depressions, however, for they are suffered by peripheral members of the international economic order, who must comply with the dictates of that order's institutions in order to receive the aid necessary to alleviate depression. Those dictates generally include austerity measures that meet with mass disapproval. Democracy must, if anything, be curbed under such circumstances, and centralized state power asserted. These and other international considerations will receive greater attention in the following chapter.

Convulsions such as a depression do not, therefore, provide a tabula rasa for aspiring democrats. But they do change the configuration of constraints under which states operate and so might occasionally offer opportunities. Still, anyone interested in democratizing the state would do better to attend to more ordinary, if far less dramatic, circumstances, to which I now turn.

Functional Indeterminacy and the Limits
to Administrative Rationality

The imperatives facing states that I have discussed suggest that if they are to survive, political forms must be functional in terms of these constraints. This point is Darwinian: Only the fittest survive. But it is not Panglossian; we do not live in a uniquely functional world. The structuralists I described earlier who write in fully deterministic terms repeat the error of Dr. Pangloss, for they fail to recognize the possibility of functional indeterminacy. In other words, for any situation there may be a number of institutional forms that are equally functional. Moreover, a substantial deviation from what is most functional may be tolerated.[4] Accordingly, corporatism (policymaking through formalized bargains among representatives of all-encompassing labor and industry associations and government) and pluralism (more decentralized and disorganized interaction of groups) might be equally effective in articulating interests. Similarly, parliamentary and presidential systems might be equally stable, as might federal and unitary arrangements. And economic systems with different degrees of government intervention might perform equally well.

The freedom that this recognition of functional indeterminacy releases should not be exaggerated—all the examples I have just given may be subsumed under the rubric of liberal democracy. But minimally, reformers may take comfort in the fact that if a particular arrangement flourishes somewhere else, it may prove functional on their own turf, too. Even structural determinists allow that the "world-historical context"—that is, the range of available political–economic models—can help explain political outcomes (Skocpol, 1979, pp. 234–35). The feasible set of functional innovations of course, is not confined to models that have already been tried somewhere else.

Functional indeterminacy means that there may be different ways for states to satisfy the imperatives confronting them. I have already noted that legitimation through the welfare state and more draconian political repression are substitutes for curbing the political instability generated by capitalism. By itself, this substitutability has little to do with the prospects for democracy, beyond highlighting the fact that there is a welfare alternative to repression. But it is also conceivable that democratization might act here as a partial substitute for welfare spending and repression. In other words, allowing ordinary people a share in decision making related to the welfare state may make them less likely to oppose the prevailing political–economic order, even if the size of the welfare state is static or contracting.

At one level, this might involve the co-optation of potential malcontents through the illusion of participation, which falsely compensates them for reductions in welfare state benefits. However, once one recognizes that there is no perfect correlation between the amount of money spent by the welfare state and the amount of social justice it delivers (see Esping-

Anderson, 1989), there is scope for more honest participatory redesign of the welfare state and its programs, even during fiscal retrenchment. This redesign might entail eliminating poorly designed or ineffective programs, or "welfare for the rich" and other privileged groups, and redirecting resources more equitably. Democratization here could never be a complete substitute for welfare, only a partial one. I am not aware of anything along these lines that has ever been tried in connection with the welfare state, but the theoretical possibility remains.

In this hypothetical case, democratization would act as a substitute for certain kinds of policy content. But democratization might also be deepened within the limits set by structural constraints on the content of policy. The history of environmental policy in the United States and Canada is illustrative of the possibilities here. Since 1970, as Paehlke (1988) notes, this history has been accompanied by extended public participation in policymaking, in the form of public inquiries, right-to-know legislation, and impact assessment (which generally mandates opportunities for public comment on environmental impact statements).

Most such extensions have done little to change the basic framework of liberal democracy. However, one type cuts a little deeper, involving face-to-face discussion among parties interested in a problem, with the intent of producing an action-oriented consensus. The interested parties might include community groups, local governments, national government agencies, environmentalists, and corporations. Such forums—"discursive designs"—usually proceed under the auspices of a neutral third party and are styled mediation, principled negotiation, problem-solving workshops, regulatory negotiation, or policy dialogue (see Dryzek, 1990, part II, for a discussion of their democratic potential). They have flourished because some policy problems may be just too intractable for resolution through conventional means, be it the give-and-take of liberal interest-group interaction, a legal system, or the delegation and division of labor of a bureaucratic hierarchy. Business firms have long recognized a related difficulty, which is why they have sometimes taken particularly obstinate or novel problems out of the corporate hierarchy, to place them in the hands of more informal, collegial, and creative "brainstorming" groups. Thus processes such as mediation and regulatory negotiation have often appeared in the vicinity of complex social problems, which suggests that established state mechanisms are not particularly good at resolving complex problems with multiple stakeholders. In this light, environmentalists and others who are unconvinced by claims to neutral expertise made by government administrators can and do press for less exclusive and more participatory styles of policy making. Administrators, for their part, may even concede that broad input is necessary in order for effective policy to be made.

The problem for states and their officials here is not just one of the limits to administrative rationality but also one of legitimacy. Liberal democratic governments today are often not very good at allocating losses to particular groups, even when the net benefit of a policy is apparently positive (see, for example, Thurow, 1980). Government agencies, corporations, interest groups, and other prospective losers can often veto such policy proposals. If these prospective losers are organized bodies of citizens, such as community or environmental groups, then governments often seek legitimacy in policy formation by recruiting citizens or their representatives for participation in discursive exercises of the sort I have described.

If these discursive innovations are involved in policymaking, the content of the policies they produce will be subject to the state-related constraints discussed earlier. But despite such restriction on their outputs, the process of these mechanisms still involves something more than liberal democratic politics as usual. Although not exactly mass participatory democracy in action, the style of interaction entails argument in terms of the public interest (as opposed to narrow self-interest), open disclosure of information, mutual education, and minimal strategizing. A depth of democratic deliberation generally missing in liberal democracy can result. Other outcomes are conceivable, too, especially if the procedure is manipulated and abused, for example, to co-opt potential troublemakers (Amy, 1987) or to justify decisions already made (Kemp, 1985). But such abuses are readily exposed, for the very claim to legitimacy of discursive designs rests on their democratic qualities. It is the power of good argument that should be decisive, rather than claims to unchallengeable expertise or formal authority. Expertise and authority may still play parts, but they must be capable of withstanding discursive scrutiny. Violation of this principle through attempts by government officials (and others) to manipulate, deceive, bias the procedure, or withhold pertinent information can be criticized by observers of these proceedings. Such exposé and criticism was especially prominent in British inquiries into nuclear power in the 1970s and 1980s.

Discursive designs can, then, operate as "worms in the brain" of the administrative state, advancing democracy at the expense of hierarchy (see Bartlett, 1990, p. 82). The advance here is generally in terms of scope and authenticity, as democratic control is extended to areas formerly the prerogative of administration, and participation can be informed and competent. Franchise is not usually advanced, for participants are drawn mostly from the ranks of the politically active.

Changing Pressures and Cross Pressures: Accumulation, Legitimation, and Environmental Conservation

Additional spaces for democratization of the state appear not only when new state imperatives emerge but also when different state functions pull in different directions. At one level, the result may produce little or nothing in the way of more democracy but, rather, just additional freedom of choice for cross-pressured public officials (see Elkin, 1985a, pp. 6–7; Lindblom, 1977). This choice may involve (say) more or less of established forms such as the welfare state: More promotes social stability, and less helps better meet market and international constraints. But larger possibilities for institutional change may open here, too. For example, as I pointed out in the previous chapter, the twin necessities of maintaining market confidence and curbing market-generated social instability can pull the Keynesian welfare state in diametrically opposite directions. Under such circumstances of a conflict between the accumulation (market confidence) and legitimation imperatives, it is very hard for that state to perform in administratively rational fashion, which requires the coordinated pursuit of an ordered set of goals (Offe, 1984). In the face of this kind of contradiction, policy responses are likely to prove dispersed, fragmented, and ultimately at odds with one another.

The resulting areas of confusion are vulnerable to action on behalf of some alternative institutional order, in that some kind of political mechanism for the resolution of conflicting imperatives and the coordination of policies may be called for. The kind that has been tried most often (with the greatest success in Scandinavia, the Netherlands, Germany, and Austria) is corporatism. Corporatism involves negotiated bargains among labor, business, and government. But whatever its virtues in reconciling the pursuit of economic growth and social justice, corporatism is not an especially democratic style of policymaking, as its processes are quite exclusionary. Some kind of democratic alternative to corporatist conflict resolution might therefore secure political legitimacy more readily in the eyes of citizens. Exactly what such an alternative might look like is less certain, and one can point to no real-world intimations, beyond the familiar variations on a liberal democratic theme. Discursive designs of the sort I discussed earlier hint at one such possibility, but so far they have been applied mostly to limited and local disputes. Later I will contend that corporatist exclusion can actually be turned to the benefit of democracy, although no such benefit is felt in the corporatist state itself.

The imperatives facing states are not necessarily constant, and shifts in their configuration have implications for what kind of politics is possible. The economic or accumulation imperative to promote economic growth and avoid recession enters only with the development of capitalism's boom-and-bust cycles. Before this development, government revenues might still vary with economic conditions, but there was little realization that government could actually do much to affect these conditions. The wrath of ordinary citizens (but not of landed elites) was less relevant, even though feudal lords often lived in fear of peasant or slave revolt. With the establishment of the accumulation imperative, the bourgeoisie could gain the access to state power previously denied to them. Thus the democratic franchise could be extended to the bourgeoisie, whose interests in economic expansion were essentially identical with this new state function.

The subsequent establishment of the legitimation imperative was accompanied by further extension of the democratic franchise and of the scope of democratic control. As I observed in Chapter 2, the defining interest of the organized working class could be assimilated to legitimation through the welfare state. Thus the organized working class could be granted a share of state power, if only within limits set by the economic imperative.

The most recent addition to the list of state-related imperatives is environmental conservation. Recognition of this imperative is less than three decades old (and still far from universal); thus uncertainty still surrounds its implications for the structure and operation of states. Liberal capitalist states took much longer than three decades to contemplate and craft effective responses to the legitimation imperative, in the form of welfare states. Recent decades have, of course, seen environmental legislation, antipollution regulation, wilderness protection, and the establishment of environmentally oriented government agencies. Yet ultimately capitalist states remain committed above all else to the pursuit of economic growth, and no state has yet found an easy way to reconcile growth and environmental conservation. "Sustainable development" remains a slogan or an aspiration, but nowhere an accomplishment.[5] Discursive designs in environmental policy of the sort I have discussed may be interpreted as an institutional response to the conflict between economic growth and environmental conservation, though they by no means exhaust the range of possibilities here. To the extent that environmental conservation can be established as an imperative, it enables effective enfranchisement in policymaking for environmentalists, just as in the past accumulation opened the door to the bourgeoisie, and legitimation to the organized working class.

Local Politics

My discussion of the possibilities for democratization of the state has so far proceeded mainly with the national state in mind. Some additional possibilities may arise at the level of local government, where the essential maintaining functions of the state are less of an issue. The tasks of keeping internal order, maintaining market confidence, and softening the rougher edges of capitalism all can be accomplished at the national level.

Some of the constraints that operate at the national level, however, can also appear locally. Local governments, no less than national ones, can make life more or less difficult for businesses operating in their jurisdiction. So, too, automatic market punishment can operate locally. In this age of footloose capital, firms can invest in the localities that give them the most favorable subsidies, regulatory relief, low wages, or tax breaks. Note, in this context, the bidding wars that large corporations now encourage among different states in the United States for new manufacturing plants. Paradoxically, the less control over business conditions that a locality has in comparison with that of the national government, the greater will be the scope for local democracy (because the economic constraint applies less powerfully).

A further paradox arises when one considers the need of all "states" (national or local) for revenue. A local government will be sensitive to local business conditions to the extent that it depends on local sources of revenue. On the other hand, if a local government is financed mostly by central government grants, it can escape this constraint. The radical policies engineered in Britain by leftist Labour metropolitan governments such as those of Liverpool and the Greater London Council during the Thatcher years of the 1980s are instructive here. Equally instructive is the fate of these policies and the institutions that produced them: An irritated central government simply abolished these local governments.

At this point, it might seem that the real scope for local innovation is quite restricted, for the more such institutions try to exercise effective control, the more constraints will come into play. However, when such constraints make themselves felt at the local level, they enter in blatant and heavy-handed fashion. To illustrate, the city of Eugene, Oregon, declared itself a nuclear-free zone in the 1980s through a referendum of its citizens. Local corporate officials and their sympathizers at the apex of the city's power structure (often the same people) claimed that the zone would drive business out of Eugene. After such a mass exodus failed to materialize, Rohr Industries, a corporation with some interests in defense manufacturing, arrived in town with a plan to build a factory. Following much publicity the plan was withdrawn, ostensibly because the terms of the nuclear-free zone would make life too difficult for Rohr, even if it undertook no nuclear weapons–oriented production in Eugene. To the proponents of the nuclear-free zone, it looked suspiciously as though Rohr never had any intention of locating in Eugene but was introduced to make an economic point and help destroy the nuclear-free zone. The zone survived, although it was weakened substantially in a referendum at the next election. The city's power structure could not simply jettison democratic control and the nuclear-free zone it produced here, for democratic forms (no less than the welfare state as discussed earlier) help legitimate political–economic structures. In local cases such as this, the issue of democratic control versus political–economic constraint comes into particularly sharp focus. In Eugene, democratic control was the loser, at least in the short term. But other outcomes are conceivable if local democrats can turn to their advantage this very obvious contradiction between democracy and political–economic constraint.

Collapsed Peripheries

One category of local—or at least subnational—politics offers more substantial opportunities for political change, although this category occurs quite rarely. If a locality collapses economically, politically, or both, some constraints on political change will be lifted. My earlier argument about the suspension of the economic constraint during depression suggested that it is replaced by equally pressing constraints related to welfare and/

or repression. But matters may prove different if only a peripheral part of a country collapses.

Consider, in this light, the case of Northern Ireland, which fell apart both economically and politically in the late 1960s. Economically, the six counties of Northern Ireland suffered from the decline of a heavy industrial base (just as parts of England, Scotland, and Wales did at the same time). Politically, the latest round of intercommunal troubles led to permanent turmoil (which also exacerbated the economic problem). The established sectarian institutions such as the Stormont parliament retained their legitimacy to the Unionist majority, but their illegitimacy in the eyes of the Republican minority could no longer be ignored, nor could their affront to international standards of fairness. Thus Westminster abolished Stormont, the B-Specials police force, and other instruments of Unionist domination.

The early 1970s began a spate of economic and political interventions in the six counties. The economic innovations were distinctly unimaginative and unsuccessful, involving large British subsidies to industrial dinosaurs such as Harland and Wolff shipbuilders and to questionable new ventures such as the DeLorean car company. The political innovations were equally unsuccessful, at least until the peace initiatives of 1994, but far more imaginative—indeed, theoretically sophisticated. They included power-sharing institutions designed to draw from both majority and minority communities, proportional representation (to discourage party polarization), constitutional referenda, and a transnational Council of Ireland to involve the government of the Irish Republic in Northern affairs. Most of these political reforms were opposed and undermined by irredentist Unionists, but the very fact that they were tried is remarkable. They were either imposed or accepted by a Westminster government that has steadfastly opposed similar changes in the political system of the rest of the United Kingdom, on the grounds that they run counter to the British constitutional tradition (which indeed they do). Parties favoring proportional representation in British elections have in fact gathered up to 26 percent of the vote in recent general elections, and opinion polls show an even higher level of public support. But the possibility of using this electoral system for Britain has never been discussed by the very Parliament that happily consented to proportional representation for elections in Northern Ireland. Even though these attempted constitutional changes fall under the general heading of liberal democracy, they imply that possibilities for democratization may be available in collapsed peripheries that are not available in the core.

Democratization Against the State

The preceding discussion suggests that opportunities for democratizing the capitalist state are often quite limited. Although not totally unshakable, the constraints on what that state can do or be prove hard to escape completely. This recognition shows that we might more profitably seek deeper democracy in venues other than the state. Here, renewed attention to the old concept of civil society on the part of political theorists is noteworthy.

By a broad definition, civil society consists of all social interaction not encompassed by the state on the one hand or the economy on the other; according to Cohen and Arato, "a sphere of social interaction between economy and state, composed above all of the intimate sphere (especially the family), social movements, and forms of public communication" (1992, p. ix). A narrower definition describes civil society as consisting of voluntary political association oriented by its relation to the state, but self-limiting in not seeking a share of state power. Civil society in this narrower sense constitutes a realm of freedom in which individuals are not forced to act in strategic pursuit of material reward (as required in the economy) or constrained by the power relationships embodied in the bureaucratic state. Perhaps the best definition of civil society in this narrower sense is in functional terms, as public action in response to failure in government and the economy. Thus, as Janicke (1994) noted, "paragovernmental" action can take place in civil society as control over certain areas of collective life is claimed back from the state.

In the West, civil society is now courted by leftists who have given up on both Marxist and social democratic strategies for gaining control of the state. The idea of civil society has also played a large part in discussions of East European politics before and after the revolutions of 1989. Especially in Poland and Czechoslovakia, civil society was the parallel polity in which democracy was practiced before 1989 and the basis for public willingness to suffer the short-term pain of economic reform for the sake of the longer-term public good after 1989 (Arato, 1993).[6]

Bearing in mind the difference between narrow and broad definitions of civil society, let me distinguish between political venues confronting the state and those existing apart from the state. Although there is no hard and fast boundary between these last two categories, by politics against the state I mean that action and interaction whose very identity is defined by its opposition to the state. Often this opposition results from states steadfastly following the imperatives introduced earlier. The most significant such opposition is that associated with public spheres, which fit the narrow definition of civil society as voluntary public association.

Public Spheres

A public sphere exists whenever individuals congregate to scrutinize freely their relationships with one another and with broader systems of political power in which they are enmeshed and to determine how they might act and interact (see Keane, 1984, pp. 2–3). As long as they confront (but do not share) state power, they possess a degree of autonomy from state imperatives, and so they can experiment with degrees of democracy generally unavailable in the state. Public spheres generally involve intense commitment by at least some participants, a willingness to defy established authority, extensive discussion and other kinds of communication, and a focus on truly public interests and concerns (as opposed to private material interests). Structural possibilities for the generation of public spheres are especially apparent whenever states adopt forms of interest representation or policymaking that exclude significant segments of their societies.

The most venerable example is the early bourgeois public sphere as celebrated by Habermas (1989), in which the emergent bourgeoisie in a number of eighteenth-century European societies challenged the feudal state. This sphere involved political activity in the form of public association and the generation of public opinion through discussions in meeting places and newspapers. Though confined to a single (and relatively privileged) social class, its workings embodied a kind of deliberative democracy of competent citizens unconstrained by the occupation of formal positions of political authority. Its members sought to develop and exercise informed public opinion in opposition to states that continued to uphold feudal privileges and limitations on liberal economic and political rights. This particular public sphere declined and eventually vanished with the bourgeois success in achieving a share of state power and with the commercialization of newspapers.

More recent examples may be found in Eastern Europe, where public spheres confronted repressive and exclusionary states of a somewhat different character. The biggest, in terms of sheer number of participants, was Solidarity in Poland, which best exemplified the uncompromising ideals of the public sphere in its early 1980s phase (see Touraine et al., 1983). At its peak in those early years, it formed a viable political alternative to the Polish state and, as such, a good example of the paragovernmental aspect of civil society to which I alluded earlier. Its members could live "as if" they were in a free country (Ash, 1990, pp. 106–8). Solidarity was, of course, interested in challenging rather than ignoring the state, and its members did have ideas about how state and economy should be organized. These ideas changed substantially over time, from an early emphasis on republican self-management to conversion to capitalism in the mid-1980s. So when offered entry into the Polish state in 1989, Solidarity's leadership did not refuse, and they readily took on all the constraints of a (proto-)capitalist state. With this acceptance, however, Solidarity lost the depth of democratic authenticity it once possessed.

Public spheres in several other East European countries followed Solidarity's life cycle on an accelerated timetable. In opposition, none had any program to seize the state (still less enter it). With the advent of the revolution, their members were generally happy to enter the power vacuum left by the implosion of the old order. Typically their best hours led up to the 1989–91 collapse of Soviet-sponsored regimes and eventually of the Soviet state itself. Following the collapse, Eastern European public spheres gave rise to hierarchical political parties, and their members took on the administration of would-be capitalist states. Even Czechoslovakia did not avoid this progression, even though the patron saint of the East

European public sphere, Vaclav Havel, became its president. Yet the oppositional public sphere is not without its legacies. The countries where an oppositional public sphere flourished (Poland, Hungary, Czechoslovakia, and the German Democratic Republic) are proving to be better equipped to negotiate political and economic transformation than are countries such as Romania and Russia where such spheres were absent or less prominent.

The history of Western Europe and North America is also well populated by public spheres confronting states that engaged in political exclusion and repression. In the United States, blacks, women, and manual workers were long excluded from liberal democratic politics. As a result, they formed what Evans and Boyte (1986) call "free spaces," involving a politics of democratic association in opposition to the state. These spaces became less easily distinguishable from conventional liberal interest-group politics with the achievement of the vote by women in 1920, of governmental acceptance of the legitimacy of labor unions in the 1930s, and of the notional political equality guaranteed by civil rights legislation in the 1960s.

Today, democratic capitalist states are confronted by a variety of public spheres. Some of these exist as a direct result of the state's following imperatives, especially economic ones, in contradiction to the wishes of large numbers of its citizens. The state so acting is a capitalist state, but hardly a democratic one, and so democracy is displaced into the public sphere. A particularly graphic example may be found in New Zealand, where in the 1980s governments formed by both major parties (Labour and National) followed radical promarket policies in contravention of their election-time promises and against the wishes of the vast majority of the population (see Mulgan, 1992). The resultant public disaffection verged on a wholesale loss of legitimacy. Some of this disaffection was channeled through a grassroots movement for electoral reform, which in 1992 and then again in 1994 carried referenda over the opposition of the major parties. This movement therefore beat a path from the public sphere to state organization, although not to a share of state power. Disaffection also produced a realignment of political forces and an organized opposition to the economic rationalism pursued by the two established parties.

Among the most visible public spheres confronting capitalist democratic states are those associated with new social movements, constituted by groups such as radical environmentalists, feminists, urban, antinuclear and peace activists, and the Greens. These movements represent constituencies excluded by established forms of interest intermediation such as welfare state corporatism (Kitschelt, 1988) or the traditionally unresponsive and "blocked" Italian state. Corporatism is predicated on the idea of a single organized association for each economic sector (usually business and labor), which is then co-opted into a formalized arrangement with government in the making of public policy. In return for this access, each sectoral group disciplines its members. Disaffected and potentially unruly "grass roots" unhappy with their distance from their sector's leadership are obvious sources of recruits for new social movements, as are individuals who find themselves unrepresented in the corporatist bargain (such as the unemployed, self-employed, marginally employed, and students).[7]

Such movements are new in at least two senses, according to Cohen (1985). First, their radicalism is self-limiting; they have no strategy to share in state power, and so they may avoid the compromised fate of the public sphere in Eastern Europe. They are more concerned with exposing power than sharing it and so do not create any unified opposition with a program like that of a political party (and in this lack of unity, they differ from pre-1989 Eastern European public spheres). Of course, this self-limitation begs the question of how new social movements might achieve substantive goals, and I will return to this issue. Second, they are permanently concerned with the definition and re-creation of their own identity. Unlike political parties, participants do not just fight about platforms but also explore who they are and what the movement means.

Beyond these two defining features, these movements may also, as Offe explained, represent a historical third force of protest politics in Western societies (1990, pp. 233–34). The first force was the ultimately successful "liberal bourgeois" protest against the old feudal regime; the second was the social democratic protest against the victorious bourgeoisie; and the third force is the contemporary protest against the mixed capitalist outcome of the second struggle. A potential reservoir of support for new social movements may be found in the long-term trend toward postmaterialist values in Western societies (Inglehart, 1990). Unlike the preceding two protests, Offe believes that the contemporary movements possess no "comprehensive vision or institutional design for a new society" (1990, p. 234). The sheer variety in and across these movements supports Offe's contention here, though there are in fact comprehensive visions aplenty, at least among Greens.

To Laclau and Mouffe (1985), the variety of which Offe speaks is explicable in terms of the variety of oppressions generated by and in mixed capitalism, related to expertise, gender, ecology, age, and even life itself (threatened at the hands of the military), as well as social class. Subjects are formed in different ways by these different oppressions, so there is no unity of oppression of the sort that once constituted proletarians in Marxist theory. To Laclau and Mouffe, multiple oppressions translate into multiple self-defining struggles, and certainly not into class-based revolution. Revolution justified by any one oppression (such as class) can no longer command anything like majority support, and so it can only perpetuate other oppressions. Laclau and Mouffe speak, too, of the linkage of different struggles in a "radical and plural democracy," though what this means in practice is unclear (1985, p. 167). Such a democracy might, however, fit well with the idea of public spheres based on ideals of respect, recognition, open communication, public deliberation, and confrontation with state authority.

For the most part, the ends of new social movements have little to do with promoting the interests of any particular class. As such, they might seem to pose a less obvious threat to business profitability—and so the state—than do the radical movements of Offe's second force, such as labor unions and socialist parties, which have sought to limit markets and expand the welfare state. Any removal of these new movements from the realm of economics might then increase their freedom to engage in democratic experimentation. It is noteworthy that their support is drawn disproportionately from individuals involved with the growing service sector, especially the information economy (Rudig, 1985), in which class struggle often looms less large than in manufacturing.

The removal of new social movements from economics and the central functions of the state should not be overstated, however. If movement projects impinge on business profitability, they will meet business resistance. Think, for example, of demands for nuclear-free zones, day care provision, and wilderness preservation. Moreover, there are reasons that movement demands often cannot easily be met by the state: These demands frequently have a transformative, all-or-nothing character. New social movements do not seek any greater share of the economic pie, or its redistribution in certain directions, or economically insignificant policies of the kind sought by more conventional single-issue interest groups (such as antiabortionists or gun control advocates). Instead, their demands entail wholesale transformation of established ways of life. As such, they are not easily accommodated by the democratic capitalist state, except on a piecemeal and often symbolic basis, as (for example) when established political parties pay lip service to environmental values. Thus their likely future is one of continued confrontation.

New social movements can, with time, lose democratic authenticity and experience deradicalization, transformation into more traditional kinds of organization, and compromise with established institutions and parties. Vivid examples can be found in connection with the German Greens (Offe, 1990). Such developments provide grist for cynics who doubt that there is anything really new about these movements (for example, Rochon, 1990). But many "realo" Greens who are prepared to go a long way toward conventional party participation—to the extent even of entering coalitions with the Social Democrats—remain aware of the continuing need for a continued "fundi" commitment as the soul of Green politics. And deradicalization of a particular organization does not exhaust the fate of the public sphere where the organization began.

Particular public spheres and social movements may rise and fall with the importance of particular issues. For example, the European peace movement declined precipitously from its early-1980s peak along with the easing of cold-war tensions and the partial removal of nuclear missiles from European soil. Such impermanence or biodegradability puzzles some observers. Przeworski observed in a note that "social movements are an ambiguous actor under democracy, and always shortlived. . . . [They] have no institutions to direct themselves to" (1991, p. 11, n. 4). Parties, unions, and lobbies have much clearer points of entry into the state.

Yet organizational permanence is less important than it might seem in assessing the significance of new social movements. As Melucci (1989) argues regarding the movements he observed in Italy, they lead a submerged but continuous existence as social networks, only occasionally manifesting themselves in overt political action. In such movements, "one does not live to be a militant. Instead, one lives, and that is why from time to time one can be a public militant" (Melucci, 1989, p. 206). Particular mobilizations may wax and wane, but the general conditions for their emergence persist.

Organizational impermanence does, of course, have its costs. Basics may need to be reinvented time and again, for lessons learned do not accumulate. Such problems are the bane of those who think of political organization in strategic, goal-seeking terms, but to think solely in these terms may be to miss a key point. To Melucci, movement members are nomads because the "journey is considered at least as important as their intended destination" (1989, p. 205).

Given the difficulties inherent in effective compromise between new social movements and the state, one possible democratic future for industrial societies would consist of public spheres and movements in permanent confrontation with the capitalist state. Karol Soltan, for one, seems to look forward to such a future, on the grounds of the positive qualities he sees in both the capitalist state and the self-limiting movements that oppose it. As he puts it, we need both Madison and Gandhi (1992, p. 4). To those who think in strategic terms, the attractiveness of this future depends crucially on the degree to which movements can prevail against state imperatives. But even if the state usually wins, movements can create an alternative space for living and democratic politics, just as Solidarity did in very different circumstances in Poland in the early 1980s.

Public spheres feature a characteristic style of political interaction in the form of egalitarian discussion oriented to action. Their contribution to democratization, therefore, comes largely on the criterion of authenticity, although they can also contribute to the extension of the democratic franchise (by involving people otherwise excluded from conventional politics) and the scope of democratic control (in both raising novel issues and extending politics beyond the state). Public spheres also contribute to democratization because they are dynamic; institutional innovation is always on the agenda, reflected most productively in their own internal organization. Their own identity is always in the process of re-creation, and concepts such as autonomy, freedom, and democracy itself can come to be defined in new ways.[8] As I suggested in Chapter 1, if there is an important sense in which one of the goals of democracy always has to be more democracy, public spheres are exemplary democratic phenomena. Particular mobilizations may come and go, but there is no reason to mourn their loss or interpret their demise as a loss of vitality in the idea of the public sphere.

Revolution

Public spheres can flourish under relatively stable political conditions, but they can also (obviously, more rarely) engage revolutionary political action, as the recent history of Eastern Europe suggests. The politically charged circumstances of revolution offer further opportunity for democratization against the state, although in a less straightforward fashion than might at first be apparent.

Revolution is often seen in terms of struggle by some organized group against the existing state. Occasionally this may be true—of the "great" revolutions, perhaps the Chinese revolution falls most clearly into this category (especially in its 1927–49 phase). Some theorists of revolution conceptualize the phenomenon in these terms; for example, Tilly (1978) defines revolution as a situation of multiple sovereignty, or competing polities.

Much to the dismay of old regime leaders, professional revolutionaries, and (some) theorists of revolution alike, it is often the case that the old regime collapses under the weight of its own contradictions, rather than as a result of the activities of its opponents, at least in what Huntington (1968) calls the "Western" model of revolution (for example, France in 1789 and Russia in 1917). This collapse of the state leaves a vacuum in which power is "left lying in the streets." And it is here that democratization can occur, not only against the state, but also in space created by the suspension of state-related constraints that go along with the suspension of the state itself.

Hannah Arendt (1962) argues that one always finds a particular kind of institution in such spaces, which today is rarely found anywhere else. She calls this the "council system." Councils are spontaneous groupings in neighborhoods, factories, or even military units that operate by means of face-to-face discussion. Her republican councils are found in the French Revolution, the Paris Commune, the Soviets of 1917 Russia, and the Hungarian revolt of 1956, among other cases. Arendt claims that these councils always discuss essentially political matters—institutional construction, freedom, matters of principle—rather than mundane issues of social administration. If she is correct on this score, then councils purchase democratic authenticity at the expense of scope (by ruling many issues off-limits). In fact, practical administrative issues were often dealt with by councils, especially when (as in the Paris Commune) they were the only remaining political authority.

A more contemporary, but equally short lived, example of an Arendtian council system may be found in the 1989 popular uprising in Beijing. The Chinese state did not collapse, but at least for a few days, it vacated the streets of Beijing. Power was indeed left lying in the streets, though only to be picked up again in ruthless fashion. Additional examples can be found in the East European revolutions of 1989, although where the public sphere ends and the Arendtian councils begin may be hard to discern in such cases, especially given similarities in the styles of political interaction found in these two kinds of phenomena.

According to Arendt, such revolutionary cases are the only appearance of authentic politics in the modern world, as opposed to the ancient Athenian *polis*, where such politics was a more permanent fixture. Unfortunately, modern revolutionary councils have shown little staying power. They have always been overthrown by a resurgent postrevolutionary state, foreign armies, or, most insidiously, professional revolutionaries like Lenin who, paradoxically, end up fighting against only the real revolution, not the old regime. The best that councils can hope for may be relatively nonviolent, but no less fatal, incorporation into the postrevolutionary state. Experience suggests that those hoping for something more than transient democratization should not pin their faith on revolution. Nevertheless, at least in the short term, revolution does provide for the possibility of authentic democracy, and this may account for the inspirational force of revolution in the human experience, as Arendt captured so eloquently. The problem is that revolutionary democracy will find itself up against not only the old regime state but also, and more important, the postrevolutionary state.

Democratization Apart from the State

The activities of public spheres and revolutionary councils inevitably bring them into confrontation with states. But democratization can proceed in nonstate venues where such confrontation is less inevitable (although it remains possible, as I shall explain). Such venues occur in connection with self-management in the workplace and community and with the feminist redefinition of what constitutes politics. There may be additional such venues, but these are the ones I will concentrate on here.

Feminism

Feminism has many faces, not all of which involve rethinking what democracy can mean and where it might be sought. But some of them do. Minimally, a liberal feminism of equal political rights for women simply asks liberal democracy to extend its reach, or its effective franchise. Among feminist political theorists, Anne Phillips (1991) sees many positive qualities in representative democracy and the basic forms of the liberal state, albeit wanting to make them more inclusive. She argues for a quota system for representation within political parties to guarantee women a certain percentage of seats in legislatures, a policy already practiced in Scandinavian social democratic parties and in 1993 adopted by the British Labour

Party. She also favors the facilitation of female participation in (conventional) politics through government provision of day care for children, parental leave, and so forth. Such measures require an interventionist but otherwise quite ordinary state.

Phillips justifies parliamentary quotas for women through reference to principles of political equality (1993, p. 99). She distances herself (see pp. 96–98) from Iris Young's (1990a, 1990b) more radical proposal that women should not be represented as equal citizens but, rather, as a group. Young believes that women, like other oppressed groups, should have not just guaranteed representation but also guaranteed consideration in policy-making through veto power over policies affecting them, along with government sponsorship of their organization. At the end of this chapter, I will return to Young's proposal for group representation. Suffice it to note for the moment that the proposals by both Phillips and Young are oriented to women's representation in the capitalist state (though more recently Young has looked beyond the state). Although potentially advancing women's policy agenda, such integration is, as I have already stated, fraught with peril for any democratizing endeavor. Moreover, entry into the state can deplete the women's movement of activists who might otherwise push for more radical changes. Something of this sort may have happened in Australia, where women have been more successful in influencing government than they have in most other countries and where "femocrats" are an established part of government (Sawer, 1991, p. 260).

Feminism is also home to radical challenges to received political concepts and categories (see Pateman, 1989). To radical feminists, the liberal guarantee of equal political rights irrespective of gender does not go far enough so long as there is sexual inequality ingrained in private life. The feminist slogan "the personal is political" refers to the degree to which power pervades all realms of life (including the patriarchal family) and so rejects the liberal attempt to establish a rigid demarcation between public life and a private realm that is no concern of the state—or of politics more generally. Minimally, this rejection demands state intervention to release the "private constraints on public involvement" (Phillips, 1991, p. 96), to which women are subjected by the domestic division of labor, and thereby more effectively extend the democratic franchise to women. More radically, the implication might be that "democratic control has to be extended . . . to the circumstances of everyday life" (Rowbotham, 1986, p. 86). Based on the criteria of democratization established in Chapter 1, scope as well as franchise becomes an issue.

What does this extension mean in practice? At issue might be the transformation of personal interactions through changes in the sexual division of labor or the structure of the family, and the institutionalization of a feminist ethic of care and nurture as opposed to competitive striving, in social life, economics, and politics alike. Jane Mansbridge claims that feminists want "to release from the realm of taboo, for incorporation into political discourse, a host of experiences and referents related to intimate personal connection" (1993, pp. 368–69). Such an incorporation would mean questioning the received notions of interest and power that pervade conventional (strategic) thinking about politics. An ethic of care dissolves the concept of "interest," and power becomes power *with* rather than power *over*. Sympathy with the needs of others would also facilitate effective democratic deliberation (Mansbridge, 1993, pp. 358–59).

What else might this kind of transformation mean for democracy? The model of female morality propounded by Gilligan (1982) and associated maternalist thinking about citizenship (for example, Ruddick, 1980) would suggest that political interaction feature concern for the concrete needs of particular individuals, as opposed to the abstract rights of hypothetical individuals found in male-ordered morality. But not all feminists are maternalists. Mary Dietz (1985), for one, argues that the kind of loving and caring mothering that maternalists see as a model for political relationships could be a model for benevolent despotism as easily as for democracy.

In regard to political theory, feminism's main contributions to the rethinking of democracy have so far come in the form of critiques, especially of liberalism. Accordingly, Carole Pateman (1988) interpreted the history of liberalism in terms of the struggle by men to impose an oppressive sexual contract on women even while they sought freedom from the state. Susan Moller Okin (1979) and others exposed the degree to which classical and contemporary works in political theory are pervaded by unwarranted sexual presumptions. Young (1990b, pp. 123–24) revealed the essentially male qualities of impartial public-spirited citizenship proposed by participatory democrats such as Benjamin Barber (1984). The product of these critiques is not a feminist model of democracy that can be summarized as easily as (say) direct democracy or participatory democracy or pluralist democracy. For the moment, feminist democratic theory consists mostly of prefaces to a model (or models) of democracy.[9]

To focus on political theory would be, however, to miss the most significant feminist contributions to the theory and practice of democratic innovation. The history of the women's movement over the past three decades reveals an interesting record of democratic innovation informing, and in turn being informed by, theoretical reflection. Carmen Sirianni (1993) provides a useful accounting of this history in the United States. The women's movement coming out of the 1960s was generally committed to radical participatory democracy of the sort that had been espoused by Students for a Democratic Society and the Student Non-Violent Coordinating Committee. Participatory democracy was especially attractive to collectives organizing, for example, health centers and battered-women shelters, to counteract the power of professional (often male) expertise. This commitment continues. Dietz added that feminist politics often features "spontaneous gatherings and marches, diverse and multitudinous action groups, face-to-face assemblies, consensus decision making, nonhierarchical power structures, open speech and debate" (1987, p. 17).

This kind of relatively open communication and discursive interaction found in the women's movement may not necessarily be distinguishable from that found in other new social movements. If one sees the political contribution of feminism in these terms, there is a danger, as Dietz recognizes, even though she herself takes such a position, that "feminist political consciousness" will be reduced to "democratic consciousness" (1987, p. 16). This reduction might be a problem for feminist identity, though not for democrats.

Feminists themselves have, nonetheless, come to question the desirability of participatory democracy. For instance, Phillips wonders whether feminists have given up too easily on liberal democracy, given that most women lack the time to attend the interminable meetings required by participatory democracy (1992, pp. 74–75). As long ago as the early 1970s, a feminist reaction against the aggressive male domination of purportedly radical democratic groups led to the formation of alternative consciousness-raising groups in which women could find "mutually supportive participation" and share feelings and experiences (Sirianni, 1993, p. 287). The hope was, and still is in some quarters, that such groups would prefigure broader political change (Rowbotham, 1986, pp. 104–5).

The "tyranny of structurelessness" found in both participatory democracy and consciousness-raising groups came in for early criticism from Jo Freeman (1975). To Freeman, structurelessness provided cover for informal but powerful elites of women, especially those with time on their hands, who were, in the name of solidarity, beyond criticism. Especially in mass meetings, an atmosphere of conformity often reigned, and dissidents were embarrassed into silence. The "personal is political" slogan could be used to subject all areas of a woman's life to public scrutiny. Jean Elshtain (1981) raised the specter of totalitarianism in this context. Not surprisingly, a reaction against structurelessness became established in the women's movement and, with it, formalization and institutionalization in the form of boards, hierarchies, and full-time staff (Sirianni, 1993, p. 297).

Such institutionalization does not necessarily mimic standard bureaucratic or liberal democratic political organization. For example, the U.S. National Women's Studies Association in the 1980s developed a system of group representation in which voting was weighted in favor of caucuses recognized by the organization's hierarchy. The justification was that oppressed groups have unique perspectives on issues affecting them, which an ethic of care demands be recognized and heard. Given the privileges now associated with victimhood, the caucuses proliferated. Some did not look very much like victims, for example, the caucus of Women's Studies Program Administrators. An ethos of special care for victims, legitimation of the special perspective of the oppressed, and guilt by the nonoppressed together worked to privilege some speakers and repress disagreement (Sirianni, 1993, pp. 301–3). In 1990 the group representation system exploded in the face of mounting demands by the Women of Color caucus which the majority eventually refused to meet, leading to resignation of that caucus (Sirianni, 1993, pp. 303–4).

A cynic might interpret this movement history as a series of object lessons in how not to pursue democracy. However, as I argued in Chapter 1, democracy is an open-ended project, and the democratic life consists largely of searching for democracy. In this light, the women's movement has led a democratic life of intertwined experimentation and critical reflection, and along the way, some experiments have necessarily been abandoned.

Some lessons have been learned. In particular, the hazards of structurelessness, expanded definitions of politics, and group representation have become apparent. More precisely, complete structurelessness, unrestricted definitions of politics, and uncontrolled group representation have been tried and found wanting. Recall that in Chapter 1, I warned against pursuing any one of the three dimensions of democratization unrestricted by respect for the other two. Mistakes on all three dimensions have been made in the U.S. women's movement: Complete structurelessness represents authenticity at all costs, and with the cover it provided for the emergence of informal but powerful elites, one of those costs was in terms of democratic franchise. The concomitant repression of dissent in the name of solidarity meant that authenticity itself was ultimately lost. Insistence that everything "personal is political" represented scope at all costs, which, as Elshtain noted, pointed toward totalitarianism and (in my terms) a wholesale loss of democratic authenticity. For its part, uncontrolled group representation represents franchise at all costs. The presentation of the demands of oppressed and thus privileged groups in nonnegotiable terms and group perspectives as impenetrable to nonmembers makes authentic democratic interchange impossible and reduces the scope of issues amenable to democratic resolution.

It is unfortunate, albeit understandable, that some of these excesses were followed by reactions that went to the opposite extreme. For example, structurelessness was widely abandoned in favor of bureaucratization. The moral of this history, therefore, is not that bureaucracy, a narrow definition of politics, and individualistic representation all should be restored wholesale. Rather, it is that if structurelessness, the politicization of the personal, and group representation are to be pursued—and there are good democratic reasons for pursuing all three—this pursuit should bear in mind that franchise, scope, and authenticity should never be sacrificed for the sake of any purported democratic benefit. Thirty years of feminism also yield some more positive lessons for democrats, especially in regard to how to go about searching for a deeper democracy, if not always in terms of the proposals that this search has unearthed.

Workplace Democracy

As a venue for democratization apart from the state, workplace democracy might seem to have little in common with feminism (although self-consciously feminist workplaces organized by women do exist). But they share a desire to politicize areas of life considered by liberals to be private and properly not the subject of political action and so extend the scope of democracy. Liberals should be doubly uneasy with workplace democracy because it impinges on the prerogatives of shareholders in private firms and thus on the right to private property that liberals hold so dear. A model of workplace democracy in which workers are the owners would remove this second liberal objection.

The basic idea of workplace democracy is quite simple: Given that work is so central to the lives of workers, they should have the same right to its democratic control as they do to democratic control in (state) politics. We may set aside for the moment the problem that actual citizen control in state politics may not be very extensive. Dahl (1985) explicitly treats the workplace as a polity, so that the same arguments that apply to democratization of any political system also apply to the workplace. It follows that the same variety of models of democracy advanced for political systems in general is also found in models of workplace democracy. So Carter finds analogues of elitist, liberal, pluralist, and participatory models in various proposals for industrial democracy (1989, pp. 285–88).

Workplace democracy does, then, cover a variety of possibilities, including profit sharing, employee ownership, employee control, and joint employee–management control. Kiloh contends that of the various possibilities, only worker self-management deserves to be called "true" democracy, for the other types can and do proceed with little input from employees in decision making (and so involve only restricted franchise within the firm) (1986, p. 38). I believe she is right, and so I will focus on self-management here. However, even self-management allows for a variety of forms of democracy, from the representative to the participatory.

This variety does not mean that there is complete, or even substantial, freedom of choice when it comes to organizing workplace democracy. There are at least three kinds of constraints that limit the possibilities here, two pertaining to the state and one to the market.

The first state-related constraint arises inasmuch as workplace democracy is intended to carry over into democratization of the polity at large. From John Stuart Mill's view of "developmental" democracy to Carole Pateman's (1970) participatory prescriptions and beyond, the intent of workplace democrats has rarely been restricted to the intrinsic desirability of this kind of democracy. Instead, the expectation has been that participation in the management of their workplace will make individuals more efficacious citizens generally, thus opening up possibilities for the further democratization of the political system—and the state. Such *state* democratization may conflict with the imperatives facing states introduced in the previous chapter, and so any workplace democratization that facilitates it may be problematic, too. As long as workplace democracy remains confined to a few isolated experiments (which is universally the case in Western countries; the biggest operation is Mondragon in the Basque region of Spain, with around twenty thousand participants), this constraint will not come into play. It will do so only if the movement should expand. The

Yugoslav experience involving more universal economic self-management might suggest that (despite Pateman's hopes) workplace democracy does not produce a particularly virtuous citizenry. But before its collapse amid ethnic warfare, the Yugoslav state was in fact more open to democratic pressure than were its east European counterparts.

A second state-related constraint arises inasmuch as the state itself *is* the workplace for large numbers of people. Public employment in advanced capitalist nations comprises between 20 and 40 percent of total employment, a fact that seems to have been missed by most advocates of workplace democracy, who confine their attentions to the private sector. The problem here for democratic theorists is that democratization of government agencies might lead to their operation in the interests of their employees, rather than the interests of the (democratic?) state that they are supposed to serve. Yet are these large numbers of workers to be denied the developmental experiences of their counterparts in the private sector? The more practical problem inherent in the pursuit of workplace democracy in the public sector is that it might produce outcomes or pressures that conflict with the need of governments to maintain a favorable climate for business investment and to operate an effective welfare state, and again one should expect the latter imperatives to come out on top in such a clash. One cannot point to any examples here, because this sort of democratization has never been consciously tried in government agencies. But one suspects that state purposes would be most easily embedded in hierarchical and centralized organizations.

Workplace democracy in the private sector faces somewhat different kinds of constraints, for firms (at least those facing an environment of actual or potential competition) must be efficient in order to survive. The peremptory goal is efficiency. No democratic firm (such as a workers' cooperative) can choose to pursue equality within the organization, social justice in society at large, environmental quality, cultural distinctiveness, or any other value if that pursuit has a sufficiently negative impact on efficiency to jeopardize organizational survival. In this context, capitalist firms may have options available to them that democratic firms do not. So, for example, the tree-planting cooperatives that once flourished in the Pacific Northwest of the United States were undermined in the 1980s by capitalist competitors. These competitors' main advantage was that they could employ illegal immigrants at extremely low rates of pay and so undercut bids from the cooperatives for reforestation contracts (for details, see Mackie, 1994).

Within this constraint—that efficiency must be pursued and achieved—it may nevertheless be the case that a form of democracy is possible in which decisions about how to operate, given the need to be efficient, can be made collectively. In this light, the prospects for the democratic firm were explored by Bowles and Gintis (1993), who are cautiously optimistic on this issue. They identified several reasons that democratic firms might be more efficient than capitalist ones, the most important of which is that workers can monitor the quality of one another's labor inputs, which is notoriously difficult for managers, especially in team production (for further argument on this score, see Schweickart, 1993, pp. 78–125). On the other hand, Bowles and Gintis admitted that there are efficiency disadvantages to industrial democracy, the most significant being the risk aversion of individuals becoming embodied in investment decisions. Economists have established that efficiency requires risk neutrality. In capitalist firms, risk taking and innovation can be enforced by wealthy owners (more willing to take risks) and financial institutions. Democratic firms are less inclined to grow beyond the point at which economies of scale are realized, because further growth might increase total profits (the capitalist's interest) but not profits per worker. Other things being equal, democratic firms should therefore be smaller than capitalist firms (Schweickart, 1993, pp. 96–98).

The critics of industrial democracy, for their part, could claim that the real-world scarcity of democratic firms is testimony to their inefficiency. Such firms are, for example, reluctant to lay off workers when times are bad. Bowles and Gintis (1993) reply that worlds of both predominantly democratic and predominantly capitalist firms are evolutionarily stable but that it is hard to get from one world to the other.

Proponents and critics of industrial democracy alike often treat "firms" in an undifferentiated fashion. However, it might be important to look at exactly what the firm is doing and producing, for some operations may be more amenable to democratic organization than others. Moreover, within the firm some activities are more readily organized along democratic lines than others. Thus anyone interested in democratic innovation in private firms would do well to focus on the kinds of activities that can be democratized within the confines of the efficiency constraint. For example, when there is considerable uncertainty as to which procedure will best achieve an agreed-upon goal, egalitarian discussion may prove useful. This might take the form of a "democracy of the experts," be they surgeons or nuclear engineers. When the tasks of an organizational unit are highly variable or its environment is uncertain, information may be more effectively generated and utilized if interpersonal relationships are egalitarian. Such arguments for organizational democracy parallel those made on behalf of (liberal) democracy by theorists such as Popper (1966) and Dahl (1989, pp. 69–70), who believe that public policy is so complex that no individual or small group can possess anything like the quantity of knowledge needed for effective problem solving. It is easy to see how such arguments might apply to units within firms (such as a design team) and somewhat less easy to see how they might apply to the overall structure of the firm.

Community Politics

Community politics occupies a somewhat ill-defined and ambiguous position in relation to the classification of sites for democratization, for it can occur in connection with, against, or apart from the state. Essentially, com-

munity politics involves localized "collective provision of services to a particular area or group" (Cochrane, 1986, p. 52), either by the group itself
or by the government's response to group pressure. The area in question
can be as small as a neighborhood or as large as a region. The connection
to service provision helps distinguish community politics from locally constituted public spheres of the sort discussed earlier and from organizations
that operate as interest groups in liberal democratic politics, although in
particular cases the distinctions here may be quite blurred.

Such projects may sometimes be sponsored by governments, as with
the Model Cities Program in the late 1960s in the United States, or the
Community Development Projects in Great Britain in the 1970s. State-
sponsored projects of this sort involve an implicit recognition by the state
of its own failure in community management; therefore, community self-
management is tried as an alternative. These projects can be more than
simple extensions of state administration, because they can soon turn
against their sponsors. If they do, the sponsors might simply abolish
them—as happened with the two programs just mentioned. Thus unsur-
prisingly, state-sponsored community politics is by no means immune from
the usual state-related constraints on political innovation. The same may
be said for projects that are initiated by or in the community but that then
develop links with states, either as conduits for the provision of government services (such as welfare, education, or health care) or as recipients
of government grants.

The prospects for democratization in state-sanctioned community
politics may be greatest in areas where the political control of the state is
weak and the local economy is a shambles. In industrial societies, these
conditions are best met in low-income inner-city areas, often populated
by ethnic minorities. Some rural areas, such as Appalachia in the United
States, may also fall into this category (see Gaventa, Smith, and Willingham, 1990). There is substantial freedom for democratic innovation
in such cases, but only if the following conditions are met. First, the fund-
ing required by the projects should be small in relation to the budgets of
the national or local government in question. Second, the demands on
conventional (liberal democratic) politics generated by the projects should
not have excessive negative implications for the basic functions of states,
national or local. For example, if a community demands control over land-
use planning in its vicinity that impinges on the profitability of the real
estate industry or the attractiveness of a city to business investors, there is
every reason to expect economic necessity to make itself felt via state action
to curb the community in question.

Given the problems—indeed, contradictions—inherent in the association of community self-control with the state, it is not surprising that
proponents of self-control often advocate democratization either against
or apart from the state. Community democratization against the state was
advocated forcefully in the United States by Saul Alinsky (1969) and actively pursued by his followers. The Alinsky model involves the introduc-

tion of an outside organizer into a community, which is to find its very identity through subsequent struggle with the established political power or some other identifiable enemy. Once that identity has been achieved, the organizer can then bow out. Judged by their results in achieving tangible goals or changing the way governments are run, the Alinsky projects of the 1960s may not have been very successful (Cochrane, 1986, p. 55). However, from the perspective of democratization, the actual impact on government policy may be less important than the creation of identity and efficacy that goes along with community mobilization. In other words, the community may be better able to control itself even if it has little impact on local or national government policy. The fact that Alinsky's movement saw the achievement of policy goals as vital to its credibility may help explain its eventual loss of confidence and impact.

Community politics seen in terms of democratization apart from the state faces no such difficulties. The idea here is for a community to provide itself with economic activity and/or political self-control, effectively creating its own sphere of social, economic, and political life. Given the reach of the state in contemporary industrial societies, there are major difficulties involved here, although, attempts have been made. In an urban context, Hess (1979) chronicled the life and times of a community experiment in the Adams-Morgan district of Washington, D.C. The idea was for participants to become as self-sufficient as possible, engaging in production and exchange within the community (even producing food in this unlikely urban location). Eventually this experiment could not withstand the long reach of the state. This reach was not directly coercive but, rather, came in the form of some of the project's more able members being unable to resist the temptation of government grants.

Murray Bookchin's (1986) "libertarian municipalism" is an anarchist program for urban community democratization, which he believes is the appropriate starting point for a wholesale democratization of society from the bottom up. Libertarian municipalism involves civic control of both politics and economics in self-governing local communities. The state's power might be confronted at some point, but the essential task is to build a political structure that acts as an alternative to the state and an economic structure that bypasses the capitalist marketplace.

Community politics apart from the state can occur in more rural settings, too. Here, the (mixed) achievements of intentional communes (of which the longest lasting have some religious dimension) would be less interesting than projects organized in connection with established communities, were it not for the rarity of the latter. If there are cultural differences between a rural population and the urban majority, self-sufficiency might look like a more plausible project. In this connection there have been a number of proposals to decrease the dependence of communities of North American Native peoples on the core of white society—and its state—through the development of renewable resource–based economies under local political control (see Berger, 1985; Dryzek and Young, 1985).

But the state's reach generally extends into even the most remote community, making it difficult to achieve even partial disengagement from commercial capitalism and from state-sponsored economic development.

Democracy Through the Arrangement of Exclusions

Deeper democratization of the capitalist state is not an impossibility, but the circumstances in which it can be pursued fruitfully and profoundly are quite rare. More ordinary circumstances allow only marginal democratization. Venues for democratization that try to stand apart from the state are not always completely beyond the reach of these constraints, but the opportunities they present for a deeper democracy are often more substantial. The most secure of all are public spheres whose very identity is defined by opposition to the state, providing that they can resist the temptations of entry into conventional state politics.

Should democrats therefore ignore the state? To do so would be a major error, for the way that interest representation is organized in the state is crucial to the degree of democracy attainable in realms that stand against or apart from the state.

My argument here begins with a taxonomy. On one dimension, states can adopt either exclusive or inclusive patterns of interest representation. Inclusive representation is open to interests defined on any basis: class, gender, ethnicity, religion, ideology, or anything else. Exclusive representation means that certain specified interests are guaranteed access to policy determination and that other interests are left out. On a second dimension, representation can be organized either actively or passively. *Active* refers to public policy consciously designed to recognize and then include or exclude particular interests. *Passive* indicates indifference to the identity of interests included or excluded. Combining these two dimensions yields a two-by-two matrix with four cells, as shown in Table 3.1.

Three of these cells describe kinds of states that actually exist. The fourth (active-inclusive) contains patterns of representation recently advanced by, among others, Joshua Cohen and Joel Rogers (1992) and Iris Young (1990a, 1990b), which I will discuss shortly. I believe democrats should favor the passive-exclusive cell, but for reasons different from those traditionally advanced on behalf of exclusion.

Historically, an emphasis on exclusion for civic benefit has been central

Table 3.1.   Patterns of Interest Representation in Capitalist States

	Inclusive	Exclusive
Active	Associative democracy, group representation	Authoritarian liberalism
Passive	Pluralism	Corporatism

to the theory and practice of republicanism. Republics in ancient Greece and Rome, Renaissance Italy, and late-eighteenth-century America could flourish as a result of their exclusion and exploitation of slaves, noncitizens, and women. Republican citizenship and public freedom for the few was bought at the expense of excluding the many. In the republican tradition, exclusion benefited only those included in the state, which was the only recognized venue for politics. Indeed, in classical times politics was, by definition, discourse about public affairs engaged by citizens of the *polis* or republic.

Among republican theorists in recent times, Hannah Arendt defends exclusion most explicitly, believing that republican politics could be for only the self-selected few. In terms of the three criteria of democratization I established in Chapter 1, she purchases authenticity at the expense of franchise (and possibly scope, as she does not believe that republics can or should discuss social issues). Arendt also recognizes that a politics of republican virtue is no longer possible in the modern state (Isaac, 1994), and the state-related constraints I have enumerated would lead me to agree. However, against Arendt I would argue that it is possible to achieve democratic authenticity without sacrificing the dimension of franchise. The democracy that results is the mirror image of classical republicanism: It is practiced among the excluded many rather than the included few. And counterintuitively, this democracy is facilitated by well-arranged exclusion.

To see why, consider the perils for democracy of an inclusive state in capitalist society. If a state is "passively inclusive" along lines portrayed by midcentury U.S. pluralists such as David Truman and Robert Dahl (before his later change of mind), there will be little space for an *autonomous* public sphere, for all political movements will be converted into interest groups—and accorded a place at the bargaining table. The policy product is at best bargained compromise with no systematic bias for or against any particular groups. Even here, there are two problems.

First is the loss of public authority and commitment to discourse regarding common ends bemoaned by republicans such as Arendt, Sheldon Wolin (1960), and Theodore Lowi (1979). All principles are converted to interests, all on the same level; so (for example) a commitment to wilderness preservation or social justice is on a par with a commitment to private financial profit. All can be bargained away. Second, the automatic constraints on state action that I have enumerated mean that the policies favored by some interests just have to be vetoed by and in the state. Moreover, as pluralists such as Dahl and Lindblom eventually recognized, against the background of a capitalist market system, the pluralist game is always biased in favor of business interests. Other interests are likely to be bought off cheaply with symbolic rewards, or co-opted. For example, as I write, environmentalists have unprecedented access to the Clinton White House, and prominent alumni of environmental organizations occupy key policymaking positions. But policy has hardly changed—which should come as no surprise, given the imperatives dictated by the transnational political economy. Meanwhile, the oppositional politics of environmentalism and the public sphere that it constitutes is impoverished. Arguably, these were in better shape (even though the environment was not in better hands) when Reagan was president and James Watt was secretary of the interior in the early 1980s.

A more actively inclusive state would generate more subtle hazards. The most explicit recent proposal for such a state was made by Cohen and Rogers (1992), whose model of associative democracy requires the state's creation and nurturing of organized interests. With Madison's "mischiefs of faction" and more recent criticisms of the destructive role of interest groups in U.S. politics in mind, Cohen and Rogers explained that the "right" kind of associations "do not arise naturally" (p. 426). Thus a state not beholden to any particular interests must engineer, certify, and promote interest associations and incorporate them into the deliberative life of the state. Legislation and other state action could, for example, reduce obstacles to unionization, centralize wage negotiations, and promote the accountability of group leadership to group members. The idea here is not just to tame already powerful interests, for "where manifest inequalities in political representation exist, associative democracy recommends promoting the organized representation of presently excluded interests" (Cohen and Rogers, 1992, p. 425).[10]

Such sponsorship was endorsed by Iris Young in her commentary on Cohen and Rogers's piece. Relating their proposal to her own earlier advocacy of group representation, Young stated that

> the state could decide to promote the self-organization of members of oppressed groups where such organization is weak, or to provide greater resources to existing associations representing oppressed or disadvantaged groups, and to create compensatory political forms to ensure that such groups have an equal voice in agenda setting and policy formation. (1992, p. 532)

Young (1990a, 1990b) defended group representation on the grounds that the ideal of universal and equal citizenship is a cover for continued oppression. In practice, members of oppressed groups do not have equal representation; they experience the world in different ways, and she believes that this difference should be recognized. Subsuming such groups under equal citizenship effectively represses their claims in a system in which the dominant perspective (white, male, and wealthy) masquerades as universal. Young believes that justice demands the political recognition and representation of group rights.

Which groups should be recognized and granted representation in these terms? Who decides? Young believes that "a public must be constituted to decide which groups deserve specific representation in decision making procedures" (1990b, p. 133). Let me suggest that the location of this "public" is crucial. If it is located in or sponsored by the state, there will be an obvious and immediate material advantage to having one's oppressed status sanctioned by the state. The result might be competitive bidding for victim status—hardly the condition of a vigorous civil society. Lest this be considered far-fetched, I would argue that such a condition often characterizes the internal politics of many North American colleges and universities, where administrators play the part of an actively "inclusive state" and the result is a pathological culture of victimhood. The history of group representation sponsored and ratified by the hierarchy of the National Women's Studies Association that I discussed in the section on feminism should also give advocates of group representation pause for thought. There, groups claiming oppressed status could use norms of care and respect for the privileged status of the victim to silence opposition. Democratic franchise may be extended, but authenticity is lost.

Rather than seek sponsorship and certification by administrative hierarchy, such groups would do better to assert and negotiate their identity, rights, and unique perspectives in civil society. With no state ratification in view, such negotiation would be less likely to freeze or falsely essentialize group identities and to distance group leadership from the constituency it purports to represent. The kind of interest certification proposed by Cohen and Rogers and endorsed by Young requires a state guided by the political theory of inclusion and deliberation but otherwise neutral across interests. This is not a kind of state that does or can exist in capitalist societies, for reasons I have discussed at length.

For their part, exclusive states can inadvertently create flourishing public spheres. Thus exclusion does not necessarily violate the "franchise" element of democratization; people and groups may be excluded from the state but not from democratic politics. The standard explanation of the rise of new social movements in Western Europe in the 1970s and 1980s is that they had to invent an unconventional oppositional politics because they were excluded from access to state power (Kitschelt, 1988). More truly pluralist state arrangements would incorporate, transform, and deradicalize such movements by incorporating them as interest groups or perhaps as factions of established political parties.

A look at the recent history of Eastern Europe shows that one of the inadvertent legacies of Stalinism was the creation of flourishing oppositional public spheres (see Bunce, 1992). In Poland, for example, Solidarity flourished as a beacon of democracy in the early 1980s precisely because it was excluded from the state and had to operate as a parallel polity. In Czechoslovakia, individuals associated with Charter 77 and, later, the Civic Forum defined their own politics of republican courage. Eastern European experience indicates, too, that if exclusion leans too far toward authoritarian repression, the public sphere can be severely squashed, if not eliminated. Clearly, the precise form taken by the exclusive state matters a great deal here. Only halfhearted Stalinism allows an oppositional public sphere; the real thing is less forgiving.

When it comes to capitalist societies, recent history reveals the availability of two main kinds of exclusive state, the authoritarian-liberal and the corporatist. Authoritarian liberalism is a term generally used to describe a market-oriented reform strategy in East European and Latin American contexts, the idea being that the transitional pain associated with marketization can be imposed most easily by a relatively authoritarian state, for the masses lack the requisite patience (Brucan, 1992). However, the term can be applied directly to the dominant political–economic currents in the Anglo-American world in the 1980s and beyond.

The United States, United Kingdom, Canada, Australia, and New Zealand all had, to varying degrees, governments committed to free-market ideas inspired by economists such as Milton Friedman and F. A. von Hayek. The kind of state to which such ideas point sits uneasily with democracy (Hayek is quite explicit in his preference for market liberalism over democracy, and Friedman had no objections when dictators such as General Augusto Pinochet in Chile took his advice and employed his students). In Britain, the Thatcherite state combined the rhetoric of economic decentralization with the reality of political centralization. Britain in the 1980s and early 1990s saw the central government assert its domination over local government, movement toward a national police force, attacks on the freedom of association of unions and others, the extension of secrecy in government, curbs on the freedom of the press to report the doings and wrongdoings of government, restrictions on the rights of defendants in the legal system, the transformation of the welfare state from a universalistic expression of social solidarity to means-tested (and mean-spirited) poor relief, and the deliberate creation of a more unequal society. Perhaps most significant for the prospects for democracy, British society became much more aggressively individualistic. The Thatcherites succeeded in breaking the power of the collectivism of the left, especially through attacks on the trade unions. But they were no less successful in their assault on the collectivism of organic, "one nation" Toryism in their own party. In 1987 Margaret Thatcher proclaimed famously that there is no such thing as society. The "mean season" (Block et al., 1987) in United States politics in the same period was subdued by comparison.

The other available model of the exclusive state in capitalist society is corporatism. Despite historical connections with Mussolini, corporatism has been pursued most comprehensively in social democracies such as Norway, Austria, Germany, and the Netherlands. Observers have debated the essence of corporatism at length (see Cawson, 1986), but a characterization in terms of tripartite power sharing among government, business, and labor will suffice here. Business and labor are organized in monopolistic encompassing bodies or federations that speak for these sectors as wholes. The essence of the corporatist compromise is that labor promises not to make life difficult for business through strikes and excessive wage demands, and business promises to support a redistributive welfare state and interventionist policies geared to full employment. Government, for its part, nurtures the compromise and participates in policy development. Policies are implemented by all three parties (for further details, see Schmitter and Lehmbruch, 1979). Corporatist states therefore play an active and inclusive role in ensuring that the representation of business and labor is encompassing, but they are passively exclusive when it comes to other interests. The only exception here is Norway, where environmental organizations such as Friends of the Earth have gained a place at the corporatist table, though only in return for their moderation.

There are several reasons to prefer the social democractic corporatist state over its exclusive alternatives here. First, corporatist states appear to be more effective problem solvers than their authoritarian liberal counterparts. There is no need to make comparative empirical assessments across every policy issue area here: All we need do is look at the criterion that the proponents and engineers of the authoritarian liberal state have themselves used to justify their efforts. This criterion is, of course, economic growth. One might question its ultimate desirability (especially in an ecological light). But if we look at the comparative performance of those Anglo-American states that pursued authoritarian liberalism in the 1980s with those European countries that did not, the evidence is clear: Economic growth since 1979 has been greater in the latter. Australia, Canada, New Zealand, the United Kingdom, and the United States all turned in a growth performance below the OECD's average for the 1979–92 period.[11] Booms in the mid-1980s under Thatcher and Reagan proved by the early 1990s to have been speculative bubbles, purchased by deep recessions preceding and following the illusory boom. Corporatist states also do better in regard to indicators such as unemployment rates and income equality (Freeman, 1989; Pekkarin, Pohjola, and Rowthorn, 1992) and perhaps even environmental protection (Janicke, 1994).

For our purposes, this issue of policy effectiveness is less important than the ramifications of the two kinds of exclusive liberal capitalist state for democracy. When it comes to democracy *within* the state, corporatism is a more democratic form of state organization than authoritarian liberalism, simply because it allows representation by and for labor, which authoritarian liberalism does not. Moreover, corporatism is more likely to produce the material equality that facilitates democratic franchise. Freeman concluded that corporatism is more intrinsically democratic than pluralism because of its greater possibility for state managers to exercise countervailing power against financial markets (although the internationalization of these markets may undermine his claim here) (1989, pp. 284–85).

In regard to democracy beyond the state, the exclusions generated by social democratic corporatism are more benign than those of authoritarian liberalism. The reason is that corporatism simply excludes individuals and groups, whereas authoritarian liberalism attacks groups and promotes and produces economically rationalistic, aggressively individualistic behavior, which is devastating for democratic politics (be it inside or outside the state). *Homo economicus* is not good for democracy. I develop this point at length in Chapter 5. Suffice it to say for the moment that democracy is not easily saved from economic rationality in the shadow of the authoritarian liberal state.

The shadow of social democratic corporatism is less deadly to democracy beyond the state. Experience shows that corporatism is compatible with a flourishing civil society, whose organizations are ignored rather than attacked by the state. As I indicated earlier, the standard explanation for the rise of new social movements in Western Europe is the exclusive form of interest representation adopted under corporatism. Feminists, ecologists, urban activists, peace movements, and others must look first to civil society rather than the state. Such movements can be found in authoritarian liberal societies too, but their existence is more precarious in societies increasingly divided into a growing and resentful underclass, on the one hand, and a majority for whom individual material reward is the main currency, on the other.

In short, there is much to be said for a state organized on social democratic corporatist lines and a parallel polity in which democratization against and apart from the state can be sought. But would not such an arrangement consign democracy to a realm of irrelevance in a society in which all important decisions were made in a state guided mostly by forces emanating from the capitalist political economy? Those who view civil society as a politics of identity rather than strategy, as a postmodern circus of endless democratic play, or as a place where people can live "as if" they were in a free society might not worry here. However, the continuing inability by democratic forces in civil society to affect what the state does might prove demoralizing. Thus the issue arises as to how the democracy of public spheres can assert itself in affecting the actions of the state while retaining its critical distance from the state. I will return to this vital issue in Chapter 7.

Democratization in capitalist societies does, then, involve a subtle interplay of civil society and the state, exclusion and inclusion. The destination is hard to predict; more important is interrogating the observable dialectics of democratization, with a view to keeping the conversation alive. Democracy is, as I noted at the outset, a quintessentially open-ended project.

4

Democracy Versus the International System

Although previous chapters have touched on the impact of international forces on the possibilities for democracy, I have not yet detailed these forces. This is an oversight shared by most advocates of democracy throughout history, who have assumed that the proper locus for democracy is some territorially bounded society and that one can address the prospects for democracy without attending to external factors. But international forces have always had a major impact on the political possibilities within states, mainly because states have always had to try to stay afloat in a dangerous world. Even the relatively self-contained city states of ancient Greece had to contend with aggressive neighbors, not to mention sundry Persians and Macedonians.

In the last few decades, the case for attention to the international dimension of democracy has redoubled with the increasing intensity of interactions—especially economic ones—across national boundaries. These interactions call into question the definition of communities whose politics we might analyze or whose democratization we might want to advocate. States, too, may be becoming less sovereign and autonomous. If the democratic ideal has always entailed the notion of a self-governing, territorially contained community, the increasing intensity and density of transnational interactions involving power, wealth, and persons will dispute the very identity of that community and so require the rethinking of that ideal (for observations on this score, see Connolly, 1991; Held, 1991, pp. 199, 204–5; Khilnani, 1991, p. 201). The implication here is not that states organized on a territorial basis are completely obsolete. Indeed, a state organized on this basis will persist as long as the residents of a territory care about attracting economic activity to it.

The upshot of these developments is not likely to be smooth progress toward a happily democratic transnational political order, for economic transnationalization imposes major constraints on the possibilities for democracy both within and across state boundaries. In particular, capital mobility means that the first priority of policymakers must be to attract investment and prevent capital flight. Popular control of policy cannot be allowed to interfere with this imperative. However, I shall argue that economic transnationalization also opens up additional room for democratization that transcends boundaries. But before turning to contemporary transnationalization (economic and otherwise), I want to consider the impact of some much older external forces on domestic democracy. These forces relate to the need of any state to survive in a potentially hostile world; they have existed for as long as states have; and they are still with us.

State Survival in the International System

In Chapter 2 I examined at some length the aspects of domestic political–economic structure that severely constrain the possibilities for democracy in the vicinity of the state. The constraints I described pertained mostly to the need for states to maintain the confidence of capitalist investors and to curb the anarchy of capitalism and legitimate the political economy in the eyes of the citizenry.

Additional constraints on the state and the political forms it can manifest become apparent once one recognizes that states face outward as well as inward: They must survive in a potentially hostile international system.[1] This assumption has long formed the core of the "realist" approach to the study of international relations (see, for example, Waltz, 1979; for a survey, see Keohane, 1983). Gilbert (1992), for one, believes that the idea of realism effectively precludes state democracy, on the grounds that a state always preparing for war and maximizing its relative position against its neighbors is in no position to tolerate popular control of its actions that might interfere with these international imperatives (see also Johansen, 1992).

A more detailed account of the survival imperative and its implications for the internal structures and processes of states and societies was offered by Theda Skocpol (1979) in the context of her theory of revolution. Unlike most previous accounts of revolution, Skocpol's theory recognizes that states face both outward, toward the international system, and inward, toward their own societies. All states, according to Skocpol, must (1) compete internationally in both military and economic terms, (2) secure order internally, and (3) extract the resources necessary to perform these first two tasks, generally by taxing their own societies. Failure to compete militarily may mean loss of territory or even complete conquest by another state or states. Failure to compete economically generally means subservience, whether as a colony, neocolony, or pawn in the international political economy. And any attempt by the state to extract resources that is successfully opposed by its own upper classes means a collapse in state authority, which is the first stage of a social revolution. Skocpol herself explains the onset of the French, Russian, and Chinese revolutions in these terms. These generalizations may become less true with time; for example, Costa Rica has done quite well for the last four decades without an army in an unstable region of the world (though it did acquire a militarized police force during the Contra war in neighboring Nicaragua). But there is no denying the historical force of these generalizations and their contemporary relevance in at least some international situations, especially in those parts of the world where military action among neighboring states is still a possibility.

Skocpol develops her account of revolution and constraints on states in the context of noncapitalist agrarian societies. In such societies, the primary source of taxation to finance the state's activities is the landed upper classes. It is when these classes successfully resist taxation that the state's authority collapses and the revolution commences. In the event of a successful revolution, any successor state faces exactly the same set of external and internal imperatives and the same penalties for failure. So Stalin's situation in 1926/27 was in many respects identical to that of the Russian czar before World War I, and he had the same choice to make: to centralize and modernize or let the regime perish. The experience of the first year or two of Stalin's forced industrialization in the Soviet Union demonstrates that at least in a noncapitalist context, a state can achieve dramatic extractive success in a declining economy if it is sufficiently ruthless in gathering revenues and extinguishing the opposition of those who object.

Thus in Skocpol's world, revolution is unlikely to produce anything much in the way of democratization; indeed, it is likely to produce only a more centralized and authoritarian state than previously, despite the intentions of the revolutionaries. The survival constraint explains why postrevolutionary regimes rarely resemble these intentions for long, if at all. Rather, revolution tends to produce only a more centralized, potent, and bureaucratic state. This generalization is confirmed in surveys of the results of actual revolutions (see, for example, Goldstone, 1986, pp. 207–317), although the post-1989 experience in Eastern Europe seems to be telling a different story.[2]

So far, the survival constraint originating in the international system would seem only to increase the probability of political and economic authoritarianism and so reduce the possibilities for democratization of any sort. This discussion has pertained mostly to noncapitalist or precapitalist societies. But capitalist states, too, may engage in draconian economic centralization, although probably only when total war is in the offing or, more likely still, when it has actually arrived. War does indeed change the configuration of the constraints on democratization in a capitalist context, often rather dramatically. But the news for democracy is not all bad.

According to one view, war is only bad for democracy. This line of thought is represented most forcefully in Harold Lasswell's (1948) dire warnings about the development of a "garrison state" in which democracy would be entirely subordinated to the need to discipline society to face external threats (for more recent echoes, see Gilbert, 1992, and Johansen, 1992). Lasswell formulated this notion in the 1930s, but he saw little reason to revise his scenario in light of World War II and the early cold war, especially in regard to the political consequences for the United States and other Western powers. Lasswell's worst fears have not been realized in the decades since he wrote, although the liberal democracies for whose future he feared have experienced some state suppression and evasion of democratic control. This has been evident especially in policy areas directly related to national security.

Historically, foreign and national security affairs have been the policy areas most difficult to bring under (liberal) democratic control. "Reasons of state" generally persuade even those governments formed by parties ideologically opposed to these reasons. So in Britain, for example, Labour governments have always maintained and extended Britain's nuclear forces, just as Labour oppositions have always called for their restriction or abolition (Smith, 1986, pp. 199–201). Realist theorists of international relations would express no surprise here, given their belief that the first concern of all states must be to survive and prosper in a hostile, anarchic environment constituted by other states, and whether or not their internal structure is democratic is essentially irrelevant to the actions they must take in response to this environment (see Krasner, 1992). Thus realists believe that the ideology of a government is irrelevant to its international behavior, unless a state is lucky enough not to be facing much in the way of hostility and constraint from its international environment. The implication here for state democracy as a whole is that the more important that foreign policy and national security become in the life of the state, then the less likely the state is to prove susceptible to democratic control. Government officials may also be tempted to interpret rather broadly "reasons of state" and associated security interests. In Britain, for example, the Official Secrets Act has been used with some regularity to silence civil servants and journalists who might have something to say that would embarrass the government of the day.

The *threat* of war, then, is not especially conducive to the maintenance and deepening of democracy and may often erode existing democratic accomplishments, mainly in the area of civil liberties. But when it comes to the *actuality* of war, the situation is a bit more complex, and there may sometimes be positive implications for democracy. One major reason for such positive implication stems from the need for the government to mobilize the society and economy in support of the war. That is, if the government seizes control of investment decisions in order to gear them to the war effort, business will be in no position to disinvest in response to policies—or institutional reconfiguration—that it does not like. Thus the economic constraint introduced in Chapter 2 is suspended for the duration of the war (see Block, 1977). Obviously it is conflicts of the magnitude of World War II that are at issue here, rather than more limited wars such as the Vietnam or Gulf wars (which, of course, were not at all limited for the countries where they were fought).

There are many different ways in which countries can experience war, and many possible implications for democracy. War means social convulsion, and the more total the war is, the more profound the convulsion will be. Hierarchical barriers to democracy can sometimes crumble under such circumstances. So, for example, in Britain during World War II, a sense of social solidarity rapidly eroded (even though it never actually destroyed) the established class structure. There was a widespread sense that participation in and sacrifice for the war effort were rightly universal, with no distinction on the basis of social class. This participation meant effort on behalf of the military, war economy, civil defense, and social welfare (the welfare state expanded in response to war-related uncertainty; see Dryzek and Goodin, 1986). One way to secure enthusiastic participation in collective wartime endeavors is to give people a share in their control. Indeed, the war years in Britain saw a degree of commitment to public ends and virtues that could be called civic republicanism in operation if Britain were not formally a constitutional monarchy. As Sir William Henry Beveridge described it in his landmark report on the welfare state, "War breeds national unity and readiness to sacrifice personal interests to the common cause" (Beveridge, 1942, para. 460). The "common cause" he had in mind was not the military effort but, rather, social welfare.

There are, of course, other ways to experience total war. Germany during World War II may have featured as widespread and deep a commitment to its war aims as Britain did, but the circumstances of the generation and the actualization of that commitment were very different. Nazi Germany extensively manipulated its population's volitions, which can hardly be described in democratic terms. And before we dismiss wartime thought control as a preserve of totalitarian dictatorships, the thorough and effective manipulation of the media by the liberal democratic governments prosecuting the 1991 Gulf War should give us pause for thought (see Kellner, 1992).

Some scope for democratic innovation during wartime does exist, as the British case illustrates, and the more extensive the war's societal mobilization is, the greater the scope for innovation will be. But that scope is limited by some considerable noneconomic constraints that war imposes on states. Obviously, the more total the war is, the more that the very survival of the state will be in doubt. Thus the state must harness its extractive powers to the full in order to finance and man the war effort. Public volitions cannot be allowed to obstruct this process, and thus there must be limits to the extent of public participation in the direction of the war effort, however enthusiastic that participation may be. The more centralized the state is, the more effectively it can prosecute the war (except in the case of guerrilla warfare). There are presumably good reasons that the military is the most hierarchical kind of social and political organization and that in total war, society itself is militarized. Historically, centralized states were largely built and shaped by the experience or threat of war (see Manicas, 1989, pp. 57–99; Tilly, 1985). States that could not craft an effective wartime response to their enemies have often succumbed to social revolution, to be succeeded by more ruthless, effective, and centralized states, as I mentioned earlier.

In short, war requires increased political control of the economy, which can temporarily suspend the economic obstacles to democratization. But there are reasons that this extended control will usually not be democratic in any simple sense. There may be some circumstances in which political control and the war effort may benefit from, or at least allow, competent public participation. However, there are many times when such participation will hinder the state's prosecution of the war, and in such cases it is the centralized state that will prevail (unless defeated on the battlefield or by revolution).

Matters do not look very different when it comes to postwar reconstruction. Although the economic constraint may remain suspended following war's end, the very need for reconstruction implies that a nation's productive capacity has been severely damaged. States under such circumstances will remain vulnerable to external pressures; war rarely dispenses with such pressures (as opposed to rearranging them). Moreover, the low level of economic activity, increasingly uncompensated by the war economy, means that just as in depressions, the welfare state enters as a necessity. Thus postwar reconstruction combines the necessitarian elements of depression (discussed in Chapter 3) and war, and there is no reason to suppose that democratization will flourish any better than it does in those two circumstances. The establishment of stable liberal democracies in Germany and Japan following World War II is not a counterexample, for these regimes were imposed by conquerors, largely in the conqueror's interest.

Outside war and postwar reconstruction, the survival constraint makes itself felt mainly as a simple reinforcement of the state's need to secure a healthy economy, which I explained in Chapter 2. The healthier the economy is, the larger will be the resource base available that states can tap to finance both external competition and the maintenance of internal order.

To summarize, states' need to survive in a hostile world has mostly negative implications for the possibilities of democracy, although there may be exceptions in regard to actual participation in total war. For many states in today's world, however, the survival constraint is still a major issue. These are the states that fall outside the club of prosperous industrial societies and that make up the Third World and the former Second World (of Soviet-style systems). With the end of the cold war, such states are likely to be increasingly ignored in the strategic designs of the powers of the industrial world and to be left to a Darwinian survival struggle in which military force is always both a danger and an option. Thus the interactions of these less fortunate states may remain consistent with a realist model of international relations. However, as Goldgeier and McFaul (1992) argue, the world that continues to exist for these "peripheral" states is very different from the world that the luckier "core" states of the global political economy are entering. This latter world brings with it freedom from the survival constraint, and some enhanced possibilities for democratization, but as I shall argue, it also brings with it additional economic constraints on these possibilities.

Transnationalization: Life in the International Political Economy

The survival constraint is not the only international force with ramifications for democracy. Economic forces matter, too. At one level, the international mobility of capital simply reinforces the capitalist market's constraints on the state, its policies, and its institutional forms, which I examined in some detail in earlier chapters (see also Bowles and Gintis, 1986, pp. 188–93). One kind of disinvestment in a society is the transfer of investment to another society. Thus if a state is pursuing policies that a business does not like, be it excessive corporate taxation, social spending, labor market regulation, or pollution control, that business can simply move elsewhere. This possibility has been present as long as there has been a capitalist international political economy.

The international system is not static, however, and so neither are the kinds of constraints it imposes. In recent decades the international political economy has changed rather dramatically in terms of the increasingly free movement of goods, services, capital, and labor across national boundaries; the globalization of financial markets; the development of international governmental organizations; the institutionalization of international regimes (especially those governing finance and trade); cultural homogenization; and easy communication. Together, these developments signify a new transnational order in which the survival constraint is withering along with the autonomy of national governments. If national boundaries become increasingly porous, survival will cease to be an issue—at least for the states of Western Europe, North America, Australasia, and East Asia that are members of the "core" of the international political economy. These core countries are free to maximize wealth rather than safety, and military force is no longer a factor in their interactions with one another (Goldgeier and McFaul, 1992).

The autonomy of core countries either is guaranteed by the transnational web in which these states are enmeshed or is already lost. In practice, it may even be hard to distinguish between these two eventualities. Competition between states becomes less important than relationships, competitive or otherwise, involving transnational entities such as the giant corporations, banks, and governmental organizations in which the states are enmeshed. What this means is that the most important international constraint on states and state-related democracy is no longer that of physical security and survival but, rather, a matter of the enormous pressures emanating from the international political economy. These pressures apply to states in both the core and the periphery. Again, the news for democrats, at least in the core, is not all bad, and later in this chapter I shall explore the additional possibilities for democratization that this emerging international order brings with it (beyond the possibilities unleashed by the withering of the survival constraint). But before doing so, I shall explore in more detail the economic transnationalization and its associated battery of constraints on democracy in both core and periphery. Perhaps the most important aspect of economic transnationalization concerns free trade, which now covers capital and finance as well as goods and services.

There is an old joke to the effect that if all the economists in the world were laid end to end, they would not reach a conclusion. However, there is one matter that just about every economist agrees on: the desirability of free trade across national boundaries. More important, the economists seem to have convinced governments on this issue (though not always labor unions and public opinion). Thus today free trade has been adopted as official policy by most governments in the core of the capitalist world order and by increasing numbers of those in the periphery. True, these governments often violate free trade in practice at the same time that they proclaim it in principle. Thus the United States government subsidizes its grain exports even as it rails against agricultural subsidies in the European Union (EU) and imposes quotas on the automobiles it imports from Japan. France, for its part, makes sure that its agricultural sector continues to get special protection even while its government pursues free trade in the context of the European Union. But for the most part these violations of free trade are in response to the concerns of domestic political constituencies, and there is every sign that free trade is expanding despite such concerns. In Europe, national barriers to trade are progressively falling under the auspices of the European Union, a process that culminates in ratification of the Treaty of Maastricht. This process is extended beyond the EU's members through a variety of agreements with would-be members and other countries. Across the Atlantic, the North American Free Trade Agreement (NAFTA) brings Canada, the United States, and Mexico together in a single market. More globally, the General Agreement on Tariffs and Trade (GATT) progressively reduces barriers to trade, especially with the culmination of its Uruguay Round, widely touted as a sure boost to the world economy.

It is slightly curious that the economic theory of free trade and its benefits was built on the assumption of the immobility of capital across national boundaries (Daly and Cobb, 1989, pp. 213–18). That is, the theory showed that nations could maximize their comparative advantage by producing what was most profitable given their endowments of natural resources, human capital, and investment capital. But free trade today means capital mobility, too (which, among other things, undermines the economist's theoretical rationale for free trade). Indeed, many large corporations now consider themselves truly transnational in the sense that no country serves as their base or headquarters. Thus they are freer than ever before to move their operations across the globe in pursuit of profit. Labor is nowhere as mobile as capital, although European economic integration means freer movement of workers across national boundaries, and in the United States there is a massive inflow of illegal immigrants seeking (low-paid) work.

Irrespective of any positive economic benefits of free trade (and even these may appear only in the aggregate, at the expense of large losses to particular categories of people), almost all the implications for democratic control are negative.

Advocates of free trade, and the market more generally, often portray their system in highly decentralized, unconstrained terms in which all actors enjoy a maximum of economic freedom. But that is a false picture. Aside from the invisible hand of the marketplace, free trade in today's world brings with it a very visible hand—wielding a sledgehammer. This is because free trade constitutes not just a market but also a regime. A regime may be the closest thing to a state that exists at the international level.

The international economic order has always been governed by one or more regimes, whose content may change over time. Regimes contain "principles, norms, and rules" together with "decision-making procedures" (Krasner, 1983, p. 1). Regimes can arise in several different ways. They can be imposed by some hegemonic power, such as Britain in the nineteenth century or the United States through much of the twentieth century. They also can be negotiated by interested parties (as in the Uruguay Round which extensively modified the GATT regime, lasting from 1986 to 1994), as well as emerge on an unplanned basis. But whatever their origin, once in existence, economic regimes severely constrain the options of the states operating within them. In part, this is simply a matter of abiding by generally accepted norms in order to secure the continued favor of others—such as trading partners—that also abide by those norms. The constraints involved also may be automatic and decentralized, as when capital and finance flee a country carrying out policies with a perceived negative impact on business profitability.

In terms of the policies that national governments pursue, the result is substantial convergence among governments of different partisanship (socialist or conservative, left or right). According to Garrett and Lange (1991), such convergence is especially likely with regard to fiscal and monetary policies, in which deviations are quickly and efficiently punished by the reactions of international bond and currency markets. They allow that there may be greater freedom on the "supply side" of economic policy, so that leftist governments in particular can and do continue to pursue corporatist strategies (in, for example, Sweden, Norway, and Austria). Such strategies involve income redistribution, restraint by labor unions, and governmental direction of training and investment in consultation with business and labor leadership. Thus, corporatist control of the economy remains an option for core countries, and in Chapter 3, I discussed this possibility under the general heading of functional indeterminacy.

International economic regimes can also contain centralized powers. Accordingly, the global trade regime established in the 1980s, characterized by a renewed emphasis on the free movement of goods and capital (and sometimes labor) across national boundaries, comes with enforcement mechanisms that can be directed against miscreants. Notably, the world debt crisis has left many Third World states beholden to transnational institutions such as the International Monetary Fund (IMF) and the World Bank, to private banks, and to First World governments. The conditions for new loans, or the rescheduling of old loans, normally require compliance with the global trade regime and local austerity for good measure. The consequence is that Third World governments accept subjection to the whims of international capital and promote export-oriented production. And it is not just Third World countries that are so constrained. First World countries that fall into financial crisis can also end up at the mercy of the IMF and its policy prescriptions. Thus even those countries that have traditionally enjoyed membership in the core of the international economic system may feel the pinch, for they are by no means immune to either financial crises to which the IMF holds the answers or, for that matter, the capital flight that punishes violators of the precepts of the trade regime.[3] And the IMF has more recently expanded its operations and its free-market policy prescriptions into Eastern Europe. The recent establishment of the World Trade Organization with global authority over a wide range of trade-related issues further centralizes power in the international economic regime. The World Trade Organization is an administrative body, with no pretensions to even the thinnest kind of democracy in its operations.

The political consequences of this kind of economic internationalization are major. Most obviously, states are not free to make decisions and policies, which instead are compelled by external forces. Moreover, within states the balance of decision-making power is changed. The dictates of the international trade regime are normally channeled through high-level executive branch officials, who then try to impose these dictates. In this light, it is not surprising that market-oriented economic reforms in Latin America and Eastern Europe are generally implemented by executive decree or rammed through reluctant legislatures (see Przeworski, 1991, pp. 180–87). Mass participation in policymaking under such circumstances is impossible. At an extreme, mass political opposition must be crushed. Indeed, several countries in the international periphery have experienced "IMF riots" in opposition to IMF-ordered austerity measures.

Bowles and Gintis argue that the more democratic a country is, the more likely it is to be shaken by the domestic political fallout of international political–economic forces. Their basis for this observation is that citizens in democracies are better able to punish rulers for poor economic performance (and, one might add, for internationally dictated austerity measures) than are subjects in more authoritarian regimes (1986, pp. 190–91). To the extent this argument holds, it would again suggest that life in the international political economy is easier for more authoritarian states.

It is not just monetary and fiscal policies that are restricted by international forces here. No policymaking area is truly immune. Consider, for example, environmental policy. If a state wishes to follow a stringent antipollution policy, it will risk driving polluting industry elsewhere. Note, for example, the high-polluting *maquiladora* industries just south of the United States–Mexico border. If a state wishes to guarantee that food supplies to its population have been produced in environmentally safe ways, it will risk being ruled in violation of free trade. In 1991, a GATT committee declared that the United States' ban on imported tuna caught in ways that caused the deaths of large numbers of dolphins contravened the GATT. If a state wishes to guarantee by law or regulation that its food imports do not contain unsafe levels of pesticides, then that, too, will be a violation of free trade. If a state wishes to subsidize pollution-control equipment for its manufacturing industry, that can be interpreted as an unfair export subsidy. More broadly, if a state wishes to follow an ecologically sustainable development strategy, it may find that this is simply not an option. A country such as Mexico, for example, which has committed itself to economic liberalization and an export-oriented economy, has foreclosed such a future, for locally grown agricultural products will not be able to compete with cheap imports produced intensively elsewhere. Peasants and other small producers are therefore forced off the land, to be replaced by internationally oriented, and ecologically unsound, agribusiness. Local people may go hungry even while food is exported. The displaced peasants move into cities (exacerbating urban pollution problems already out of control) or across the border. Yet once the commitment to free trade is made, there is simply no alternative. (In the Mexican case, the environmental side agreements negotiated as amendments to the North American Free Trade Agreement in 1993 speak only to the issue of pollution, not sustainable development.)

A similar story could be repeated for other policy areas. If we stay with development, strategies that would involve import substitution, public ownership, satisfaction of basic needs, diversification of a nation's economic base, local control of investment decisions, or the managed growth of internal markets are either precluded or available only at a terrible cost (see Keohane, 1984). If we turn to industrial relations and labor policy, we will find that free trade can easily be turned against labor. The more mobile capital is, the more credibly businesses can threaten their workers with relocation to a country with lower wages (for a case study, see Gaventa, 1990). Again, the growth of the *maquiladora* industries in Mexico is part of this development: Their operations are owned by companies whose market is the United States but that are taking advantage of lower Mexican wages, as well as lax environmental regulation and work-safety laws. Capital mobility is an excellent union-busting device, although strong labor unions in corporatist countries may be able to prevent capital flight. Labor mobility is almost as good a device, especially if the labor in question migrates illegally. Illegal immigrants are in no position to unionize and (at least in the United States) are prepared to work for lower wages and in more dangerous working conditions than are their American counterparts. Companies that employ illegal immigrants are therefore at a competitive advantage (see Mackie, 1994).

Free trade as it involves the movement of capital and, to a lesser extent, labor across national boundaries is, then, a recipe for the equalization of wages across countries. The leveling will take place only downward, which means that in the core countries, material inequality is bound to increase. Such a development is highly destructive of community in these countries, as Daly and Cobb (1989) argue at length. But it is no less destructive of democracy, which cannot easily flourish under conditions of ever-increasing material inequality.

It would be possible to multiply examples of the effects of free trade in different policy areas, but the general point should be clear: The emerging international free-trade regime is severely eroding the autonomy of states. States simply must abide by regime dictates (including, but not limited to, the explicit instructions of the World Trade Organization), and if democratic control of any sort gets in the way, it will have to be overruled.

Transnationalization is, then, proceeding mainly under the auspices of economic actors and forces. But the free-trade regime does not exhaust these forces, economic or otherwise. At least in some regions of the world, we are witnessing the more formal integration of a number of countries and the creation of international political authority. That process is best developed in the case of the European Union, which, aside from facilitating trade among its member countries, is also creating a central power to rival that of these states. European financial integration, despite the 1992 collapse of the Exchange Rate Mechanism, might eventually centralize control of the community's money supply. Signs of a European protostate are also manifest in the EU's evident desire to engage in a communitywide, vaguely Keynesian fiscal policy. In other words, recession would be countered by deficit-financed EU expenditures spread across member nations. This kind of intervention would resemble the kinds of counterrecessionary policies normally thought to be the preserve of states. Any such European protostate would, of course, severely constrain the policies and erode the sovereignty and autonomy of the member states (conservative Euroskeptics, especially in Britain, are very sensitive to this possibility). In the long run, this protostate would also be subject to all the state-related economic constraints on political structures and public policies discussed in earlier chapters.

In short, economic transnationalization brings with it a weakening of the survival constraint on the possibilities for democratization, at least in the core states. But it also brings a battery of political–economic constraints that apply to both the core and—still more powerfully—the periphery. The periphery of the international system is doubly disadvantaged in the democratization stakes because much of it still faces the survival constraint.

Economic transnationalization and its constraints on democracy cannot be wished away or easily countered by the policies of particular nation-states. Block (1992) seeks to salvage the autonomy of states, and the prospects for democracy within states, through governmental imposition of controls on the movement of capital across national boundaries. Such controls would inhibit capital flight in response to policies or reforms unpopular with investors. To the same end, Daly and Cobb recommend government enforcement of "balanced trade" in goods and services, in order to prevent the surpluses and deficits on current trading accounts that are needed to finance the import and export of capital (1989, pp. 209–35). But it is hard for any state to go it alone in such respects, for it would immediately feel the impact of the enforcement mechanisms embedded in the international trade and financial regimes that, as I have noted, are not limited to capital flight. As Block recognizes, controls on capital flows would have to be negotiated at the international level and to secure the agreement of most if not all the major economic powers. In other words, what Block and Daly and Cobb want is a wholly different global regime for trade and finance, one that would reinstitute the autonomy of nation-states.

Although not completely inconceivable, it is highly improbable that the clock could be turned back in this fashion. In this light, democrats should not just regret the world that has passed but also anticipate the world that is emerging, in order to move it in a democratic direction. Fortunately, the contemporary transnationalized political economy does indeed open up some more positive possibilities for democracy and democratization, to which I now turn.

Conceptualizing and Actualizing Global Democracy

If, as I noted earlier, transnationalization undermines the ideal of a territorially bounded, self-governing community, where else might the energies of the advocates and analysts of democracy be directed? It is easy to say that the nation-state as traditionally defined should not be the exclusive or even the primary focus, but having ruled it out, a large number of possibilities remain. For example, Gilbert (1992) calls for a "resistant citizen project" (p. 33) of "democratic internationalism" to counter the militaristic forces highlighted by realist accounts of the international system (Gilbert ignores the implications for democracy of economic transnationalization). He has in mind the international peace movement of the 1980s and particular organizations such as European Nuclear Disarmament. Connolly (1991) speaks in vague terms of a "democratic politics [that would] flow below, through and above the level of the state" and of the "extra-state pluralisation of democratic spaces" (p. 481) in the service of a "cosmopolitan democratic imagination" (p. 464). More oriented to conventional political authority than Gilbert and Connolly, Pogge (1992) calls for the vertical dispersal of sovereignty to "nested territorial units," some below and some above the level of the state. Pogge's model is essentially federalism writ large.

The idea of a "cosmopolitan" democratic order is given a bit more content by David Held (1992). To Held, the creation of such an order is absolutely necessary if democracy of any sort is to remain relevant in the future, as the locus of political control is increasingly eluding states. He believes, too, that the states system and notions of state sovereignty with which we are currently stuck nearly preclude democratic control across boundaries (and that the model of international relations specified in the Charter of the United Nations has not made much difference here). Held's proposed "cosmopolitan democracy" would somehow bring transnational affairs (such as international financial or environmental policy) under democratic control and allow nongovernmental organizations a greater role in "international civil society" (p. 33). Institutionally, the cosmopolitan model would contain regional parliaments (such as the existing European Parliament), international courts, a strengthened global assembly of nations (to improve on the United Nations General Assembly), as well as transnational "social spheres" independent of governmental control. Held also allows for "referenda of groups cutting across nations and nation-states" (1991, p. 233).

A still more radical revision of the existing states system in the name of international democracy was proposed by Burnheim (1985, 1986). Burnheim advocates "demarchy" for all levels of social organization, including the international one. Demarchy consists of a system of authorities, each governing a functional area (such as pollution problems or transportation). The geographical scope of these authorities would be entirely variable and dependent on the characteristics of the issue area in question, and need not correspond to state boundaries. Some authorities could even be global in scope. Their leadership would be selected by statistical representation, analogous to the way that juries are usually chosen. These leaders would be selected by lot (not by voting) from among those with a demonstrated material interest in the issue in question.

Burnheim's model is ingenious and has all kinds of attractive properties. It bypasses all the practical difficulties associated with electoral democracy on a potentially global scale and avoids the degree of authoritarian central control that a "world state" of the sort advocated by global federalists would connote. Indeed, it would dissolve the authoritarian and warlike proclivities of existing states by dissolving the states themselves (Pogge, 1992, p. 61, has a similar hope for his nested authorities). With no unitary notion of state sovereignty, individual loyalties would not be to a single state but, rather, to a multiplicity of authorities. This situation would resemble that of the Middle Ages, when individuals divided their loyalties among local leaders, kings, and popes (Held, 1991, pp. 223–24). To date, however, there is little sign that transnational bodies have benefited from the kind of loyalty shift projected here.

The main problem with Burnheim's model lies in its inattention to the real-world constraints on democratization in the international system. Burnheim himself admits that demarchy has a utopian cast (1986, p. 232). Held's cosmopolitan model is less utopian but still ambitious, making few concessions to political feasibility—again, as Held himself admits (1992, pp. 37–38).

In other words, these two models tell us less than they might about the actual possibilities for democratizing the international system. Counterposing an ideal system of any kind to the status quo may in fact lead one to be too pessimistic about the possibilities for such democratization. In fact, I would argue that these possibilities are substantial and greater perhaps than the prospects for any deeper democratization of domestic political systems (that is, within the confines of nation-states). My relatively optimistic evaluation rests on two observations. The first is that over the past few decades the international system has seen truly innovative institutional changes of a scope beyond that of any domestic political system. The second is that the decentralized character of the international system means that there is no state analogue at the system level, and thus one fewer impediment to democratization. Of course, some major constraints on global democracy remain (as I have already pointed out).

The institutional innovations that have occurred in the international system since 1945 have not necessarily advanced democracy. Yet they are none the less instructive for anyone interested in global democratization, for they have not just "happened"; they have been consciously shaped in the service of particular ideals, and this shaping has been sensitive to real-world constraints.

The principal ideal that has inspired global institutional reshaping is liberalism, not democracy. Liberalism as an international political philosophy features free trade, human rights, international rules and institutions, and, ultimately, peaceful cooperation. But as long as it remains idealistic, liberalism is unattractive because naive, likely to believe that free trade automatically promotes peace or that institutions can be designed in any way one wishes. Keohane (1990), for one, therefore prefers a more sophisticated "reformulated" liberalism, which adopts an "ameliorative view of progress" (p. 174). This reformulated "liberalism only makes sense as an explanatory theory within the constraints pointed out by Marxism and realism," two alternative theories of the international system (p. 192). (Keohane should have said "normative" rather than "explanatory" here, to avoid giving the impression that he is arguing from values to facts.) In Keohane's view, both Marxism and realism stress constraints rather than possibilities (of course, Marxism can be interpreted very differently). Marxism emphasizes the ability of global capitalism to constrain policymakers through the ever present threat of capital flight, a force that I have already discussed at length. Realism, for its part, points to the necessity that states promote their security and power in a hostile, anarchic environment. Keohane prefers and argues for liberalism precisely because it offers hope rather than despair, positing that human agency really can change the basic contours of international politics for the better. In Keohane's terms, liberalism has "imaginative flexibility" (1990, p. 193). Sophisticated liberalism can highlight the fact that despite the terms in which their adherents sometimes cast them, neither Marxism nor realism is deterministic. (Gilbert's unsophisticated democratic internationalism tries to argue the same point in relation to realism, as I stated earlier.)

Keohane praises the achievements of reformulated liberalism in constructing the post-1945 international economic order, which includes institutions such as the General Agreement on Trades and Tariffs, the Bretton Woods monetary regime, and the European Union. According to Keohane, this set of exercises in institution building and rule making succeeded because it was sensitive to the issues of sovereignty and state power stressed by the realists and to the realities of the global political economy as highlighted by the Marxists (even though Marxist political economy played little part in the deliberations). The resulting institutions are far from perfect. In particular, they have secured only cooperation and prosperity for some, but not social justice, let alone global democracy. However, this limited aim itself can be justified through reference to Marxist insights into the futility of pursuing social justice in the world capitalist system.

It is a straightforward matter to contrast this successful realistic episode in institution building with an unsuccessful idealist contemporaneous exercise. The United Nations exemplifies liberal idealism, committed (at least in principle) to human rights, peace, and cooperation. But its designers erred in their insensitivity to the power-seeking imperative highlighted by the realists. Thus the United States tried to line up the organization on its side in the early years of the cold war, but later the tables were turned by an anti-American majority in the General Assembly. Marxist insights into the constraints of international capitalism have been ignored in the UN's pursuit of social justice in the international arena (which is not to say that the quest should be abandoned). Though not a chronicle of unrelieved disaster, the UN's record of idealistic liberalism is distinctly spotty compared with that of the realistic liberalism in international economic institutions. And this record suggests, too, that idealistic liberals who today want to extend the role of UN-like global institutions (for example, Held, 1992) would also do well to attend a bit more closely to constraints emanating from the transnational political economy and system of nation-states.

The establishment of international trade regimes in the post-1945 period hardly constitutes a pinnacle of democratic achievement; indeed, these regimes have done much to restrict the possibilities for democracy both within and across state boundaries. However, other kinds of regimes have developed in the international system as well, covering everything from the atmosphere to the deep-sea bed to outer space to Antarctica to fisheries to human rights to regional seas. Whatever their other qualities, these regimes do not impose any antidemocratic political–economic constraints on states or other actors in the international system, nor do they contain centralized power of the sort embedded in the World Bank or the International Monetary Fund. Instead, they can offer relatively high levels of cooperation across state boundaries, with a minimum of central coercion (regimes can be imposed and enforced by some hegemonic power, but none of those I just mentioned fall into this category). For example, the regime that operates in association with the 1959 Antarctic Treaty operates through negotiation across its member states, with substantial input from transnational scientific communities and (more recently) environmental organizations.

Regimes, however decentralized and noncoercive, are not necessarily democracies. They can be authoritarian, as when they are imposed and operated by one dominant power or a small group of powers. They can be formulated, perpetuated, and operated by states alone and allow democratic participation only indirectly, through the ordinary political structures of the states involved. However, regimes can also constitute sites for democratization within the international system—just as states have constituted sites for democratization within national political systems.[4] Democratization can enter in terms of both who may get to participate and how they get to participate.

In terms of who may participate, it should be remembered that transnationalization undermines the notion of a territorially bounded, self-governing community. Thus one should not expect—or seek anything like or anything analogous to—universal suffrage for all the citizens of all the countries that are subject to a particular regime. Many, perhaps the majority, of these people will not even know that the regime exists. Thus "suffrage" and "majority rule" are not relevant concepts. More important is the possibility for participation by those people who are (or could be) aware of a regime's existence and who do have some concern with it. So the "franchise" criterion is still at issue here. Such participation can be achieved through nonstate organizations—international nongovernmental organizations, or INGOs as they are usually known.[5]

Although INGO members are self-selected, their involvement constitutes democratization on at least two of the three criteria introduced in Chapter 1. More people are participating than would otherwise be the case, so franchise is advanced. And democratic authenticity benefits because the INGOs operate in the open and have a stake in educating the public on the issue area or regime in question. Thus they provide a channel for more authentic citizen participation than do states, which in their international dealings are disposed toward secrecy, guided by "reasons of state," among which public opinion rarely looms large.

INGOs can sometimes play major roles in regimes, especially those that do not involve military affairs or international trade and finance. For example, in regard to human rights, Amnesty International is a major source of information on rights abuses, of expertise on arrangements for rights protection, and of embarrassment for rights violators. In the international whaling regime, organizations such as Greenpeace and Friends of the Earth International play significant roles. They are a very visible presence at meetings of the International Whaling Commission (IWC), and not just outside the doors of the meeting place. Their presence extends to membership of some of the smaller state delegations to the IWC. International governmental organizations (IGOs) evidence much less potential for democratic participation. IGOs are established by treaties between states, and the opportunities for democratic participation that they exhibit are entirely indirect, through any democratic features of the states that are party to them.

In regard to how participation might occur in the inception and development of international regimes, there is substantial advantage in the fact that the international system is highly decentralized, with no single locus of authority analogous to the state. Technically, this system is an anarchy (Bull, 1977; Young, 1978). In the past, international anarchy often meant living under the continual threat of violence, and so transnational democracy was barely conceivable. But as I stated earlier, the core countries of the international system have largely escaped that kind of world. Thus international anarchy can now mean substantial scope for experimentation with institutional forms. I noted in earlier chapters that any extension of democratic control that threatens state imperatives (pertaining to economics, welfare, internal order, and, now we can add, survival in a potentially hostile world) is automatically obstructed and punished. But if there is no state in a political system, then there will be no state-related imperatives and so no obstruction and punishment for democratization.

This condition perhaps explains why institutional arrangements featuring decision making through free discussion oriented toward consensus have made more of a mark on the international system than on politics in states. Elswhere, I referred to these as international discursive designs (Dryzek, 1990, pp. 90–108). They have appeared mainly in the vicinity of international disputes, as conflict-resolution mechanisms. Examples include problem-solving workshops bringing together representatives from hostile states (such as Britain and Argentina over the Falkland Islands following the 1982 war), transboundary commissions concerned with natural resources, informal seminars progressing in conjunction with international conferences (such as the UN Conference on the Law of the Sea), and the mediation of various kinds of international disputes.

Such examples hardly constitute transnational participatory democracy in action, and they may be subject to distortion and manipulation by established centers of power (such as states and multinational corporations). But they offer hints to how transnational democracy might proceed, especially in the style of interaction—decision through uncoerced communication and free consensus—that forms their claim to legitimacy, even if it does not always describe their actual operation. The point is surely for anyone interested in transnational democracy to expand on and deepen this kind of interaction.

In the context of international regimes, one can imagine these kinds of discursive designs appearing as the decision-making components of established regimes, as means for creating regimes (as alternatives to more traditional kinds of negotiation and imposition), and as means for transforming the structure of regimes (Dryzek, 1990, pp. 92–93). So far, any application along these lines has been highly limited, but the opportunity is there for an expanded discursive democratization of the international system and its component regimes. According to some accounts, authentic democracy is secured by egalitarian deliberation about collective interests, not elections, party or interest-group competition, voting, or representation (see, for example, Cohen, 1989; Miller, 1992; also Chapter 5). In this light, the particular possibilities for deliberative democracy in the international system take on added significance for the prospects for democracy in the world more generally.

The possibilities for global democratization that I have described include the democratization *of* political authority. But just as democratization can proceed against the state in domestic political systems (as I observed in Chapter 3), so democratization can proceed against political authority in the international system. The public spheres that I discussed in Chapter 3, whose identity is constituted by their opposition to the state, have their direct counterparts at the international level.

Transnationalization is not just economic transactions across national boundaries, however dominant in the scheme of things economics may sometimes seem. Transnationalization can also include the movement and exchange of people, ideas, principles, jokes, cuisine, radio and television signals and programs, letters, telephone calls, faxes, electronic mail messages, newspapers, magazines, works of art, performances, symbols, and even diseases (such as AIDS). Thus transnationalization generates forces that both oppress and constrain democratic possibilities—notably free trade and its associated economic regimes—and the conditions for opposition to oppression and constraint.

Like their domestic counterparts, international public spheres are characterized by egalitarian discourse, a focus on public interests (now defined internationally), and a willingness to defy established authority, be it the authority of states or international bodies such as the IMF or multinational corporations. Again, the more exclusionary that these states or bodies are, the better that the international public spheres will flourish.

Some international public spheres are direct counterparts of domestic social movements of the sort discussed in Chapter 3. And just as public spheres are rooted in civil society, so international public spheres can be grounded in the idea of international civil society (Lipschutz, 1992). The environmental movement, feminism, and the peace movement operate at the international as well as the domestic level. In domestic politics, such concerns may be manifested in conventional interest-group or political-party activity as well as more uncompromising opposition to the state. Similarly, in the international system these concerns may be manifested through organizations that try to work with states and international authority and through movements or networks that work against such authority. Particular international nongovernmental organizations, like the German Greens and other domestic parties and organizations, may contain both "realo" and "fundi" wings (see Chapter 3).

There will rarely be a one-to-one correspondence between a particular INGO and a particular public sphere. Thus the international public sphere made up of indigenous peoples and their sympathizers and advocates is something more than the World Council of Indigenous Peoples, and the public sphere pertaining to universal human rights is more than Amnesty International. International public spheres can even exist in the absence of formal organizations. For example, the students and others rebelling against the Chinese state in Beijing in 1989 in the name of democracy were clearly part of such a sphere (as faxes flew between them and their sympathizers in the outside world). The fact that these rebels were not entirely sure what democracy should mean is not a matter for ironic commentary (of the sort that appeared in the Western media) but, rather, entirely what one would expect of authentic public spheres. Identity questions—in this case, "What does democracy mean to us?"—should always be on the agenda of such spheres. The Chinese state and its leadership were certainly aware of the power of this particular international public sphere, regardless of its lack of formal organization.

One of the best recent examples of an international public sphere is the Global Forum organized in parallel with the United Nations Conference on Environment and Development in Rio de Janeiro in 1992. This forum featured thousands of activists from around the world (again, they were self-selected) linked with a broader global network of participants before, during, and after the conference.

International public spheres, then, can give practical expression not only to a "democratic politics of disturbance," to use Connolly's term (1991, p. 473), but also more substantial challenges to state and international authority. They should remind us once again that the essence of democracy can be insurgency against power unjustly constituted and exercised, as well as any more formalized set of institutions for popular control.

Conclusion

For better or worse, international forces have a major influence on the prospects for democracy. Historically, that influence was due mostly to the fact that the international system was a dangerous place where violent conflict often threatened. An effective response to threat generally meant centralization in state authority, so that the international dimension of political life contained only bad news for democracy (ameliorated by only an occasional, and still highly problematic, loosening of constraints on the possibilities for democratization during wartime).

This "survival constraint" remains a fact of life for most states on the periphery of the international system, in what used to be called the Third World and in much of the former Second World. To the extent this constraint remains, one should not expect to find much in the way of deepening democracy in the periphery beyond some diffusion of basic liberal democratic forms, which appear not to interfere with war-making capabilities. The periphery is in even deeper trouble in regard to democratization because of the constraints inherent in life at the edge of the transnational political economy and the imperatives that the international trade regime imposes on peripheral states and societies.

The core states of the international system—in Western Europe, North America, Australasia, and East Asia—have for the most part escaped the survival constraint. Their enmeshment in international regimes, though still imposing major constraints, is less paralyzing than in the periphery. Thus when it comes to the possibilities for *domestic* democratization, life is happier in the core than in the periphery. Yet this life is far from democratic bliss, as even core states are increasingly forced to follow policies dictated by international trade regimes and other economic forces.

Given these constraints on democracy emanating from the international system, it might seem surprising that possibilities for transnational, even global, democratization really do exist. The reason that they do is that the same lack of central authority that has traditionally made life in the international system so uncertain and dangerous now appears as one less constraint on the possibilities for democratization. Thus when international political authority is constructed, especially in the form of nonmilitary and noneconomic international regimes, it can be open to variety in regard to both who can participate (franchise) and the terms of their participation (authenticity). An authentically democratic discursive style of interaction can sometimes be found. In addition, decentralization combined with the increasing intensity of noneconomic and nonmilitary interactions across national boundaries is conducive to democratization against the established power of both states and international authority. This possibility for the development of international public spheres underscores the fact that in international society no less than in domestic politics, democratization is a matter of insurgency as well as participation in established authority.

5

Democracy Versus Economic Rationality

The macrolevel forces discussed in the previous chapters on the state and the international system do have a major bearing on the prospects for democracy. But these prospects also are shaped by the dispositions of the persons who make up any actual or potential democracy. Any democratic project based on erroneous conceptions of how people do or could act should be treated with extreme skepticism, if not ruled out entirely. This chapter moves to this microlevel of analysis to consider the implications for democracy of the fact that people in Western industrial societies and beyond are increasingly motivated by economic calculation. Such persons prove to be bad for democracy.

Many observers see human capabilities and dispositions in set, single terms; in other words, they believe there is such a thing as human nature, which does not vary across time and space. With such a conception in hand, it is possible to reason toward explanations and evaluations of, and prescriptions for, political life.

The problem here is that different analysts and observers have come up with very different conceptions of human nature. Darwinian biologists believe that human beings, like all other creatures, are guided by their genes. Behavioral psychologists view humans as stimulus-response machines. Maternalist feminists see women and perhaps (someday) men as essentially nurturing in their relationships with others. Some sociologists see people in plastic terms, as molded by their social environment. But by far the most influential model today is the one that describes human nature in terms of rational self-interest. There are good reasons for this model's popularity, not the least of which is its consistency with some powerful political trends, which I will describe shortly. I shall argue that this model subverts democracy of any sort and that its expansion is a major threat to democracy and democratization. This chapter therefore addresses the issue of how democracy might be saved from economic rationality and what the resulting kind of democracy might look like.

Economic Rationality and Its History

The idea that humans are essentially rational and self-interested is held most dearly by economists. Economic rationality specifies that human beings are both rational and egoistic. They are rational in the instrumental sense of being able to devise, select, and effect good means to clarified and consistent ends. They are egoistic in the sense that the ends in question relate to self-interest. This model is not, however, the exclusive property of economics. There is an increasing tendency on the part of many people, social scientists and others, to apply the model to areas of life other than narrowly economic transactions, such as politics, culture, friendship, war, and the family.

I stated in Chapter 2 that it is a mistake to see human nature in fixed, unitary terms. Instead, human subjectivity is better conceptualized in more open-ended and multidimensional terms, with different dimensions coming to the fore in different times and places, perhaps invoked by different institutional arrangements. But in our time and place, economic rationality has become increasingly pervasive, and nowhere more so than in the English-speaking countries. The Reaganism that dominated the United States and the Thatcherism that dominated the United Kingdom in the 1980s were economistic ideologies that assumed and advocated the wholesale pursuit of naked material self-interest. In both societies, rational egoism was legitimated and promoted by public policy—in privatization, welfare state retrenchment, deregulation, the introduction of market competition within the public sector, quasi-market schemes to pursue policy objectives, attacks on collective bodies such as trade unions, denigration of public service and civil servants, and direct appeals by politicians to personal financial self-interest. The consequences were felt beyond the City of London, Wall Street, American savings and loan banks, British housing markets, homeless shelters, and riot-hit cities, which were the most visible sites of rational egoism run wild. Politics, too, was changed. So, for example, Sears and Funk reported that in the United States from the 1950s to 1980 there was little correlation between personal wealth and voting intention— in other words, voting behavior was not in general determined by financial self-interest (1990, p. 161). But between 1980 and 1984 this correlation jumped from .08 to .36.

With the departure of Reagan and Thatcher, the movement toward the universalization of economic rationality seemed to falter in both the United States and the United Kingdom. But the momentum was maintained in the Antipodes, where New Zealand was administered an extreme dose of economic rationalism (see Mulgan, 1992) and Australia experienced a watered-down version (see Pusey, 1991). In both cases, economic rationalism was instigated by a nominally social democratic government. In New Zealand, a more avowedly free-market conservative successor then accelerated the trend.

More insidious still is the messianic zeal with which Anglo-American economic rationalism is now being exported. As a result, the post-Soviet market-oriented reforms in Eastern Europe have "Made in America" stamped all over them and are often escorted to their destination by carpetbagging social scientists (see Przeworski, 1992). Organizations such as Institutional Reform and the Informal Sector (IRIS), funded by the United States Agency for International Development, based in College Park, Maryland, and controlled by economic rationalists, tries to convince other countries that their problems lie in government and excessive organization by interest groups, and their salvation in the market and private property. One effort in this respect involved an expedition to Costa Rica, to try to convince this most stable, democratic, and prosperous of the Central American countries that it is doing worse than it thinks and that its government is controlled by politicians and bureaucrats who profit themselves at the expense of the nation.[1] It is curious that even as economic rationalism is losing some momentum in its Anglo-American home, its export prospects have never looked brighter.

These recent developments are extreme expressions of longer-term trends toward the rationalization of society, noted in the early twentieth century by Max Weber, and the commodification of ever more aspects of life, noted even earlier by Marx. Habermas (1987) referred to these trends as the "colonization of the life-world" by money and power, in which everyday communicative interaction is increasingly displaced by and subordinated to commercial control in the interests of profit and to bureaucratic control in the interests of power. Of these two aspects of rationalization, it is commercialization or commodification that now has the upper hand, although as I shall argue, commodification may itself require concentration of state power.

What this brief account of the rise and stabilization of economic rationalism in the Anglo-American world suggests is that the amount of economic rationality in any society can vary over time and that its quantity seems to have increased in recent years. Before turning to the substantial implications of economic rationality for contemporary democratic politics, an exploration of some deeper history is in order, to underscore the fact that there is nothing natural, still less universal, about rational egoism in human social, economic, and political life. This history will also show that economic rationalization was once good for democracy, even though it has now outlived its usefulness.

For insight into the history of rational egoism, I look first to that fountainhead of economic reasoning, Adam Smith. Smith is best known today for his celebration of the invisible hand of the marketplace, especially in terms of how individuals pursuing their own advantage promote as a by-product *The Wealth of Nations* (Smith, 1976a). However, Smith, like his Scottish contemporary David Hume, treated economic rationality as only a contingent feature of human interaction. Economic rationality did not come to the fore until the rise of what Smith called commercial society (Hont and Ignatieff, 1983, pp. 9–10), which we may call capitalism, and even then this development did not penetrate all realms of life uniformly. Before the development of capitalism, other motivations predominated. Noneconomic motivations recognized by Smith and Hume included grief, shame, vindictiveness, identification with a group or leader, anger, envy, and glory (Holmes, 1990).

It was precisely because of the destructive nature of many of these alternative motivations that Smith and Hume welcomed the development of commercial society. As Hirschman explained, "Political arguments for capitalism before its triumph" (1977) emphasized its reinforcement of relatively innocuous self-interested calculation, to the simultaneous detriment of dangerous passions such as religious zealotry, fame, honor, factional advancement and, most important, glory (a particular worry of Thomas Hobbes). Thus rational egoism promised a society of safety and peace, a way to rescue Europe (and possibly the world) from strife and turmoil. This calming effect of rational egoism explains why it could find so much favor among humane and progressive writers in the seventeenth and eighteenth centuries (Holmes, 1990, p. 276). The argument was resuscitated by Mueller in 1992 in support of a minimal liberal democracy featuring sporadic participation. Mueller argued that if people are mostly selfish and apathetic, the polity they constitute will be a fairly safe, if not very inspiring, place (1992, pp. 991–92).[2] Hume and Voltaire, for their part, also offered self-interest as an alternative to Christian self-abnegation; according to them, an assumption of self-interest enables one to start caring about oneself and others in this world (Holmes, 1990, pp. 281–82). Humans became repositories not just of original sin but also of defensible worldly desires.

Historically, then, self-interest—and the commercial, capitalist society that secured it—were good for democracy. Holmes contended that the universalization of the self-interest assumption to all persons was an "egalitarian and democratic idea" (1990, p. 283), for if everyone, and not just kings, princes, or popes, had interests, then everyone was worthy of concern. Thus Hume and Smith could be attracted to such universalization, even though it contradicted the recognition of multiple human motivations appearing in their more subtle and reflective moments. Hume and Smith were liberals rather than democrats. Nevertheless, universal self-interest is good for democracy because the more interests apply to everyone, the more they will conflict and the more attractive that democratic means will become to resolve conflict. Gone are aristocratic leaders who can claim to speak for the common good, for they too are recognized as having only particular interests, like everyone else.

If we add here the impetus that capitalism gives to democracy by creating a working class in whose interests it is to fight continually for more democracy—in the hope that it will lead to more in the way of material equality (Rueschemeyer, Stephens, and Stephens, 1992)—then it will become apparent that the simultaneous and related ascents of capitalism and economic rationality were good for democracy. However, today economic rationality has run wild to the point that its expansion is destroying democracy.

This last development also was anticipated in the work of Adam Smith, who of course believed that rational egoistic behavior is collectively beneficial when expressed through market transactions. But he could also be quite cynical about the motivations of businesspeople, politicians, and bureaucrats. In regard to politics, Smith believed that the "interested sophistry of merchants and manufacturers" is generally used to try to secure government protection against competition and thus to increase profit. This view of the political behavior of business is shared by those more contemporary market advocates Milton and Rose Friedman, who cite Smith approvingly on this score (Friedman and Friedman, 1979, p. 30). But Smith was more subtle than the Friedmans in recognizing all kinds of undesirable moral consequences of the unrestrained pursuit of self-interest, not just for politics, but also for the individual person so behaving. Thus to Smith, rational egoism was a decidedly mixed blessing, even though in his own historical context he thought that the benefits of its expansion— even universalization—would outweigh the costs in economics and possibly even in politics, interested sophistry notwithstanding. But our context may be sufficiently different that this assessment should be revised. To see why, we need only look at the findings generated by the "public choice" school of thought to see what happens when economic rationality is allowed to run unchecked in politics.

Public Choice and Its Critique of Politics

Public choice assumes that individuals are just as economically rational when they act in political settings as when they act in the marketplace. Thus the basis of this kind of analysis is deduction regarding political phenomena from an assumption of universal rational egoism. Some practitioners—notably the Virginia school of public choice associated with James Buchanan, Gordon Tullock, and their colleagues—begin with the economist's leaning toward free markets, and a general suspicion of anything and everything done by government. Others have less overt pro-market sympathies to begin with and concern themselves with modeling the properties of political interactions, sometimes in very intricate mathematical terms. In American political science, the most high-tech analysis of this latter sort is based at the University of Rochester, although its tentacles have spread widely.[3] The following discussion will ignore some of this more abstruse high-technology mathematical modeling but otherwise seeks a degree of comprehensiveness in its coverage of public choice analysis as practiced in Virginia, Rochester, and elsewhere in the world.

Public choice practitioners can assert the objectivity of their field in terms of a claim that all they do is deduce the consequences for politics from a justifiable behavioral assumption. This behavioral assumption is not only parsimonious but also, it is claimed, free from "romantic and illusory notions" about how individuals and collectivities behave politically, and it is "surely more consistent with the political reality" (Buchanan, 1991, p. 217). Furthermore, it is said, "the *theory* of public choice, as such, is or can be a wholly positive theory, wholly scientific, and *wertfrei* in the standard meaning of these terms" (Buchanan, 1991, p. 217, italics in original; see also Mitchell, 1988b, pp. 102–6; Riker, 1982b). Thus in its self-image, public choice is concerned first and foremost with *Government as It Is* (to use the title of Mitchell, 1988a).

Despite this self-image of a value-free, positive science, the conclusions of public choice, inasmuch as they draw lessons for the real world of politics (and they usually do), have a definitely political cast. Public choice practitioners are mostly committed to classical liberalism's tradition of limited government, constitutional restraints, and the free market. There are a few exceptions to classical liberalism in public choice, several of which I will discuss later.[4] Among the most visible are rational-choice Marxists such as John Roemer (1986) and Jon Elster (1985). However, Roemer and Elster do not use rational-choice reasoning to justify socialism, even though they are socialists. For Roemer and Elster, public choice theory is simply a source of insights into problems in Marxist theory, such as the choice of production techniques by entrepreneurs and collective-action problems in class formation and strategy.

What, then, explains the overwhelmingly classical liberal evaluative and prescriptive conclusions reached by a school of thought that pays tribute to the canons of positive science? Let us look at the comprehensive critique of political life constructed by public choice.

Public choice has described in great detail the nefarious effects of economically rational individuals pursuing advantage through political mechanisms. Arrow's (1963) theorem, one of the starting points for the field, pursues this theme at a high level of abstraction, showing the impossibility of devising satisfactory collective choice mechanisms that do not lapse into either dictatorship or the manipulation of agendas.[5] This Nobel Prize–winning effort effectively founded the subfield of social choice theory, which explores the properties of the various means (such as voting systems) that societies can use to aggregate the preferences of their members to arrive at choices for the society as a whole. Building on this social choice tradition, Riker (1982a) attacked a whole series of democratic doctrines on the grounds that "social choice theory reveals populism to be inconsistent and absurd" (p. 241). He tried to demonstrate that there is no vox populi independent of the mechanisms that aggregate preferences.

Such mechanisms can produce vastly different results from identical distributions of preferences across the persons in a society.

Social choice theory from Arrow on has shown that all collective choice mechanisms are bedeviled by cyclical collective preference orderings and other paradoxes, making consistent social choices impossible (provided, of course, that individuals actually behave in the way that social choice theory says they do). In the presence of cyclical majorities (that is, a majority prefers A to B, B to C, and C to A), the alternative chosen depends solely on the aggregation rules of the political mechanism at hand and cannot be justified in more general terms. Those with the power to manipulate rules and agendas are therefore at an enormous advantage, as they can ensure that their favored alternative will be chosen. There is nothing sacred about (say) majority rule or unanimity or any other constitutional rule, and Riker, for one, offers no reason for preferring one over another. All can be manipulated, and all can be the target of strategic behavior. Consider the case of a cyclical majority, in which A is preferred to B, B to C, and C to A. Partisans of option C can get C chosen by trying to ensure that the voting begins (by majority rule) with a choice between A and B. B is then knocked out, leaving the field clear for a showdown between A and C that C will win.

Not every public choice theorist accepts Riker's blanket dismissal of all voting rules. For example, Buchanan and Tullock (1962) criticize only majority rule for its Pareto suboptimal and oppressive exploitation of minorities. A change is a Pareto improvement if at least one person is made better off and nobody is made worse off. A situation is Pareto optimal when no individual can be made better off without making some other individual worse off. The criterion is much favored by welfare economists, who generally argue that perfect markets produce this kind of outcome. Buchanan and Tullock argue that Pareto optimality can be achieved when all individuals are free to exchange goods, services, money, or votes in an effort to improve their lot. Under majority rule, those voting for the minority position receive nothing in return for their vote, and so the result is not a Pareto improvement. Buchanan and Tullock prefer a voting rule of unanimity, at least at the level of constitutional choice, under which every individual's vote must be bought with something in return.

Public choice practitioners have developed critiques of many other kinds of political arrangements. Niskanen (1971) interprets bureaucracy as an arena in which bureaucrats maximize their budgets, constrained only by the need to demonstrate some minimal level of output. To Niskanen, bureaucrats are as self-interested and rational as anyone else, and so they pursue career advancement, income, and prestige, all of which are positively associated with the size of their bureau's budget. Niskanen's analysis found favor in U.S. politics in the 1980s, and Niskanen himself became head of President Reagan's Council of Economic Advisors. His analysis is of obvious comfort to anyone hostile to bureaucracy, and it helps legitimate across-the-board budget cuts, for it implies that agency budgets will always be too large and that cutting can proceed with no impairment to the level of service delivered.

In a similarly cynical vein, Fiorina (1977) contends that the U.S. Congress generally creates programs that do little for the public interest (however defined) but that yield tangible rewards to the constituents of particular members of Congress, irrespective of the cost to taxpayers. In addition, the intercession of a member of Congress is ideally necessary for these benefits actually to reach constituents, for this helps the reelection chances of members. Again, the prediction is that most federal government programs will not be in the public interest and even are quite likely to have negative net benefits.

Friedman and Friedman (1984), for their part, target "iron triangles" of self-interested politicians, bureaucrats, and lobbyists in conspiracy against the public interest, diverting and wasting public resources. Iron triangles almost always prevail because they have a monopoly on expertise and influence in a particular policy area (such as agriculture or defense). Ordinary taxpayers have a diffuse interest in all policy areas but no incentive to attend to any one area. So again, one should expect bad, costly public policy to be the norm.

Tullock, Buchanan, and other Virginians portray an out-of-control state leviathan that has grown to the point that it can now create demands for its own services—for example, in the electoral behavior of bureaucrats, who can help elect politicians who promise to finance the programs that employ the bureuacrats. Recent Virginian public choice interprets politics as a negative-sum game in which the costs of action (mainly to taxpayers and consumers) always outweigh the particular benefits accruing to self-interested political actors (Mitchell, 1988b, p. 108). Politics is thereby also an intrinsically irresponsible game in which all actors seek benefits for themselves while imposing the necessary costs on others.

Olson (1983) argues that the self-interested political actions of unions, cartels, and other "distributional coalitions" can create a "sclerotic" society of complex understandings in which the creative destruction necessary for vigorous economic growth cannot occur. These understandings cover employers and employees, protecting the position of particular groups of workers and other segments of society. But they also reach into government, which can give its blessing to certain practices (such as tariffs on imports) that restrict the free market and hurt society as a whole even though they benefit particular groups of workers and corporations. Olson believes that this sort of process is especially advanced in the longer-lived and stable liberal democratic societies, such as in Britain and the United States. According to this view, war and revolution are ultimately good for economic growth because they shake up society and destroy established groupings. Obviously, Olson's analysis provides an easy justification for attacks on trade unions as being bad for economic growth.[6]

In the words of Barry and Hardin (1982), public choice paints a picture of "rational man and irrational society"—or, as they might have said, irrational polity. Among other things, the tradition would seem to have demonstrated the impossibility, incoherence, or undesirability of democracy. All that might remain is a very thin liberal representative democracy, which Riker defends on the grounds that it preserves some basic freedoms, and "it does not require that the outcome of voting make sense" (Riker, 1982a, p. xviii). To Riker, elections are useful not because they give any kind of mandate to government, but because they protect citizens against tyrants, who can be thrown out of office. Unfortunately, Riker's own analysis implies that this is very weak protection for citizens, because "if outcomes are arbitrarily connected to the preferences of the electorate, we cannot infer from his removal from office that an officeholder's conduct was in fact disapproved of by the voters" (Coleman and Ferejohn, 1986, p. 22). Thus in Riker's world, even his minimalist conception of liberal democracy is ultimately useless.

As I mentioned earlier, there are a few exceptions to this general hostility to politics and democracy by public choice practitioners. Notably, Brennan (1989) argues for social democracy, believing that the "romance" disparaged by Buchanan can inform the rational choices of voters and politicians. His argument starts with the public choice demonstration of the inconsequential nature of voting; precisely because voting is inconsequential, voters can use it to express their ethical preferences. This expression is costless because of the near-zero likelihood of one's vote proving decisive. Moreover, rationally ignorant voters should not even bother to calculate the cost to themselves of (say) a welfare program. Politicians seeking election must therefore espouse moral principles, rather than merely promise rewards to constituents. As Brennan points out, all this is a far cry from markets, in which the expression of altruism is both costly and likely to be ineffective due to free riding by others.

Brennan's argument for social democracy is not convincing so long as it stays within public choice parameters, for politicians who followed public choice's hyperrational model could espouse ethical principles without having to believe them. Brennan suggests that successful politicians would do well to believe such principles (1989, p. 62), but only a non-public choice supplement, such as cognitive dissonance reduction, would rescue his argument here.[7] Without such an account, one can expect politics to be largely fake, symbolic action. Moreover, Brennan does not address the social choice literature on cycles and paradoxes, which would still exist in his politics of ethical preferences across policy alternatives. And his defense of democracy requires that politicians espouse ethical positions either because they are unfamiliar with or reject the public choice account of politics or because they understand this account so well (better, indeed, than James Buchanan!) that they realize they must behave as Brennan prescribes. Either one of these possibilities is surely an insecure foundation for a public choice argument for democracy. I am not suggesting that Brennan's argument fails but simply that if it is to provide real sustenance for democracy, it must step outside the public choice paradigm (I will return to this point shortly).[8]

Brennan's efforts notwithstanding, a battery of chastening results for politics in general and democracy in particular remains. But this battery stands only as long as democracy is interpreted as a device for preference aggregation under conditions of noncognitivism in individual preferences, instrumentally rational behavior (Bohman, 1990, p. 107), and self-interest. (Noncognitivism means simply that values and preferences should be understood as given, formed independently of and before the choice at hand.) This interpretation captures quite well what liberals mean by democracy: "In the liberal view, the aim of democracy is to aggregate individual preferences into a collective choice in as fair and efficient a way as possible" (Miller, 1992, p. 55).

In most (but not all) Virginian public choice, it is self-interest that does most of the damage. In other words, problems arise because actors pursue private advantage, be it budget size or material benefit, not because of the simple fact of this pursuit's instrumental nature. Social choice theory, in contrast, remains skeptical of politics and democracy, irrespective of the content of actors' preferences; here, instrumental rationality and noncognitivism do the damage, even if actors pursue their conceptions of the public interest. As long as these preferences or conceptions differ across individuals, their political interactions will remain bedeviled by the cycles, paradoxes, and Pareto suboptimalities highlighted by Arrow, Riker, Buchanan, Tullock, and others, which I mentioned earlier. Noncognitivism means that the persons involved cannot escape these problems by subjecting their preferences to rational scrutiny and possible adjustment in the interests of determinate collective choices.

Responses to the Critique of Politics

The world according to public choice is, then, one in which democratic politics is distorted, paradoxical, and counterproductive in all kinds of ways. How can we respond to this multifaceted critique of a politics of unconstrained economic rationality? One response would be simply to dismiss the critique out of hand, on the grounds that individuals do not behave like this.[9] Along these lines, Carole Pateman concluded that "Riker's social choice theory neither confronts nor defeats radical democratic theory, nor offers any comfort, because it is largely irrelevant" (1986, p. 46). Pateman's dismissal rests on her hope that radical democratic politics would feature completely different kinds of persons and interactions. But there is no denying that economic rationality does indeed capture one (nearly universal) aspect of human character, one whose quantity has increased in recent years to the point that it threatens to dominate politics. Thus simple dismissal is an inadequate response.

Two more productive kinds of response to the critique of politics are possible. The first—proclaimed most openly by the public choice practitioners themselves—would take universal rational egoism as a given and try to design institutions to harness this behavior to the common good. The second—into which even public choice practitioners sometimes slip in their less guarded moments—would treat economic rationality as a contingent and variable feature of political life and promote alternative kinds of rationality—and democracy. I shall argue that the first option is counterproductive and incoherent and the second constitutes the proper and effective response to the problems on which public choice has concentrated (and sometimes helped create).

In regard to the first option, how might institutions be designed so as to channel economically rational behavior to the common good? The answer to economists from Adam Smith on has been clear on at least one point: Promote free markets. This prescription is echoed in the work of public choice practitioners who suggest that as many social functions as possible be entrusted to the private sector. In practical terms, this prescription translates into wholesale privatization of government operations, of which countries throughout the Western industrial world have seen a great deal in recent years. Operations that have been shed by governments include airlines; telecommunications; car, steel, and beer manufacturing; and oil, gas, water, and electricity supply. Deregulation of the economy, too, would follow from this prescription, and so in the United States, for example, the deregulation movement since the mid-1970s has been extended to banks, freight transportation, airlines, and telecommunications.

Even the most zealous privatizer and deregulator, however, cannot deny that some functions must continue to be performed by governments. But this zealot might also argue that these functions themselves can often be organized along quasi-market lines. The items to be traded in quasi markets are created by government rather than by firms. So, for example, in 1989 the Thatcher government in Britain determined that the next best thing to a politically infeasible privatization of the National Health Service was to introduce competition within a government-financed system. Following a proposal by Enthoven (1985), health authorities were directed to purchase services from providers such as hospitals that could compete with one another. This kind of market is unusual in that it is not the consumers of health care who exercise the purchasing power but the public-sector managers acting on their behalf.

Other policy areas are suited to different kinds of quasi markets. In the area of pollution control, for example, public choice economists have advanced proposals for markets in pollution rights. The key to this kind of *Free-Market Environmentalism* (Anderson and Leal, 1991) is the establishment of private property rights to all aspects of the environment: land, trees, clean air, fish, clean water, and, most notably, the right to pollute. A government agency could establish the total quantity of pollutants desirable for a particular watershed or airshed, divide this quantity into a number of pollution rights, and then hold an auction for these rights. Once sold by government, these rights could then be traded among polluting firms. It is not hard to demonstrate that this approach would be more efficient and cost effective in curtailing pollution than the more traditional regulatory approach employed by antipollution agencies in most industrialized countries. That is, decision-making power would be taken out of the hands of government bureuacrats and placed in the hands of corporations, which have every incentive to find the least-cost combination of pollution-abatement technology and continued pollution, the latter paid for by the purchase of pollution rights. Some experiments along these lines have been sponsored by the United States Environmental Protection Agency, under the heading of emissions trading.

Privatization and quasi markets can go a long way toward the reorganization of government activities (in economic theory, if less often in political practice). But politics, and all its perversities as highlighted by public choice analysis, still cannot be eliminated completely by such measures. At this point, public choice theorists who despair of collective political choice ever being at all rational if left to its own devices can move to the constitutional level of analysis. The hope here is to identify constitutional arrangements that would harness the behavior of economically rational actors toward collectively beneficial ends. This kind of public choice analysis is known as constitutional political economy (Brennan and Buchanan, 1985; Hardin, 1988). Its practitioners draw a sharp distinction between "constitutional" collective choices, which they hope can be rational, and "in-period" collective choices, which can be rational only to the extent that matters were properly arranged at the constitutional stage. The constitutions in question might specify voting rules, separation of powers, the relative authority of different branches of government, limitations on the scope of government, the proper domain of different kinds of rights, and even the tolerable level of budget deficits and taxation rates. The hope is that some kind of rational agreement may be possible at the constitution-making stage, although constitutional political economy is adamant that the individuals involved in constitution making are no less economically rational than those involved in any other kind of political interaction.

Do these attempts to save politics and democracy from rational egoism through the intelligent deployment of rational egoism succeed? There are two reasons why the efforts fail. The first is apparent as soon as we recognize that the amount of economic rationality in society is variable. If so, then efforts to channel economic rationality to the common good—whether through privatization, quasi markets, or constitutional political economy—may have the effect of simply producing more in the way of economically rational individual behavior, thereby making matters worse than they were before.

Claus Offe's discussion (1987) of the widespread loss of support for the welfare state beginning in the mid-1970s in many countries is illustrative of what can happen here. As ideological attacks on the welfare state intensified (prompted in part by public choice analysis) and as governments pursued market-oriented reforms, the perceptions widened that the welfare state was not a solid rock of common community endeavor in which one could trust one's future. Accordingly, people became increasingly aware of the need to secure an individual future and to calculate more consciously the costs and benefits to themselves of particular programs and policies. In other words, their behavior became more economically rational, and the result was that the welfare state got into still more serious trouble, as it became increasingly subject to problems such as individuals' free riding on the efforts of others. People no longer regarded the welfare state as an expression of community solidarity but, rather, as a set of programs to be supported, exploited, undermined, evaded, or attacked as expedient for each person. And as each person sees such attitudes becoming more widely held by other members of society, it seems to become increasingly risky for that person to remain committed to the old welfare state alliance (Offe, 1987, pp. 534–35). The "calculative attitude toward individual and short-term costs and benefits is therefore nothing that is inherent in human nature or an eternal standard of rational action; to the contrary, it is the product of the disintegration and decomposition of cultural and structural conditions that constrain and inhibit such utilitarian orientations" (Offe, 1987, p. 525).[10]

The decline in social solidarity and the concomitant rise of the calculative behavior of which Offe speaks are reinforced by individuals' actual experience of markets in more and more areas of life. In markets, people respond to decline in an organization's performance by taking their business elsewhere. In democratic politics, the proper response includes giving voice to complaints. Thus the more people experience markets, the more likely they are to become creatures of exit rather than voice (to use the terms of Hirschman, 1970), and the less conducive their behavior will be to the operation of democracy (Bowles and Gintis, 1986, pp. 134–35). Exit here might take the form of opting for private alternatives to welfare state programs, seeking cleaner air by moving to the suburbs, not paying taxes, or simply not voting in elections.

A similar story could be told in connection with quasi-market mechanisms for pollution control. Such mechanisms fail to stigmatize pollution as morally wrong, which is why many environmentalists oppose them, despite the direct effects of these mechanisms in controlling pollution in cost-effective ways (Kelman, 1981). If markets in pollution rights were to be adopted more widely, so would the idea that pollution is a morally neutral commodity to be bought and sold on the market like any other. Thus the strategic pursuit of material self-interest would be legitimated still more strongly. Environmental policy would no longer be an expression of a common citizenship and trusteeship toward the environment but, rather, just another area in which economic calculation is to prevail—and to wreak the political havoc that public choice analysts have so vividly described.

This havoc may be intensified in the environmental area because many environmental problems are the result of individuals' pursuing their material self-interests in an instrumentally rational fashion. The "tragedy of the commons" popularized by Garrett Hardin (1968) is a case in point. It is always in the rational egoist's interest to exploit further the commons (be it grazing land, a fishery, or an ecosystem), because he or she receives all the benefits of this increased exploitation, whereas the cost (in terms of damage to the quality of the resource) is shared across all other users. Thus any policy that promotes rational egoism in the vicinity of environmental problems is likely to exacerbate the tragedy of the commons and related problems. Market expansion has just such effects (see Dryzek, 1987, chap. 7).

The effects of the diffusion of markets can be intensified by the diffusion of public choice analysis. The language we use to describe and analyze institutions has major consequences. Kelman (1987b) pointed out that the spread of public choice analyses beyond the academy corrodes trust and civic virtue within government. If he is right, the importance of public choice is not just that its hypotheses might be true but that they might become more so (helped perhaps by individuals trained in public choice attaining high rank in government). If one fears the potentially dire consequences of such developments as demonstrated by public choice itself, then the alternative to Kelman's studied naïveté about the "public spirit" he believes already pervades government and politics is to seek self-denying rather than self-fulfilling hypotheses in public choice analyses. In other words, the practical task becomes one of determining how public choice predictions might become *less* true through awareness of these predictions by participants in politics.[11] Unfortunately, as Offe's (1987) analysis of the loss of support for the welfare state indicates, the opposite can easily apply: Awareness of the predictions makes them more true. The solution here is to stress the contingency of these predictions, alternative rationalities that could negate the predictions, and institutions that might embody these rationalities. This solution requires stepping outside public choice, beyond the idea of harnessing economic rationality, and I will return to it shortly.

Attempts to harness economic rationality in political behavior toward the public interest may often prove counterproductive, inasmuch as these attempts end up producing more of the problems they set out to solve. But there is a still more fundamental reason to distrust this kind of strategy: The whole idea is deeply contradictory. When prescribing institutional arrangements to channel rational egoists toward the public good, someone must do the channeling. But who exactly is to undertake this task? In the world portrayed by public choice, those doing the channeling must themselves behave according to the precepts of economic rationality. Thus the constitutional political economy of James Buchanan and others holds that "no theory is of any interest if it cannot be implemented by *Homo economicus* agents" (Hardin, 1988, p. 515). At another level, such agents cannot possibly implement prescriptive public choice theories. The reason is that in making institutional prescriptions to limit the leviathan of government through constitutional restraints, to replace voting with demand revelation, and so forth, public choice practitioners assume the existence of some public-spirited policy engineer. Conceptualized as a single individual or policy dictator, this engineer violates the self-interest postulates of public choice, not to mention a host of secondary assumptions concerning budget-maximizing behavior, self-interested reelection proclivities, and the like. If this engineer is conceptualized in collective terms, in addition it will be paralyzed by the cycles and paradoxes in social choice and by the collective-action problems and irresponsibilities that the tradition has so carefully enumerated. As I have already noted, Buchanan and others draw a sharp distinction between "constitutional" and "in-period" collective choice. They hope that constitutional choice will entail such uncertainty about the effects of different arrangements on particular persons' well-being that each will behave impartially. But this hope itself contradicts the public choice literature on "rent seeking," which argues that individuals will seek rules favorable to themselves (Vanberg and Buchanan, 1989, p. 53).

The result is that public choice prescriptions can be implemented only by people who violate public choice assumptions in their own behavior by not acting in either instrumentally rational or egoistic terms. Perhaps the best example of such a dynamic in operation came with the wave of deregulation in the United States that began in the late 1970s. As Quirk (1988) argues, deregulation was very much a triumph of "the politics of ideas." Key political actors, especially members of Congress, became increasingly convinced of the benefits to the public of deregulation, especially in terms of improved service and lower prices. Appropriate legislation was passed and implemented against the opposition of the regulated industries and regulatory agencies, and without much in the way of a groundswell of diffuse public support. In short, beliefs and ideas proved decisive in determining the content of policy—a far cry indeed from the political world as portrayed by public choice, in which members of Congress respond only to special interests and reelection desires.

Thus practical public choice must treat its postulate of self-interested maximization as contingent and open to change, for otherwise its prescriptions cannot be implemented. This conclusion highlights the fact that coherent democratic politics of any sort is possible only to the extent that economic rationality is not allowed to colonize politics and is kept firmly in its place by other kinds of rationality.

This need to keep economic rationality out of politics was recognized long ago by Adam Smith. In the *Wealth of Nations*, Smith both celebrated rational egoism in the marketplace and warned against its presence in politics. The practical challenge is how to secure the benefits of the unconstrained pursuit of self-interest in economics while avoiding the moral and political hazards so generated. In Smith's other major work, *The Theory of Moral Sentiments*, he argued for the cultivation of a very different kind of behavior. Smith's ideal in that work was the "impartial spectator."[12] The impartial spectator is capable of balancing self-interest with the interests of others. Smith believed that by inculcating the key virtue of sympathy, the ability to imagine oneself in the place of others, citizens could become more like impartial spectators (Phillipson, 1983, p. 183). Smith proposed establishing an ethical realm in which the impartial spectator would flourish and restrict self-interest.

Unfortunately, Smith died before he could write the full "account of the general principles of law and government" promised at the end of *The Theory of Moral Sentiments* (Smith, 1976b, p. 342), which might have explained how such ethical improvement in society might be accomplished. However, he was essentially optimistic on this score, for "it was Smith's view that the scope for prudence and wisdom increased rather than diminished with the development of society into its more complex forms" (Winch, 1983, p. 260).

I believe that the most appropriate kind of rationality to seek here is *communicative* rationality and that the scope for this, too, increases as society develops into more complex forms. Communicative rationality in turn suggests a distinctive model of democracy, which is discursive or deliberative in character and much more than a mechanism for the aggregation of individual preferences.

From Economic to Communicative Rationality

According to Jurgen Habermas (1984), modernity brings increasing potential for the exercise of two sorts of reason. The first, instrumental reason, is the sort normally assumed by public choice to exhaust the concept of rationality. Many critics of modernity, notably Max Weber, Max Horkheimer, and Theodore Adorno (for example, Horkheimer and Adorno, 1972), contended that this kind of behavior encompasses the sum of modern rationality and that the world will only see more of it. The likely consequence is Weber's "polar night of icy darkness and hardness" in which the triumph of instrumental rationality is realized in public and private bureaucratic–authoritarian structures, in which the only kinds of interpersonal interaction are command and manipulation.

Habermas argues that these critics of modernity have missed the increasing potential for a second, more congenial, kind of rationality, communicative rather than instrumental in character, and organized around talk rather than strategy. Communicative *action* is oriented to reciprocal understanding and the coordination of actions. Politics is inconceivable without some measure of communicative action, if only so that strategic actors can understand what kind of game they are playing against one another. Is the game competitive, cooperative, zero-sum, or positive sum? Are the stakes territory, votes, money, prestige, or power?

Communicative *rationality* may be defined in terms of free, competent, and informed linguistic interaction, in the absence of strategizing, hierarchy, deception, and self-deception. As such, it is a property of collectivities rather than the social isolates of public choice. It advances, though is never fully realized, along with "modern structures of consciousness" and the decline of myth, religion, superstition, unthinking compliance with traditional norms, and so forth. This kind of rationality is appropriate to the interactions of competent, reflective, critical, and social individuals. These individuals are never social isolates, and so the conditions of their action and interaction can be more or less reasonable. Depending on the social conditions in which they move, their actions might be governed by anything from repressive causal influences to enlightened recognition of their place in a web of political relationships. Their rationality has cognitive, moral, and subjective aspects, not just instrumental ones. In other words, the development of worldviews, ethical positions, and identity contributes to and helps constitute an individual's rationality (Bohman, 1989, p. 270; for a discussion of how democratic interaction can contribute to this process, see Bowles and Gintis, 1986, pp. 145–51). Above all, rationality means the competence to decide when it is appropriate to act instrumentally, in conformity with social norms, or dramaturgically as an expressive subject—and the ability to judge these qualities in others (White, 1987, p. 117). This communicative competence is, then, a matter of intersubjectivity and social interaction, not just isolated subjectivity.

With a little effort, public choice arguments can be extended in the direction of communicative rationality and so away from noncognitivism (the idea that individuals' preferences and interests are beyond the reach of reason). One such argument may commence with Brennan's (1989) case for "romance" in politics, which I introduced earlier. Brennan, recall, claims that public choice assumptions predict the expression of moral principles by voters, and response by politicians. Extending this argument, we can say that the more that politics becomes characterized by instrumental rationality in decentralized settings, the greater the potential for ethical discourse will be. But that discourse cannot emphasize myth, tradition, utopian values, and an unproblematically benign government. To survive in a world of competent, instrumentally rational political actors, this discourse must be rational in character. To use the term *communicatively rational* here, one must step outside the rational choice paradigm. Brennan, for one, seems ready for such a step when he suggests that successful politicians must actually believe the principles they espouse and therefore not engage in deception or self-deception.

A somewhat different and more explicit opening from public choice to communicative rationality was constructed by Vanberg and Buchanan (1989). They proposed that ethical discourse of the sort predicted by Brennan is unlikely, on the grounds that when it comes to politics, people can only disagree and at best merely reach expedient compromises over their different interests. However, Vanberg and Buchanan argue that individual preferences have not just an "interest-component" but also a "theory-component." By "theory" they mean a knowledge of causal relationships. At the level of constitutional choice, the theory-component consists of a person's beliefs regarding how particular arrangements will affect his or her interests. Although Vanberg and Buchanan assume that people are quite sure of their interests, they can be highly uncertain when it comes to the theory-component. This uncertainty inhibits collective constitutional choice simply because individuals do not know whether alternative constitutions will hurt or benefit them. According to Vanberg and Buchanan, rational discursive scrutiny of the sort that Habermas postulates can help here by enabling individuals to seek and share information about the likely effects of constitutional options (1989, p. 59). "Constitutional agreement can be facilitated by a process that systematically encourages critical examination and discussion of alternative theoretical constructions" (p. 60). With this conclusion, Vanberg and Buchanan dispute the contentions of many of their public choice colleagues that "political rhetoric is mere camouflage, concealing real interests . . . [and that] it is ultimately only interests and the power behind interests that count in the political process, while arguments and reason lack any power of their own" (p. 60). Although they argue in static terms, it is again quite straightforward to add a dynamic extension: The more complex a society becomes, the greater the uncertainty will be in the theory-component of choice, hence the greater the need for rational discourse.

While applauding the efforts of Vanberg and Buchanan, there is no need to accept their noncognitivism and concomitant dismissal of normative discourse. And if we add Brennan's account of the place of ethics in politics here, we will find that the leading public choice practitioners have constructed warrants for communicative rationality that involve facts *and* values, truth *and* morality.[13] An increasing number of cracks seem to be appearing in the citadel of economic rationality. Thus an embrace of communicative rationality requires just a few more steps along the road already taken by these practitioners. Equally important, we can draw on the extensions of these public choice arguments to which I pointed to see exactly why the potential for communicative rationality in politics can be expected to expand with the growth of instrumental rationality attendant on modernity.[14]

Despite the opening to communicative rationality made possible by Brennan and Vanberg and Buchanan, there remains an essential tension, not an easy complementarity, between instrumental and communicative rationality. We can profitably reinterpret a great deal of public choice in the terms established by a focus on communicative rationality here. To be more precise, public choice's exposé of democracy, government, and politics stands only as long as people behave in certain restricted, instrumentally rational and self-interested, ways. This kind of action is not the only sort available in modern politics.[15] Instrumental rationality has its proper place in economics, science, technology, and even politics, and indeed its refinement is one aspect of social development. But there are realms in which instrumental rationality needs to be regulated by communicative rationality. One of these realms is politics, as public choice has demonstrated so well in its catalog of horrors that exist only as long as individuals behave in strictly instrumental, self-interested, maximizing ways.

The point is surely to avoid these dire results by asserting the preeminence of communicative rationality. To do so would curb self-interest and noncognitivism, by making values subject to rational public discourse, and instrumental rationality, by highlighting a different kind of political interaction. As Miller (1992) explained, this kind of public discussion helps dissolve the dismal results of social choice theory. For those persons whom social choice theory sees as caught up in cycles and paradoxes from which there is no escape can now at least discuss their common problem. Several escape routes are then possible. Public discussion may lead to the elimination of some privately held preferences that will not sustain public scrutiny, even in the eyes of those who previously held them. Thus the range of options in a collective choice is likely to be narrowed, and fewer opportunities will arise for cycles. Cycles are created mostly when several different dimensions of disagreement are combined into one collective choice. Discussion may promote "a general willingness to break the decision down along its several dimensions, on each of which we should expect to find a winning position. Putting the bits together again, we would have an overall result which can fairly be said to represent the will of the majority" (Miller, 1992, p. 65).

However, it is conceivable, as Przeworski observed, that the information communicated in deliberation may actually increase the probability of cycles, by inducing individuals to change their orderings across alternatives in a socially awkward direction (1991, pp. 17–18). But deliberation does more than simply increase information while leaving basic preferences and interests undisturbed. Its cycle-busting qualities depend on the possibility for a deeper scrutiny of interests and of the dimensions of collective choice. In other words, effective deliberation is not just a matter of talk but also of communicative rationality.

Skepticism of the effects of discussion on social choice is also evidenced by Knight and Johnson (1992), who charge that the inclusive discussion of the kind sought by proponents of deliberative democracy threatens to increase the number of perspectives involved and so unsettle shared understandings and multiply the possibilities for instability and ambiguity in social choice. The Knight and Johnson argument against extending democratic participation to previously unrepresented individuals and interests echoes that of the ungovernability theorists discussed in Chapter 2 (and, for that matter, antidemocratic philosophers through the ages). As such, their argument is really against democratic participation in general, rather than democratic deliberation in particular. Indeed, one would expect it to apply with more force to liberal democracy, to which strategic action and preference aggregation are more central. But their criticism underscores once again the point that the consequences of extended participation depend on the terms of that extension. Extended deliberation will dispel the dismal predictions of social-choice theory only if it is accompanied by communicative rationalization.

In this alternative type of interaction, collective choice would proceed discursively rather than strategically. Cognitivism would limit, if not dispel, the dismal predictions of social choice theory by making options and the reasons for them the subject of debate rather than simple voting, strategy, and manipulation. And the public discourse of communicatively competent actors would constrain free ridership, rent seeking, and the other irresponsibilities enumerated by Virginian public choice.

Any response here to the effect that strategic rationality and the pursuit of private advantage are indeed universal, preeminent, and inescapable now takes on an ideological cast; that is, it ascribes inevitability to what is in reality open to change. Such thinking would also be untrue to the classical liberal lineage of public choice, in which individual freedom looms large. Individuals who are treated as inevitably engaging in instrumentally rational maximization are not in fact free to choose something else.[16] All they are free to do is select options from within a feasible set using a particular decision rule. They are not allowed to pursue a communicative resolution of the problem at hand or to redefine its character so that it would no longer entail strategic action in their relations with others.

How, when, and why do people interact in communicatively rational, as opposed to economically rational, ways? There is a literature in experimental prisoner's dilemmas that shows one way in which economically rational individuals can transcend their limits. The prisoner's dilemma underlies many of the collective action problems highlighted by public choice. In its simplest presentation, the dilemma arises when two persons are faced with a simultaneous choice. If both choose to cooperate, each will receive a moderate benefit. If both choose to defect, each will receive a moderate loss. But the highest benefit is gained by the person who defects while the other cooperates, and the biggest loss is sustained by the individual who cooperates while the other defects. Thus it is always individually rational to defect; but if both individuals defect, the result will be, of course, collectively irrational. Thus the basic finding of public choice: "rational man, irrational society" (Barry and Hardin, 1982).

Experiments with one-shot (that is, not iterated or repeated) prisoner's dilemma games show that there is a baseline cooperation rate of around 20 to 30 percent; that is, 20 to 30 percent of participants behave in economically irrational fashion by not taking the dominant defect option. The proportion of cooperators increases dramatically if the experimental conditions are changed slightly, principally through the introduction of a period of discussion among the participants before their making their still independent choices about whether to defect or cooperate with one another (Dawes, McTavish, and Shaklee, 1977; Orbell, van de Kragt, and Dawes, 1988). It should be stressed that the incentive structure remains the same, so that it is still economically rational to defect once the discussion ends and the time for choice arrives.

The reason for this result is that a period of discussion enables (even though it does not guarantee) the group's interactions to be governed by communicative rather than instrumental rationality, which continues to affect the content of motivations once the discussion is over (remember that communicative rationality refers to reciprocal understanding and the coordination of actions). The implication here is not that talk always promotes cooperation. Conversation can, of course, engender antagonism, even violence. The point is that when the structure of the situation is such as to make mutual gain possible yet problematic, then discussion generally helps. Under communicative rationality, good arguments can get the better of strategic calculation. And arguments based on interests common to the group—"generalizable interests," or, in the language of microeconomics and public choice, "public goods"—are normally more acceptable than arguments based on self-interest. Discussion can invoke different kinds of motivations than one finds in isolated individual behavior.

Orbell, Dawes, and van de Kragt (1990) explain discussion's stimulation of cooperation on the grounds that it provides opportunities for making promises about how people will act in a subsequent (prisoner's dilemma) choice. But promise making can have this positive effect only to the extent communicative rationality prevails, free from deception and strategizing. Even after promises have been made and recognized, it is still economically rational to defect in the one-shot prisoner's dilemma. This is another example of work that starts within a public choice paradigm but must move outside, and even undermine, that paradigm—in this case, in order to explain observed phenomena. Again, the movement is in the direction of communicative rationality.

Even when discussion is not available in prisoner's dilemma experiments, participants may still be able to communicate with one another through the cooperate/defect choices they make. This possibility is especially prevalent in iterated or sequential prisoner's dilemmas, in which participants play numerous rounds of the game (via computer). Hurwitz (1991) demonstrated that subjects signal to one another through choosing and so exhibiting particular sequences of plays and responses. Rather than taking the strategic structure of the game as given, they actually negotiate with one another and change the meaning of the game as it progresses, even though they cannot talk or even see one another. As Hurwitz argues, such negotiation defines communicative, not strategic, rationality.

Before leaving the prisoner's dilemma, I should point out that such experiments have produced another stable result worth mentioning. Undergraduate students of economics consistently take the defect option at a much higher rate than do students of other subjects, or nonstudents. Although this might seem to be a trivial result, it underscores my earlier point about the negative implications for society and politics of the diffusion of economic and public choice interpretations of the world.

The result of all these exits from public choice to communicative rationality is that even when political life is stripped down to its bare strategic essentials, as in prisoner's dilemma games, it cannot be understood without appealing to some notion of communicative action. So when it comes to thinking about communicative rationality, the issue is not one of imposing this particular style of interaction on politics but, rather, of making the most of a style that is always and already there.

From Liberal to Deliberative Democracy

What is at stake in the encounter of economic and communicative rationalities is not just a definition of rationality but also a definition of politics and democracy. If we truly wish to banish from political life the dismal predictions of public choice analysis, a liberal conception of democracy will be inadequate. To liberals, the point of democracy is to aggregate preferences that are formed privately, outside politics; I have argued that public choice has inadvertently shown that such a conception of democracy cannot be sustained. Communicative rationality points to a more authentic democracy (it has less to say on matters of democratic franchise and scope). The kind of democracy consistent with communicative rationality, and so capable of overcoming the problematic politics portrayed by public choice, is *discursive* or *deliberative* in character. Its essence is free discussion about points of conflict oriented to some kind of agreement, and in that discussion preferences can be changed and not just aggregated (see Cohen, 1989; Dryzek, 1990; Miller, 1992).

How might communicative rationality and its associated discursive model of democracy be promoted, and economic rationality and its associated liberal conception of democracy be attenuated, in the practical task of shaping and reshaping political institutions? I have already stated that the task is promoting the communicative dimension of politics inevitably present in some degree. Institutional design starts to look very different from constructing devices with rules for the aggregation of preferences of social isolates.

Different institutions can invoke different kinds of motivations and interactions. This recognition can draw support from the apostate James Buchanan, fresh from winning the 1986 Nobel Prize in economics: "The whole point of constitutional inquiry is the proposition that the constraints, rules, and institutions within which persons make choices politically can and do influence the relative importance of separate motivational elements" (Buchanan, 1986; quoted in Mansbridge, 1990, p. 21). The elements that Buchanan had in mind are pecuniary self-interest and conceptions of the general interest. Developing the renegade Buchanan's point, institutions that promote instrumental rationality and the pursuit of private advantage in competitive, hierarchical, or adversarial procedures should be criticized, limited, and (if possible) abolished. Hierarchy implies the attempted manipulation of some people by others, and instrumental guerrilla warfare by subordinates. Competitive and adversarial procedures incite individual persons and other actors to strategic action against others. Most Western political systems can be described as "adversary democracies" (Mansbridge, 1980), and so a thorough overhaul might be desirable. Committee hearings, parliamentary debates, public inquiries, administrative rule making, environmental impact assessment processes, and judicial scrutiny of policy all generally proceed in an adversarial fashion.

The alternatives to hierarchical and adversarial institutions emphasize discussion oriented to consensus. Examples include alternative dispute resolution, mediation, and various other kinds of third party–facilitated conflict-resolution procedures of the sort I discussed in Chapters 3 and 4. The oldest public institution in liberal democracies that works by deliberation oriented to consensus is the jury. There have been some recent attempts to extend the main principles of the jury—selection of participants by lot and reasoned deliberation—to questions of public policy. In Germany, "planning cells" have been organized along these lines to contemplate issues such as energy policy planning. In Minnesota, the Center for New Democratic Processes (working with state agencies and interest groups) has sponsored "citizen panels" on issues such as agriculture and water quality (see Crosby, Kelly, and Schaefer, 1986). Like a trial jury, a policy jury hears presentations from experts and advocates before commencing deliberation and then reaching a recommendation (and thereby the elements of adversary democracy are retained). Statistical representation (that is, by lot) fits nicely with a commitment to communicative rationality because it is less open to manipulation by money and political strategizing than are more familiar forms of representation such as elections or self-nomination by the leadership of organized interests.

Such discursive institutions can still be subject to subtle manipulation by the vestiges of hierarchy and strategic action. Critical scrutiny can expose such attempts to manipulate discursive exercises toward symbolic participation that buys off potential troublemakers cheaply. Of course, the constraints on state-related democratization introduced in earlier chapters are likely to obstruct political reform along these lines. And antagonistic conflicts of interest generated by the capitalist political economy may not always be amenable to communicative resolution. Discursively democratic exercises located in autonomous public spheres (such as new social movements) confronting the state are less easily subverted and manipulated, even when they are less obviously connected to political authority (see Chapter 3; also Dryzek, 1990, pp. 37–38, 48–50).

Conclusion

There was once a time when economic rationality battled the forces of organic hierarchy and aristocratic and religious privilege. In this struggle, economic rationality and democracy often were compatible and complementary, although prescient observers such as Adam Smith could already discern signs of contradiction. Matters today are very different. Economic rationality has run wild to the point that it threatens to consume democracy of any sort. Public choice theory has demonstrated the impossibility of political order, democratic or otherwise, founded on unconstrained rational egoism.[17] The direct implication is that capitalist democracy is producing its own grave diggers.

Marxists once believed that capitalism's grave diggers would come in the form of the industrial proletariat, acting in concert to overthrow the capitalist system that generated it. But that kind of class solidarity has receded and, along with it, any chance of proletarian revolution. Today's grave diggers are individual people, not collectivities of any sort, and they are digging a different grave. In behaving more and more in exactly the way that capitalist economists say they should, and cheered on by the likes of Ronald Reagan and Margaret Thatcher and their ideological heirs, these individuals are thoroughly undermining the liberal conception of democracy. Economic rationality run wild is as deadly to liberal democracy as it is to any other kind of democracy. The grave is for democracy, not capitalism.

I have said that political interaction can never be interpreted in purely strategic terms; some modicum of communicative action is essential. But as economic rationalization undermines the communicative dimension of politics, egalitarian communication is increasingly displaced by authoritarianism. At the end of the line is the authoritarian liberal dystopia of an aggressively individualistic society policed by a highly centralized state. It is no coincidence that economic rationalization and state centralization advanced together in Thatcherite Britain in the 1980s and beyond.

In this light, hope for the future of democracy in capitalist times lies in the activation and institutionalization of communicative rationality, and the associated conception of democracy as public deliberation rather than preference aggregation. This is not a utopian project, for it can be grounded in kinds of social interaction that already exist and in forces I have identified that are conducive to such interaction. Nevertheless, when applied to state structures, the project remains problematic for all the state-related constraints on democratization explored in earlier chapters. Applied to public spheres in civil society the project is safer, for the idea of civil society makes sense only as a rejection of economic rationality. But the project still is vulnerable to the increasing commodification and privatization of all areas of life, to authoritarian liberal policies attacking democratic association, and to increasing material inequality. Thus the state and its policies cannot be ignored, and the democratization of civil society through the activation of public spheres should not rest content with a self-limiting politics of identity and disturbance. How state actions may be influenced without falling prey to state-related constraints will be addressed in Chapter 7. But first, I must demonstrate that conceptions of politics in terms other than those of capitalist democracy underwritten by economic rationality actually do exist in the public at large, and this I shall try to do in the next chapter.

6

Democracy Versus Ideology

Capitalist democracy has, on many accounts, vanquished its competitors at the level of human belief as well as political–economic structure. In Chapter 2, I observed that this apparent victory has been achieved in part because of the lack of ideas about practical alternatives to capitalist democracy and still less about alternatives that might actually work better in important respects. I also argued in Chapter 2 that the power of this development is redoubled to the extent that liberal democratic ideology creates a powerful discourse. *Ideology* and *discourse* are related concepts, and both have a variety of meanings.[1] For my purposes, a *discourse* may be defined as a system of possibility for apprehending the world, constituted by common capabilities that enable readers and listeners to assemble words, phrases, and sentences into coherent and intelligible wholes (or *texts* as they are sometimes called; see Dryzek, 1988, p. 710; van Dijk, 1985). Discourses are social constructs that enable their adherents to ascribe meaning to observed phenomena. With this definition in mind, it is possible to gain access to some powerful tools of discourse analysis, which I will use in this chapter.

To underwrite an end to any profound experimentation with political alternatives, the dominant discourse would have to be capable of disarming or absorbing all opposition. Whether there are, or have been, discourses this powerful is an empirical question. Michel Foucault (for example, 1980), for one, thinks that discourses of this scope do indeed exist. But whether single or multiple, dominant or subversive, discourses help condition the way people think, their identity, and their standards of judgment. In this sense, the discourse of liberal democratic capitalism can provide criteria for comparing the political–economic system of capitalist democracy with its competitors. This discourse is also very good at assimilating critics, as I also pointed out in Chapter 2. Thus at first glance the discourse of capitalist democracy seems capable of disarming opponents. Here, Marxists will recognize the idea of "hegemony" introduced by Antonio Gramsci: class rule not through coercion but through the dissemination of beliefs and values that systematically favor the ruling class. My own analysis does not turn on the presence of any ruling class or other material determinants of the content of discourses (although I admit that such things may exist in conjunction with the forces of economic rationalization described in the previous chapter).

If capitalist democracy does indeed constitute an internationally dominant discourse, it does not quite follow that no institutional tinkering is possible, for this discourse does allow variations on its theme. These variations may come in the form of different voting systems, relations of government to key interest groups, parliamentary structure and rules, the distribution of power across the various branches and levels of government, and so forth. The allowable variations are probably smaller in regard to the economic system than to political structure; as Przeworski observed, "Market ideology seems to have attained uncontested intellectual hegemony" (1992, p. 46).

Such possibilities for political tinkering notwithstanding, it remains true that if the discourse of capitalist democracy were truly encompassing, then the sort of analysis that appeared in the previous three chapters—devoted as it was to identifying democratic alternatives to the dominant political–economic order—would be a waste of time. Even if such alternatives were structurally possible and information about them were disseminated, people would never actually choose them, even if it were in their interests to do so. Their standards of judgment as determined by capitalist democratic discourse would block such a choice.

I shall argue in this chapter that capitalist democracy does constitute a discourse, that it is a powerful one in many respects, but that it is not hegemonic. In Chapter 2, I stressed the assimilative capacity of liberal democratic capitalist discourse. Here I will examine the obverse side of that capacity, which allows possibilities for dismembering this discourse. Alternative discourses of democracy do exist, and they prove to be something more than simple variations on a liberal democratic theme. I shall make this case through reference to that home (and now leading exporter) of capitalist democratic discourse, the United States. The United States proves to contain a surprisingly rich variety of alternative discourses, four of which I identify here in a study of how people actually conceptualize democracy and their place in it. These four discourses are contented republicanism, deferential conservatism, disaffected populism, and private liberalism. If alternatives are available in the United States, then surely they are available anywhere.

With the search for democratic alternatives in mind, the key here is to map the prevailing constellation of political discourses in order to locate those that challenge the dominant political order. Especially pertinent would be discourses registering motivations that cannot be reduced to economic rationality. To be of interest here, these alternative discourses do not have to constitute fully formed and comprehensive counterparts to the political status quo. Even if they are tentative and incomplete, these alternatives still might be pressed into a productive conversation with imaginative proposals for different kinds of democracy.[2] Ideally, such a conversation would also take into account the kinds of structural constraints and possibilities that I discussed in previous chapters. I shall return to the posibilities for such a conversation in the concluding chapter.

Capitalist Democracy as a Discourse

What are the essential components of the discourse of capitalist democracy? To answer this question, it is necessary to identify the key elements that characterize any political discourse. These elements constitute a checklist for the analysis and comparison of discourses. The vital elements of a political discourse are as follows (see Alker and Sylvan, 1986; Dryzek, 1988, p. 711; Seidel, 1985):

1. An ontology, or set of entities recognized as existing (for example, individuals, classes, nations, races, genders, genes, interests). Likewise, some entities will be denied recognition; for example, liberal discourse has traditionally denied the existence of social classes defined by their relation to the economic means of production.
2. Assignment of degrees of agency to these entities. Some will be construed as autonomous subjects, which can act (for example, Marxists conceive of classes in this way). Others will be seen as objects, which can only be caused or acted on (vulgar Marxists see the state as fully controlled by the dominant class).
3. For agents, some motives will be recognized, others denied. Relevant motives might include material self-interest, historical destiny, altruism, shame, civic virtue, anxiety, subconscious desire, repressed sexuality, impartiality, survival, and reproductive success.
4. Conceptions of natural and unnatural political relationships (*natural* here can mean inevitable *or* proper, the latter not necessarily being observable). Such relationships include taken-for-granted hierarchies based on age, education, birth, gender, wealth, social class, and the like. Other possibilities might be competitive, cooperative, harmonious, or adversarial relationships. For example, fascist discourse regards violent conflict as natural between races and nations.

How should we interpret the discourse of liberal democratic capitalism in terms of this checklist? The ontology consists, first and foremost, of individuals, who in turn are viewed as structured bundles of beliefs, opinions, and attitudes that are formed in their private experiences. Entities such as social classes, society (in the organic sense of anything more than an assemblage of individuals), "the people" and "the state" are not recognized. This denial is rarely made explicit, although in 1987 Margaret Thatcher did announce that "there is no such thing as society." The only collective actors recognized by the discourse and irreducible to their component individuals are firms and interests; the latter may be organized into (say) pressure groups and political parties. The discourse ascribes agency to all the main entities in its ontology: individuals, firms, and interests.

In regard to motives, the capitalist democratic discourse sees all action in instrumental terms. That is, individuals, firms, and interests have ends and pursue actions with ends in mind. The ends in question primarily concern material self-interest, but more altruistic ends are not ruled out, nor is, for instance, a simple desire to see a position prevail. Although at first sight unremarkable, the motives recognized have major implications, as political behavior is seen as coterminous with other kinds of behavior. Politics pertains to the pursuit of interest and advantage, not to the *formation* of opinions or the *discovery* of preferences or the *re-creation* of relationships.

The relationships regarded as natural by the discourse of capitalist democracy are made up of a mixture of competition, hierarchy, equality, and antagonism. Competition exists in both politics (across individuals and interests) and markets (across individuals and firms). Within firms (and, for that matter, other organizations), hierarchy based on wealth and expertise is regarded as natural. Within politics, hierarchy in terms of control of political power is seen as equally natural; ordinary people possess far less in the way of power than do political leaders. And if Pateman (1988) is right, liberal political equality (for men only) is predicated on patriarchy in the private realm. Equality in both politics and economics comes in the form of equality of opportunity—but not of material condition or political influence. Antagonism across persons, including those in government, requires that individuals have a range of rights for their protection against others.

These, then, are the bare essentials of the discourse of liberal democratic capitalism or, for short, capitalist democracy. The discourse does not rule out some degree of political change. Thus those would-be democratizers Samuel Bowles and Herbert Gintis state that their "conviction is that elements of the now-dominant liberal discourse can be forged into powerful tools of democratic mobilization." In particular, they have in mind the extension of liberal conceptions of rights, but they hope that this mobilization "if successful, is almost certain in the long run to burst the bounds of the liberal discourse itself" (1986, p. 175). It is possible that they may be too pessimistic about the short term or too optimistic about the long term. It all depends on whether the discourse really is "now-dominant" or hegemonic, as Bowles and Gintis aver, or if, on the other hand, there are cracks in it or even alternatives to it. These are empirical questions. So let me turn to the country where the hegemony (such as it is) began: the United States. Surely, if there is no hegemony here, then there is no hegemony anywhere.

Capitalist Democracy in the United States

The United States has always been unique among Western industrial societies in its lack of a serious socialist alternative (despite the millions of votes amassed by Eugene Debs in presidential elections early in the twentieth century). To Dorothy Ross (1991), this has been viewed since the mid-nineteenth century as a matter of "American exceptionalism": The nation's endowments of economic opportunity and republican government enabled avoidance of the poverty and class struggle that beset Europe. In these terms, Louis Hartz celebrated the liberal tradition in America (1955), which supposedly conjoined capitalism and democracy in a harmonious manner seen nowhere else in the world. According to this account, the country's absence of a feudal past meant that the assertion of rights was never a radical or revolutionary act but simply the affirmation of an egalitarian and competitive political–economic order. Hartz believed that once they had shaken off their feudal heritage and its legacy of class struggle, other countries could also follow the path charted by the United States.

Hartz is undoubtedly Panglossian in his ascription of social harmony to the United States and its history, although his account perhaps made some sense in the 1950s, that most stifling of decades. The 1950s also gave birth to the "end of ideology" thesis (see Bell, 1960; Lipset, 1960; Shils, 1955), which held that ideological conflict in the United States had been replaced by a pragmatic, problem-solving focus within a consensus on capitalist democracy as the appropriate political–economic system. That decade also spawned a new theory of democracy. So-called empirical democratic theory flowered when new technology, most notably the opinion survey, enabled summary judgments concerning the capabilities and dispositions of mass publics. The theory was "empirical" in that it relied on social scientific information about the real world of politics.

The opinion research findings were, at first sight, disturbing rather than comforting to friends of American democracy: For the most part, ordinary people proved to be politically ignorant, potentially intolerant, inconsistent and unstable in their opinions, and influenced by social and psychological forces beyond their conscious control.[3] However, empirical theorists such as Dahl (1956), Sartori (1962), and Eckstein (1966) could eventually draw comfort, and not anguish, from these findings. The key was to recognize that the optimal amount of participation by the masses was not unlimited. Too much participation could lead to instability and violence, of the sort seen in Germany's Weimar Republic. In this scenario, apathy could be regarded as functional, a sign of support for the system, rather than alienation from it (Samuel Huntington echoes this point in his contribution to Crozier, Huntington, and Watanuki, 1975, p. 114). According to this account, the masses possessed, and should possess no more than, limited and indirect influence in politics, but this did not make the system any less democratic. Existing institutions in the United States political system (and perhaps some others) seemed to provide the optimal level of mass access to politics, especially through channels constituted by interest groups. Equally fortunately, mass publics in the United States and Great Britain proved to have just enough faith in their capabilities, tempered by just enough deference and parochialism, to accept and support the limited participation that their systems allowed (Almond and Verba, 1963). Thus there seemed to be no difficulty in measuring "democracy" in terms of degree of proximity to the Anglo-American ideal. The effect on the degree of democracy of factors such as level of economic development (Lipset, 1959) and mass attitudes (for example, Cnudde, 1971; Prothro and Grigg, 1960) could then be investigated.

At first, the years were not kind to either the end-of-ideology thesis or the empirical theory of democracy. The micropolitical foundations of the empirical theory were questioned (though very politely) within the community of survey researchers, some of whom began to discern more in the way of instrumental rationality in the political behavior of the mass public (see, for example, Fiorina, 1981; Nie, Verba, and Petrocik, 1976). However, as Kinder observed, these revisionist accounts involved no more than a marginal adjustment to a dismal account of mass political capabilities (1983, pp. 393–97). The political events of the late 1960s and 1970s were more serious challenges to the end-of-ideology thesis and the empirical theory of democracy, calling into question both the stability of U.S. political institutions and their ability to accommodate new pressures and demands from below. The empirical theory of democracy seemed to run out of energy in this period, and some of its adherents changed their minds about actual and desirable democratic orders (for example, Dahl, 1982). Its critics, for their part, relished exposing its ultimately ideological commitments to the status quo in Anglo-American politics (for example, Dunn, 1979, pp. 25–26; Pateman, 1970, pp. 1–17; Skinner, 1973). But no new empirical theory of democracy has arisen to supplant that developed in the 1950s and 1960s. The weight of survey research findings supported no alternative account, at least until the very recent efforts collected by Marcus and Hanson (1993); the "old" empirical theory is still entrenched in the U.S. politics textbooks;[4] Sartori (1987, 1991), for one, remains unrepentant; and its essential elements reappear (if unacknowledged) in minimalist accounts of democracy such as those of Riker (1982a) and Mueller (1992).

If the empirical theory of democracy does no more than linger on, its cousin, the once-ridiculed end-of-ideology thesis, has found renewed life.

It is not quite true that the supposed end of history merely updates the end of ideology (as some unsympathetic political scientists with long memories have suggested). Rather, the end-of-history thesis has a global purview, whereas the end of ideology was presented only as an American phenomenon, at least in the first instance. Moroever, Fukuyama (1992) has a historical depth and ambition that the more limited focus of Bell (1960) and his colleagues lacked; Fukuyama explains exactly why we have come to this resting place, rather than treating it as a purely local and empirical phenomenon (see Chapter 2). It would perhaps be more accurate to say that the end of history subsumes the end of ideology, for ideological dispute is just one aspect of the history that Fukuyama believes we have buried.

Despite their ups and downs, which I have noted here, American exceptionalism, Hartz's liberal tradition, the end of ideology, the empirical theory of democracy, and the end of history all are manifestations of something very continuous. This continuity rests on the belief of intellectuals that there is a large measure of public consensus on, stability in, and effectiveness of the basic institutions of the U.S. political economy. The consensus here allows for substantial disagreement on the content of policies, even on constitutional questions (such as those pertaining to the proposed balanced budget amendment to the U.S. Constitution or the equal rights amendment). The important point is that there seems to be nothing to offer in the way of alternatives to the basic discourse of capitalist democracy as I defined it earlier.

Or is there?

A Reconstructive Approach to Democratic Discourse

Many of the accounts of unity in the U.S. political culture and its discourse of capitalist democracy are constructed from the armchair. When social scientists have lifted themselves out of the armchair, they have often used methods and tools that are not very good at disclosing alternatives to the dominant discourse. Foremost among these tools is opinion survey research, which tries to elicit from its respondents unambiguous answers to carefully specified questions. The trouble is that inherent in the survey instrument is a discourse replicating many of the features of the discourse of capitalist democracy that I described earlier (see Dryzek, 1988). Moreover, the researcher's own preconceptions are a big obstacle in survey research. As Sullivan, Fried, Theiss-Morse, and Dietz explained,

> The problem lies in investigating concepts in a particular way, by operationalizing them in an *a priori* manner that can severely and arbitrarily restrict the domain within which people can respond. Given this *modus operandi*, investigators are not likely to learn much from the subjects of their inquiry, other than whether people generally respond as predicted by researchers' hunches

or theories. A richer process of learning and discovery by truly *listening to* respondents' views is precluded. (1990, p. 3, italics in original)

The alternative followed in the remainder of this chapter is to approach in *reconstructive* terms the study of mass dispositions and capabilities and associated discourses of democracy. Reconstructive science is concerned with the social competences of individuals and the corresponding grammars of human interaction. Its categories are sought in how its subjects apprehend the world, downplaying as much as possible (though never actually eliminating) the analyst's prior expectations. The findings thus generated should therefore be a more secure foundation for theorizing about democracy than the findings or assumptions generally used by democratic theorists.

Perhaps the best-known discussion of the idea of reconstructive science is Jurgen Habermas's idealization of the theories of Lawrence Kohlberg on moral development, Noam Chomsky on linguistic competence, and Jean Piaget on operational thought. Habermas (1979) claims that these theories are universally applicable and above reproach, that they capture the true nature and development of essential human capabilities. But Habermas's argument on this score is almost certainly false. These three theories can be, and have been, disputed and so merit a status little different from more familiar kinds of social scientific theory (Alford, 1985). Moreover, their categories are specified in the theorist's interpretation of some ideal subject and how he or she should develop, rather than by the subjects themselves.[5]

We[6] offer here a more truly reconstructive approach that lets the subjects speak for themselves about their interactive competences, and the categories—in our case, political discourses—that these competences help construct. Thus in speaking of the competences of individuals, we are not holding them up against a yardstick external to them. Our notion of reconstructive science is, instead, somewhat different from that of Habermas, for we afford less license to the analyst to reconstruct the competence of an ideal subject. Our concern is with actual subjects, and we try to minimize the influence of our preconceptions concerning the content of their competences.

The idea that the analyst should attend closely to the subjects' own constructions of politics has in the past been advanced most forcefully in ethnographic studies involving intensive interviewing of a small number of subjects, notably those of Lane (1962) and Hochschild (1981).[7] While applauding the ethnographers' intent and recognizing their accomplishments, we try here to be still more truly reconstructive. To make sense of the conversational data they collect, ethnographers must creatively impose coherence on subjects' orientations and dispositions. This creative act is inevitably personal, partly intuitive, and unconstrained. In contrast, our methodology is explicit, public, constrained by statistical results, and replicable in its reconstruction and measurement of the subjects' orientations, thus affording less interpretive latitude to the analyst. In addition, our methodology is capable of yielding surprising results that directly oppose the analyst's own intuitions and expectations. We do not claim that our kind of reconstructive inquiry is the only proper way to understand human political disposition and action but simply that it has distinct advantages over speculative philosophical assertion, unconstrained ethnographic interpretation, and restrictive opinion survey research.

In proceeding in reconstructive terms, our concerns lie in uncovering the *dispositions* of individuals (that is, their opinions about matters of fact and value relevant to democracy) and their *self-described capabilities* as potential members of a democratic order. Dispositions and capabilities are, of course, intertwined, and we do not attempt to measure them separately. Rather, it is individual persons' *interactive* competences that are our concern, and these competences have no existence independent of a person's orientation to his or her social context. In other words, the way in which people construct reality is inseparable from the roles they think they can, do, and should play in relation to that reality.

In the next section we describe in some detail our reconstructive methodology. Readers more interested in the results concerning the discourses of democracy that exist in the United States than in how we arrived at them may want to skip this methodological section.

Q Methodology and Political Discourse Analysis

To ascertain the discourses of democracy present in the United States, we use the best-developed approach to the study of human subjectivity, Q methodology, which is ideally suited to the measurement of patterns embedded in language.

Q methodology was invented by the psychologist William Stephenson (see especially Stephenson, 1953). A Q study begins by modeling subjects in terms of their reactions to a set of statements about a given domain. Unlike more widely applied methods such as survey research, Q is not concerned with patterns across variables (for example, the association between issue attitudes and vote choice) but, rather, with patterns within and across individuals. To this end, the whole subject is modeled at once, as a respondent's reaction to any one statement makes sense only in the context of his or her reactions to every other statement in the set. We compiled 64 such statements, which our subjects were asked to order in a quasi-normal distribution (that is, with relatively few statements in the extreme categories and relatively many in the center of the distribution). The extremes of the distribution were coded $+6$ for "most agree" and -6 for "most disagree," with 0 indicating indifference. This ordering of statements that a subject produces is called a *Q sort*, and it represents the subject's orientation to the domain in question, as represented by his or her pattern of reaction to the 64 statements.

This orientation is produced through reference to language the subject is likely to use and understand, not in terms of categories developed by the investigator. As Kitzinger explained, "The theoretical basis on which Q methodology is founded relies on the axiom that researchers should acknowledge and present the reality constructions of different women and men without prejudging or discrediting them, and without insisting on the superior (more 'objective') status of the researcher's own construction of reality" (1986, p. 153). Q is therefore a reconstructive methodology, albeit an imperfect one because it is the researcher who defines the domain of the study. In our case, we defined the democratic domain or concourse just as specified in Chapter 1, as concerned with the collective construction, application, distribution, and limitation of political authority, and we collected only those statements that fell within this domain.

It is possible to compute a correlation coefficient between the Q sorts of any two persons. A correlation of 1 would indicate perfect agreement, and -1 would represent perfect disagreement. But the most common approach to statistical analysis of Q sorts is to summarize the pattern of agreement and dispute across all the subjects at once using factor analysis. So those people who load highly on any one factor reveal a high level of commonality with one another and dissimilarity with people who load highly on other factors (or negatively on that same factor).[8]

The statements that someone is asked to order in a Q sort are drawn from a concourse of verbalizations in which that person has some interest. A *concourse*, as noted at the beginning of Chapter 1, is the sum of communication or "the volume of discussion on any topic" (Brown, 1986, p. 58) representing an interplay or running together of positions, ideas, and opinions. More formally, a concourse can be operationalized as the population of statements about some topic. The analyst draws a representative sample of statements from the concourse at hand (in our case, democracy), with the intention of using them in a Q study.

Fidelity to our reconstructive principle requires that the statements selected by the analyst and presented to the subjects for ordering be drawn from those actually made by individuals involved with the concourse. We gathered around 300 statements from newspapers, magazines (of many different partisanships, ranging from the John Birch Society's *New American* to the leftist *Guardian*), voter's pamphlets, quotation dictionaries, the verbatim reports contained in the ethnographic studies of Lane (1962), Hochschild (1981), Bellah, Madsen, Sullivan, Swidler, and Tipton (1985), and Reinarman (1987), and discussion groups on democracy for which we recruited people through newspaper advertisements.[9] Again, our reconstructive commitment meant that we did not edit statements beyond occasionally substituting a noun for an *it*.[10] Some statements were ambiguous, but that is the nature of political language. Am-

biguity is resolved by each subject and reflected in his or her placement of
a statement in relation to other statements. Of the 64 statements we
eventually used, 20 came from ethnographic studies, 17 from magazines,
15 from our discussion groups, 5 from newspapers, 4 from voters pamphlets, and 3 from quotation dictionaries. In keeping with our earlier
point that reconstructive science treats competences and orientations as
inseparable, we sought statements that refer to the individual making
them as well as to the world "out there." An example of the former kind
of statement is "I don't feel that I'm that knowledgeable about things. If
I knew a lot more actual facts and everything, then I might be able to
strike up a conversation about politics."

To reduce the 300 statements to a manageable 64, a procedure is
necessary that is as independent as possible of the analyst's particular interests. Complete independence is, of course, impossible, given that we
had to make judgments in selecting statements in the first place (based on
whether they belonged in the democratic concourse), but Q moves further in this direction than do procedures such as survey research. Brown
justified a rough-and-ready approach to statement sampling on the
grounds that "there is no standard Q sample for a concourse. Any suitably comprehensive sample is adequate for purposes of experimentation"
(1986, p. 73). Although we generally do not dispute Brown's point
here, we believe we can do better in regard to the analysis of essentially
political discourses, such as that pertaining to democracy, for the
following reasons.

Concourse is a more inclusive category than *discourse*, which is why we
introduced it. If a discourse is hegemonic (as Michel Foucault and his
followers often suggest when they describe the history of Western societies), there will be only one discourse in the concourse; that is discourse
and concourse will be identical. On the other hand, it is possible that more
than one discourse will be present in a concourse. According to Hajer, "In
politics we characteristically deal with mixes of elements drawn from different discourses" (1993, p. 46). Later we will demonstrate that such is
indeed the case when it comes to democracy in the United States. The
situation when several discourses coexist may be described as one of *partial
intelligibility* across different discourses. In a political context, for example,
we might speculate that socialists and conservatives inhabit different discourses. It may be that the same words, phrases, or statements—for example, "democracy demands diversity"—may mean different things in
different discourses. To liberals, the diversity in question would represent
points of view; to partisans of political correctness in U.S. universities,
diversity would have to encompass the race, gender, and sexual preferences
of the people involved (ordinary opinion survey research is exceptionally
bad at picking up on such subtleties). Partial intelligibility means that communication across the discourses at hand is possible but problematic. Just
as when speakers of different languages try to communicate, translation is
possible, but some meaning is inevitably lost.[11]

How do we make sure that the key points defining and separating the different discourses are generated and identified? Our answer is that we should be guided by the four categories of political discourse analysis introduced earlier. Thus we sought statements pertaining to ontology, agency, motives, and relationships regarded as natural. The details of statement selection are relegated to a footnote.[12]

The sample of 64 statements was administered to 37 subjects. Our guiding principle in subject selection was diversity, so that if a discourse (however marginal) exists, we would be likely to locate it. Some of our subjects were identified on the basis of known political commitments: We sought peace, civil rights, environmental, labor union, religious, and business activists; Republicans; Democrats; Libertarians; liberals; conservatives; socialists; and feminists. The remainder of our subjects were chosen with an eye to maximizing social variety. We sought white- and blue-collar workers, the retired, rich and poor, males and females, voters and nonvoters, members of different ethnic and racial groups (African American, Asian, Latino, and white), adherents of different religions (and of none), urban and rural residents, and residents of different states. Our limited resources meant that we could not contact subjects from across the United States; rather, our subjects were concentrated in California, Oregon, Washington, Wisconsin, West Virginia, Maryland, and North Carolina.

Q is an intensive form of analysis and always works with small numbers of subjects. Although one can never claim that one's subjects are statistically representative of some larger population, that is not the point. The patterns that Q methodologists find in a small group of subjects can be expected to reflect the structures existing in some larger population of subjects (Brown, 1980, pp. 66–67). Therefore a discourse identified in a small-n Q study generally is a genuine representation of that discourse as it exists in a larger population of persons, and this is the kind of generalization in which we are interested. Or to put it another way: Our units of analysis in regard to generalization are not individuals but discourses. And we soon get to a point that adding individuals to a study does not yield any new information unless the extra individuals are truly different—another reason for stressing diversity in subject selection.

Like most successful sciences, Q has confidence in its individual observations (in contrast to surveys and statistical studies that utilize large numbers precisely because they have little confidence in individual observations). We cannot say just what proportion of any larger population subscribes to the discourse in question, although that question could be answered easily, if expensively, by a sample survey of the United States population (see Sullivan et al., 1990).

We identified four discourses of democracy through a factor analysis of the Q sorts of our 37 subjects.[13] An idealized Q sort can be computed for each discourse; this represents the way a hypothetical individual loading 100 percent on a factor would order the 64 statements, and it forms the basis for our interpretation of each factor. Table 6.1 shows the scores of all 64 statements on the idealized Q sort for each of the four discourses (factors A, B, C, and D).

Table 6.1. Statement Scores on Each Factor

Statement	Factor			
	A	B	C	D
1. I don't think freedom has anything to do with democracy.	−4	0	−6	+2
2. Democracy is never easy to define. The meaning of the word changes with the vagaries of time, place and circumstance.	0	+4	0	2
3. Democracy is a governmental form, not necessarily having anything to do with society as a whole or the way society works.	−4	−2	−3	+1
4. Democracy is an empty vessel into which one can comfortably fit socialism as well as freedom, a corrupt society as well as a healthy people.	−1	+1	−1	+4
5. Community means people who interact at a personal level; have shared identity, values, and traditions; and possess the power to make decisions about their common values.	+4	+4	0	+4
6. Citizenship is a man's basic right for it is nothing less than the right to have rights.	+2	−1	0	−1
7. Any citizen who can read and wants to take the time can make a good decision among candidates for an office.	+1	−3	−1	0
8. Mass democracy depends on an informed and active citizenry.	+6	+3	+3	−2
9. To try to find the public good, I would try to ask questions about how this or that would affect the community twenty five years from now. Not whether such and such a regulation will affect somebody else's pocketbook.	+1	+5	+1	−1
10. If I wanna say my mind that's fine. But I also have the right not to listen, and that's what the First Amendment gives me.	+1	0	0	+5
11. When the president does it, that means it's not illegal.	−6	−6	−5	−5
12. Democracy means my right to choose what's best for me and the public at large.	+4	0	+4	0
13. Work and family are the center of our lives, the foundation of our dignity as a free people.	+2	−1	−3	+6
14. Democracy demands diversity.	+5	−1	+2	+1

Table 6.1. (*continued*)

Statement	Factor			
	A	*B*	*C*	*D*
15. Men are not created equal. They have different intelligence; they're born into different situations. What "all men are created equal" basically means, of course, is whether you're white or black or poor, you should have your equal say, your equal education, be treated equally.	+5	+5	−2	+1
16. I think the rights of the individuals add up to majority rule.	+1	+1	−4	+2
17. You can have a socialist society and have the government elected in a democratic election.	+1	+1	+2	+5
18. A market economy, a democratic legislature, an independent judiciary, and constitutionally guaranteed rights are the only proven foundations for sharing power.	+1	−2	−1	+3
19. Democracy sure does not exist in its pure form today.	0	0	+1	+3
20. I have a big problem identifying with hundreds of millions of anything—people, flowers, cars, miles. I can see the community around me.	−2	0	−2	−3
21. We the people have not chosen the freedoms that we have.	−3	−1	−2	+2
22. I don't feel that I'm that knowledgeable about things. . . . If I knew a lot more about actual facts and everything, then I might be able to strike up a conversation about politics.	−3	+1	−4	−4
23. Not everyone is going to be represented, there are always those people who fall through the cracks.	+1	+6	0	+3
24. If things don't get done, it's because the people don't go out and do it. The power is with the people.	+3	−1	+4	0
25. I'm interested in the national economy and our defense ability, not all these crappy issues like human rights.	−6	−5	−4	−4
26. I don't think it's possible to have a democracy of three people without greed being the main factor.	−4	+1	−4	−2
27. In essence, the government doesn't really care about what I say.	−2	+2	−1	−1
28. All governments, and the elites that live off them, want to control public opinion.	−1	+1	+4	+1

Table 6.1. (*continued*)

Statement	Factor			
	A	B	C	D
29. Elected officials are better able to make decisions for voters than voters themselves.	-3	-4	-5	-6
30. Now we are pretty much all equal. I don't think the people stand for NOT being treated equal any more.	-2	-6	-6	-3
31. The daily lives of all citizens are deeply affected and changed by the decisions of government.	$+3$	$+6$	$+2$	$+6$
32. I can get pretty confused when I listen to political speeches. A guy gets up and sounds like he's the best there is. The next guy gets out and makes a bum out of him. You don't know who to believe.	-2	$+5$	-1	-1
33. A free press protects our basic liberties by serving as the watchdogs of our nation.	$+5$	-2	$+5$	-2
34. If I can find something that's good for the average person, that's good for democracy.	-1	-2	-2	-1
35. Democracies can make mistakes, but they have the unique advantage of a way to make corrections before it is too late.	$+3$	-5	$+1$	$+1$
36. Government can't be too powerful because the government is the people.	-3	-3	-2	-3
37. A lot of government's problem is too many chiefs.	-1	0	0	0
38. Anybody can stand on the street corner and under the constitution voice pretty much anything, and that's a problem.	-5	-4	-5	-3
39. We should be critically concerned about the drop-off in democratic participation in the United States, and about who is voting (the educated and economically well-off) and who is not voting (the poor, the young, minorities, and the least educated).	$+3$	$+2$	$+6$	$+3$
40. America has deteriorated in the direction of a democracy as we have become a government of men instead of a government of law.	-3	0	$+3$	$+3$
41. In a systematic way, the rights of individuals have been curtailed in this country, not for the benefit of the whole nation, but in conformity with a narrow interpretation of a vocal conservative minority.	0	$+2$	$+5$	-1

Table 6.1. (*continued*)

Statement	Factor			
	A	B	C	D
42. A major problem with democracy is that many people do not know what they want.	−1	+2	−3	0
43. Violence is a just and legitimate reponse to the economic, political, and military violence employed by the state.	−5	−2	+1	−5
44. I'd like to hear all points of view. Sometimes it's confusing, but I'd rather like that.	+2	+3	+1	−3
45. The way that democracy is manifested in our culture, some people are more equal than others. It becomes a double standard very quickly.	+2	+3	+6	0
46. I don't think social class is important.	0	−4	−2	0
47. The government is like a domineering mother. It takes away all the people's incentives and tries to do everything for them. You know what it's like for children who have been dominated all their lives by a strong, powerful mother. They become near vegetable cases. It's the same with government.	−4	−3	0	+4
48. The impersonal hand of government can never replace the helping hand of a neighbor.	+1	+2	+3	+5
49. Politicians should not be allowed to get away with lying as a form of free speech.	+4	+3	−1	0
50. Religion should be banished from politics because a democratic politics is based not on truth but on justice.	−2	−1	0	−4
51. All voters should be allowed as much information as possible to make their choices. Any attempt to regulate political literature and speeches is a move against our First Amendment freedoms and toward totalitarianism.	+6	+4	+2	+2
52. Our system of social justice must be, and is, based upon natural human rights.	+3	−5	+1	+1
53. The future of democracy? Bleak. It's just gonna get worse, unless things get really bad and people start protesting again.	−2	−1	+3	+2
54. If everyone put what money and/or time they could into political campaigns and causes, we would all be better off.	0	−4	−1	−5
55. If you want the state off your back, put your feet to the pavement.	0	−3	+2	−1

Table 6.1. (*continued*)

Statement	Factor			
	A	B	C	D
56. We should relocate power away from elites and the federal government and return it to the community level.	−1	0	+1	+4
57. You're part of society. Everybody has to do something to help society.	+2	+4	+4	−2
58. I think we should take a good look at future candidates and ask questions about him that are for the good of the people and not just big business.	+2	+3	+5	+1
59. All that is needed is for governments to be honest, for those governments need the people.	0	+1	−1	−2
60. Democracy is best, it's something we should strive for.	+4	+2	+3	−1
61. We can build a world where it is self-evident that all people are created equal.	−1	−3	+1	+1
62. Under communism the state would supply all the money for you. Everyone would be working for the state, there wouldn't really be no rich people in it. That would be good, if everyone is on kind of an equal level.	−5	−2	−3	−6
63. The family—like most traditional institutions—simply needs to be made more democratic.	0	−1	−3	−4
64. The perfect society is everybody living in accord, going about their own business and having separate interests, but that hopefully these interests all mesh nicely, they aren't bumping into each other and conflicting.	−1	+1	+2	+2

Alternative Discourses of Democracy

The most parsimonious form in which to present the four discourses is with a label and a narrative for each. The numbers in brackets in each of the following narratives refer to the statement numbers in Table 6.1.[14] The four discourses, each of which embodies a conceptualization of democracy, are as follows:

Contented Republicanism (factor A). We live in a democracy, which is fortunate because democracy is, without doubt, the best form of government (40, 60). Democracy is a way of life, not just a political system; it is bound up with our freedoms, and though fallible, democracy can correct its mistakes (3, 1, 21, 35). Thus there is no need to fear an excess of democracy or to fear for the future of democracy (53). This future depends on the citizenry's remaining active and involved in politics (8). There is no difficulty here, for politics is an uncomplicated activity in which everyone can and should be involved, although it would be good if the poor and less well educated were to participate more (39). Political equality is important and easily achieved and does not require social and economic equality (15, 61, 30). There is such a thing as the people, and power is in its hands (24). This is a diverse society, but that is good for democracy (14). It is our common citizenship that unites us, not communal traditions; citizenship is basic to our way of life (6). Politics need not be based on greed or self-interest, for democratic debate can help establish an identity between what is good for me and what is good for society (26, 12). The importance of this debate means that there should be no restraints on the availability of information, that a free press is crucial, and that we should not tolerate lying in politics (51, 33, 49). Thus government should be seen not as an adversary but as the institution in which our citizenship is embodied, although, of course, government can become too big and intrusive and so may need constitutional restraint (47, 36). The government does listen to me, and there are few limits to my capacity to exercise political influence (27).

Deferential Conservatism (factor B). Politics is only for the few. Not everyone is capable of making good decisions; people do not know what they want; and not everyone can be represented (7, 42, 23). Thus human frailty makes democracy problematical and hard even to define (26, 42, 2). Although this difficulty in defining the concept means that democracy does not necessarily bring bad things, democracy is not particularly valuable or effective either (12, 35, 60). Certainly, democracy should not pervade society, and it does not necessarily have much to do with real freedom (1). It is undesirable for people to get any more involved in politics. Citizen activism is not a good thing (54, 55), nor are the liberal values of a free press, independent judiciary, social justice rooted in basic rights, or the market very attractive (18, 33, 52). To me, politics is remote and confusing (22, 32, 2). But this does not matter, because government does not listen to people like me, anyway (27, 32). However, there is no need to fear government; we should rely on elites to govern and hope that they are honest (47, 55, 49). Such elites will be able to look out for the long-term interest of society, which matters more than short-term economic concerns (9). This is an unequal, class-divided society, and little can or should be done about that (15, 30, 46, 61).

Disaffected Populism (factor C). We do not live in a democracy, as power is in the hands of conservative, corporate elites and a government that represses the people (41, 28). This is a highly unequal society, especially in terms of political influence, and calling it a democracy does not change that (30, 45). Over time, democratic control has deteriorated, and the future of democracy will be bleak unless people wake up and do something about it (39, 40, 53). The freedoms that are central to democracy have been curtailed (1, 41). It is up to the people to rise up and challenge this situation; they have the capacity to do so (55, 24, 42). The power of big business and corporate elites should be restricted (58). Thus equality and true democracy are possible and desirable, even though we are very far from them today (8, 15). Ordinary individuals are well motivated, and they should attend to politics rather than be preoccupied by work and family (26, 13), though politics cannot and should not be all-consuming. Community does not matter much, and so it does not matter at what level of government power resides (5, 56). More important is the people acting together, confronting government rather than occupying institutional roles within it. In this critical sphere, a free press is essential (33). One should not necessarily condemn political violence when it is undertaken by the oppressed (43). I have complete confidence in my own political capabilities and in those of citizens more generally (22).

Private Liberalism (factor D). We do not live in an especially democratic society, and not everyone can be represented (19, 23). But this is no cause for concern, for democracy is of no particular value, given that it can encompass both desirable kinds of government and undesirable forms such as socialism (60, 17, 4). Government itself is something that need not be central to society (3). Moreover, society should not be central to individuals, who do not have to consider themselves part of, or contribute to, society (57). Individuals should be free to pursue their own interests, but democracy will not guarantee that freedom (1, 21). It is the private realm that really matters—work and family are the most important things in life, and one should rely on friends, neighbors, and the market rather than government (13, 48, 18). Interests defined in the private sphere are paramount, and this is why (for example) it is fine for religion to motivate political action (50). Government, however democratic, has intruded too far into this private realm; government should be small and subject to separation of powers and constitutional restraints (31, 47, 18). Furthermore, power should be moved back to communities, away from the federal level (56). Active citizenship is not important or desirable, and individuals have every right to ignore politics; it would be undesirable for people to put more time and effort into politics (8, 10, 54). I'm not interested in public debate, and so I do not care unduly about a free press (44, 33). This lack of interest is not because I lack confidence in my own capabilities, but because politics is not central to life (22).

These, then, are our four discourses of democracy. The ontology, ascription of agency, motivation, and natural relationships associated with each discourse are further summarized in Table 6.2. The four discourses are divided on the basic issues of who or what constitutes a recognizable

Table 6.2. Analysis of Four Discourses of Democracy

	Discourse Element			
Discourse	*Ontology*	*Agency*	*Ascribed Motivation*	*Relationships Seen as Natural*
A. Contented republicanism	The people	Everyone	Public good	Political equality, harmony between public and private interests
B. Deferential conservatism	Society, elites	Elites	Mysterious	Hierarchy
C. Disaffected populism	Corporate and governmental elites, the people	Currently elites, properly the people	Elite—own interest; people are properly radical	Currently class conflict, properly radical equality
D. Private liberalism	Individuals, government	Individuals (but not necessarily in politics), government	Material self-interest	Separateness of individuals, conflict between individuals and government

political entity, which of these entities can act, their reasons for action, and the kinds of relationships that can exist between entities. Thus A's contented republicanism recognizes an unproblematic harmony encompassing active individuals and an active people, private and public realms. Consequently, A's democratic enthusiasm is unbounded, treating political equality is an accomplished fact. But this enthusiasm is not quite Panglossian, inasmuch as it seeks still more extensive participation, to which it perceives no structural impediments. Politics for contented republicanism is a matter of honest talk about the public good, coextensive with individual activity and social life.

Although both A and B accept the broad political status quo, in other respects they could hardly be more different. B's deferential conservatism constitutes a discourse that accepts that political hierarchy is natural and whose commitment to democracy is correspondingly problematical. Although B seems to assent to democracy as an abstract symbol, its more specific judgments are not easily described as democratic in any definition of the term. Political agency for B can only be a property of elites, which rules out any measure of active citizenship, political equality, and public participation. Individuals loading highly on B have little faith in their own competence as political actors. Perhaps the most that can be said for B's democratic commitment is an expectation of honesty by elites and a desire to be able to listen effectively to political communication. B cares little even for liberal constitutionalism and liberal freedoms.

C's disaffected populism is as eager for political equality as is A's contented republicanism. However, C believes that society is currently divided by class and repressive, such that mass action against political–economic elites is called for. C is an insurgent democrat's discourse, tinged with liberalism in its commitments to human rights, a free press, free speech, and individual differences and is less liberal in its ascription of agency to the people. The popular struggle that C seeks must contend with not only a repressive system and the forces that perpetuate it but also two discourses that would oppose such a struggle. Nor is the tactical question here made any easier by the fact that this opposition would come from the very different perspectives of the deferential conservatives and the private liberals. The contented republicanism of factor A would not necessarily oppose all of the ends of C's struggle, but it would question the need.

The private liberalism of discourse D has a guarded view of democratic possibilities, stemming from the fact that it sets individuals apart from one another (partially excepting friends and neighbors) in pursuit of personal advantage and in conflict with government. As a result, D is energized mostly by the need to establish and protect the private realm against social sanction and government interference. Like B, D is not interested in extensive political participation, although for different reasons. B's deferential conservatives have little faith in the competence of themselves and others, whereas D sees no limits to this competence but believes it should be used for nonpolitical pursuits. D has much less faith than B does in the benevolence of political elites and so accords far greater importance to constitutional forms that might constrain elites.

We should note further that all four discourses are united on a number of points. All disagree strenuously with Richard Nixon's remark that "when the president does it, that means it is not illegal" (11). None claims to be hardheaded enough to confine its concerns to defense and economics, as opposed to social justice (25). None believes that democratic representatives are any more capable of making choices than ordinary voters are (29); thus—surprisingly—none is really a discourse of *representative* democracy. None wants to restrict freedom of speech or information (38, 51), and all profess to care about declining voting participation (39), (although B's concern is marginal). All are anticommunist, though based on a reading of communism that no Marxist would endorse (62). None believes that we live in a truly equal society (30). None has unlimited faith in the benevolence of government (36).

Our results do not allow us to generalize about how the discourses relate to social and political characteristics in the population at large. However, looking only at our subjects, it is striking that the four discourses cut across standard social and political categories. Table 6.3 reports the loadings of our 37 individuals on the four factors. Individuals with statistically significant (at the .01 level) loadings on contented republicanism included a "conservative" real estate developer, a "liberal/feminist" administrator, an "open-minded" army sergeant, a "liberal Democratic" union official, and a "slightly right of center" store detective. Those loading heavily on deferential conservatism included a "concerned but not active, confused" artist/teacher, a "Democratic" accountant, an "independent conservative" retired engineer, and a "moderate liberal" bowling alley employee. Disaffected populism attracted a "politically independent" tree farmer who volunteers for the League of Women Voters, a (different) "Democratic" union official, an anarchist bookshop owner, and a "Republican" medical salesperson. And private liberalism drew a "libertarian" public relations worker, a "nonpolitical" waitress, a Forest Service employee who "don't know nothing about politics," and a "constitutional conservative" computer analyst. (These quoted political descriptions are as supplied by the subjects themselves.)

Table 6.3. Subjects' Factor Loadings

	Factor			
Subject Self-Description	*A*	*B*	*C*	*D*
1. F, tree farmer, independent	49*	15	73*	1
2. M, real estate developer, conservative	68*	18	29	26
3. F, union representative, democrat	27	2	60*	39*
4. F, public relations, libertarian	15	−4	20	56*
5. F, administrator/consultant, liberal/feminist	65*	16	38*	11
6. F, teacher/freelance artist, concerned/confused	3	61*	15	32
7. M, self-employed, free-market socialist	24	22	26	26
8. F, accountant, liberal Republican	36*	42*	14	34*
9. M, army sergeant, open-minded	65*	10	13	21
10. M, manager, conservative Republican	52*	19	33	27
11. M, office manager, liberal	68*	20	−1	17
12. M, computer programmer, moderate liberal Republican	57*	25	16	20
13. M, health care provider, independent	58*	−10	43*	32
14. F, waitress, not political	20	42*	−4	47*
15. M, bookstore owner, anarchist	10	5	46*	13
16. M, pharmaceutical salesperson, Republican	37*	10	66*	7
17. F, clerical, conservative	16	39*	1	36*
18. M, union leader, liberal Democrat	64*	14	21	20
19. F, office manager, radical	−11	35*	44*	13
20. M, retired, open-minded	65*	7	20	42*
21. F, Forest Service employee, don't know nothing	11	21	47*	69*

Table 6.3.   (*continued*)

	Factor			
Subject Self-Description	A	B	C	D
22. F, no employment, indifferent/ ignorant	43*	31	20	14
23. F, craftsperson, liberal	53*	46*	25	27
24. F, insurance adjuster, conservative	73*	27	19	22
25. M, accountant, Democrat	14	64*	18	−12
26. F, student, liberal Democrat	27	7	24	39*
27. M, contractor, liberal	18	24	0	42*
28. F, clerical, conservative	40*	27	11	17
29. M, student, moderate Democrat	51*	1	18	9
30. F, student, socialist liberal	27	8	56*	21
31. M, computer analyst, constitutional conservative	12	8	8	51*
32. F, student/teacher/organizer, democratic socialist	51*	24	46*	−5
33. M, store detective, slightly right of center	51*	−4	24	35*
34. M, retired engineer, independent conservative	49*	49*	5	25
35. M, bowling alley employee, moderate liberal	32	48*	32	7
36. F, homemaker, conservative	17	12	4	33
37. F, secretary, liberal	46*	38*	−4	17

M = male, F = female.
* Loading significant at the .01 level.

Democratic Discourse and Democratic Possibilities

What does all this tell us about the possibilities for different kinds of democracy? The first implication to stress is that there is no hegemonic discourse of democracy present in the United States, and so no associated foreclosure of democratic possibilities.[15] Discourses are, of course, conditioned by the institutional and cultural context in which they arise, but nothing we found represents a simple reflection of the political–economic status quo. It is quite striking that our results indicate that several very different conceptualizations of democracy are present even in the United States and that there is no consensus around capitalist democracy. Indeed, we could find no simple discourse of capitalist democracy that was at all prominent. Two of our discourses support the status quo in U.S. politics, but neither does so because of the liberal and capitalist nature of this situation. Deferential conservatism supports the status quo because it allows elites to govern, and contented republicanism because it allows for citizen participation and civic virtue.

The ideational foreclosure postulated by the end-of-ideology argument, the empirical theory of democracy, and the end-of-history thesis does not exist. There are indeed coherent alternatives available.[16] We found no discursive foreclosure at all in regard to the basic parameters of democratic government; moreover, the content of the discourses that do exist bears little relation to what the various "endists" have said must be true. For its part, the empirical theory of democracy is undermined by the interest of at least two of our discourses in extended, direct, competent citizen participation. Disaffected populism would seek to use such participation to destabilize the political system. But such destabilization would be the last thing on the minds of contented republicanism, which clearly does not point to the instability teetering on authoritarianism inherent in extended participation, as feared by the empirical theorists of democracy.

How can we explain this divergence between our results, on the one hand, and the conjectures of American exceptionalists, believers in the dominance of the liberal tradition such as Hartz, empirical democratic theorists, and proponents of the end-of-ideology and end-of-history theses, on the other? The answer is that all these people approach the American public with very blunt instruments and a concomitant incapacity to make fine distinctions. This problem is most evident in approaches that rely on survey research findings. For example, Almond and Verba (1963) reached conclusions about the American citizen (in comparison with those in other countries) based on the percentages of people who replied in certain ways to their survey questions (concerning, for example, belief in the possibility of getting something done through government action). Thus they could see only singularity when in reality there was multiplicity. This applies also to all those armchair theorists who portray only a single American political culture. For example, Lowi (1979) suggested that pluralism (which stresses the competition of interest groups in an open liberal democratic context) is the ideology of what he called the Second American Republic. We discovered no support for the kind of ideology of pluralism to which he referred, which indicates either that pluralism was only an ideology of social science intellectuals, and not ordinary people, or that Lowi's second republic has passed (the first edition of his book appeared in 1969).

In the light of our finding that four distinct discourses of democracy are present in the United States, the error of all these observers was to have stirred the four discourses together and picked out bits from the resultant stew that supported their view of the world. One can indeed pick out components from the discourses that together would constitute the capitalist democratic discourse as defined at the outset of this chapter. From private liberalism could be taken those persons whose beliefs, opinions, and attitudes are fully formed in their private experience; rejection of the idea of social classes and any organic properties of society; market competition; and antagonism across individuals (and with government), necessitating that they have rights. From deferential conservatism could be taken an essential faith in the elites that govern the system, and a corresponding recognition of the dangers of excessive public participation. From deferential conservatism and contented republicanism could be taken strong support for the political status quo. From contented republicanism and disaffected populism could be taken the desirability of some level of popular participation and political equality, and the idea that individuals can be capable citizens.

But to pick and choose in this fashion is illegitimate. The idea of a discourse is that it forms a coherent whole; one cannot take some bits from it and leave others behind, for each bit makes sense only in relation to all the others. Thus those who have portrayed mass consensus in the United States on capitalist democracy have oversimplified a complex reality. Or at least they have oversimplified a reality that is *now* complex. I suspect there was always more to this reality than a single discourse, but I have no direct evidence from earlier eras on this score.

Surprisingly, some theories of democracy that have never sought grounding in opinion studies or other empirical research fared somewhat better in the light of our results than the supposedly realistic theories just criticized. There is no one-to-one identity between any of the four discourses and any one such democratic theory, but some useful connections can be drawn. These connections might fruitfully be used as correctives to the theories in question, which stand little chance of ever being put into practice if they cannot find a discourse to support them. The tradition of democratic theory is often criticized as utopian (Dunn, 1979, p. 26) or alienated from the conversation of democratic political development (Gunnell, 1986; Ricci, 1984, pp. 319–23). Connections to live discourses of democracy could help cure this alienation.

A theory of democracy is viable to the extent that there is a discourse or combination of discourses to which it can relate. The absence of any such relation undermines the model of democracy at hand *precisely because the model claims to be democratic*—that is, capable of generating some degree of mass approval. This does not mean that all democratic theories should submit themselves to a simple discursive popularity test and withdraw from the field if they fail. Even if a theory can find no discursive confirmation, its partisans can still seek to engage a particular discourse or discourses in productive conversation that can transform both discourse and theory. The four discourses identified do not define rigid boundaries outside which fruitful democratic theorizing cannot occur. Moreover, the presence of several persons with significant loadings on two factors indicates that in contrast to the world as portrayed by Foucault and the poststructuralists, there is not necessarily radical discontinuity across discourses, for such individuals have access to both the discourses in question. Assuming that this pattern is not just a methodological artifact, it provides some hope for theorists interested in articulating alternative or novel democratic theories, because it implies that potential audiences are not completely imprisoned by prevailing discourses. But this possibility does not

exempt theorists from needing to engage somehow the existing discourses.[17] Stretching a point, this pattern in which some people have significant loadings on more than one discourse also suggests that even the
rational egoists of factor D have access to more disinterested motivational
wellsprings (for more direct evidence on this point, see Dryzek, 1990, pp.
182–84).

An engagement between theorists and discourses might begin by not-
ing that our discourse A bears some resemblance to the classical republicanism that began in ancient Rome, flickered in Renaissance Florence and
seventeenth-century England, and influenced the founding of the United
States. This tradition is conventionally defined in terms of commitments
to a mixed government (or separation of powers), the rule of law, and,
above all, an active, virtuous citizenry (see, for example, Canovan, 1987).
Republicanism as a distinctive tradition waned by the twentieth century,
although its emphasis on positive freedom, civic virtue, and personal fulfillment through public life reappeared in the work of Hannah Arendt in
the 1950s and 1960s (for example, Arendt, 1958). Arendt's political philosophy is as much a lament for republics past as a hope for republics future.
A more applied republicanism (if not by that name) was advanced in Kelman's (1987a) highly optimistic interpretation and positive evaluation of
U.S. politics. Our contented republicanism shares his assessment that politics is already pervaded by public spirit and that all that needs to be done
is make the most of it.

Both discourse A and the classical republican tradition value active
citizenship and public life, and both abhor the politics of self-interest.
However, unlike the classical tradition, our contented republicanism evi-
dences no fear of democratic excess. This fear underpins the classical stress
on mixed government which, especially in James Madison's corrective to
the tradition, puts active citizenship in a decidedly unheroic and subor-
dinate place. In contrast, our contented republicanism favors a degree of
popular activism greater than even Arendt would seek, given her belief that
even the best of republican politics is only for the self-selected few. Moreover, contented republicanism shows no special commitment to Madisonian checks and balances. But despite any differences here, our results suggest that a revival of long-unfashionable classical republicanism might find
a receptive audience.

As a reluctantly democratic discourse, B came as a surprise, although
there are many similarities between our deferential conservatism and
the classical conservative tradition founded by Edmund Burke. B is very
Burkean in its acceptance of the political ways that help constitute a society's tradition, its awareness of imperfection in human nature, and its deference to authority—hoping perhaps for Burke's "true natural aristocracy"? B's commitments to community, liberty guaranteed by authority
and order rather than abstract natural rights of the sort advanced by liberal
philosophers, and limited expectations for governmental action also are
Burkean. Nonetheless, B departs from classical conservatism in its lack of

interest in the decentralization of power to the local level and in its un-willingness to concede that elected representatives know better than their constituents. Nor does B seem to value diversity as a protection against the leveling tendencies of mass society and so departs from twentieth-century classical conservatives such as Ortega y Gasset.

Since Burke's day, classical conservatives in the Anglo-American world have accepted the advance of democracy. Our deferential conservatism's acceptance of that advance seems at best begrudging, and in that respect it is similar to the conservatism of the European continent. A rare U.S. intimation of B's deferential conservatism may be found in Robert Frost's announcement that "I have given up my democratic prejudices and now willingly set the lower classes free to be completely taken care of by the upper classes" (1973, p. 127).[18] It would be hard to find a U.S. political theorist or public intellectual who would put the matter this bluntly, al-though hints may be found in the paleoconservative journal *Chronicles*. U.S. paleoconservatism has, for the most part, abandoned the local com-munity and adopted the nation as its locus of identity, a move that reso-nates with B's seeming lack of interest in decentralized power within the nation-state. B's combination of a lukewarm endorsement of some of the forms of democracy and suspicion of its substance also has substantial af-finities with the viewpoint of the ungovernability theorists that I discussed in Chapter 2. Recall that these theorists are aghast at the political and economic problems caused by an excess of participation, and so they favor a democracy more firmly under the control of political elites. So Samuel Huntington looks back with fond memories to the days when the United States "was governed by the president acting with the support and co-operation of key individuals and groups in the Executive Office, the federal bureaucracy, Congress, and the more important businesses, banks, law firms, foundations, and media" (Crozier, Huntington, and Watanuki, 1975, p. 92). Huntington concludes that "in many situations the claims of expertise, seniority, experience, and special talents may override the claims of democracy as a way of constituting authority" (p. 113). The masses, for their part, are to be consigned to "apathy and noninvolve-ment" (p. 114).

The disaffected populism of discourse C has some similarity to the theory of participatory democracy, in that both envision extended, ener-getic, competent, and public-spirited citizenship. However, C's critique of injustice and repression in existing society is more uncompromising than many participatory theorists would allow. For example, Barber (1984) speaks mainly in terms of reforming liberal politics, in particular by taking advantage of advances in communications technology. Like most partici-patory democratic theorists, Barber favors extended citizen involvement in public affairs as an intrinsic good linked to personal fulfillment. In con-strast, C's real motive for extended participation is the need to attack the world's injustices. Thus C advocates participation for instrumental reasons contingent on the prevailing amount of repression. Many theorists of participatory democracy, such as Barber, might therefore be happier with the attitude toward the intrinsic merits of participatory citizenship evidenced by the contented republicanism of discourse A. The puzzle here for Barber and others is that the very discourse that is closest to their ideals sees absolutely no need for the reforms they recommend. C's account of repression and struggle is perhaps more consistent with participatory theorists such as Poulantzas (1980), who have been influenced by Marxism and so see the need for participatory innovations that confront the state as well as reform it (although we should note that C proclaims anticommunism). C also departs from participatory democratic theory in ascribing little importance to community and in recognizing that one should not expect too much of people's participatory energies.

D's private liberalism was unsurprising in that liberalism looms large in the U.S. political tradition, and liberals have always championed a private realm against excessive governmental interference. But in its thorough denigration of public life, D rejects many of the elements of Lockean and Madisonian liberalism. Liberalism has generally prized government by reasoned deliberation, especially in connection with the legislative branch. In the twentieth century, this view has been well represented by theorists such as John Dewey and Karl Popper. Although for the most part "modern liberalism questions political authority, but typically seeks to reform it rather than merely to evade it" (Zvesper, 1987, p. 285), D's private liberalism really does want to escape politics. D does not necessarily object to the symbols of democracy but is far more energized by the need to banish government from the private realm than by concern as to how any such government might proceed. Thus D bears a definite resemblance to the ideas of libertarian philosophers such as Murray Rothbard and Robert Nozick. Such libertarians might, however, be uncomfortable with D's acceptance of religion as a motive force for political action, with its recognition of local community (though not of society) and its seeming lack of concern for a free press and associated political liberties. In its selective radicalization of the liberal tradition in favor of *homo economicus*, able to calculate and pursue self-interest, D has some affinity with the economic rationalism and market-oriented public choice analysis discussed in Chapter 5. Having discarded liberal ideas of civic virtue, D can join these schools of thought in their scorn for politics of all sorts (not just democratic politics), and in their enthusiasm for the capitalist market.

Conclusion

When it comes to the language of democracy, it is easy to be cynical. Thus Dunn believes that "democratic theory is the moral Esperanto of the present nation-state system, the language in which all Nations are truly united, the public cant of the modern world, a dubious currency indeed" (1979, p. 2). As noted in Chapter 5, most public choice practitioners see language as just so much camouflage for the real stuff of politics. From a very different theoretical perspective, Edelman (1987), too, believes that political language systematically cloaks power in order to secure compliance and subservience.

In this chapter I have suggested that close attention to the language of democracy can in fact be highly productive. The findings are rooted in the way people "out there" really do talk and think about democracy, about themselves, and about what it means to act politically (or apolitically). There is also a sense in which they have been generated in reflexively democratic fashion. In other words, the conceptions of democracy that the four discourses represent do not emanate from the minds of professional theorists and analysts (such as myself) but, rather, from interactive encounters between analysts and subjects and their language.[19]

The fact that political language is important does not mean that language is all that matters or that any of the various discourses of democracy can be implemented at will. Yet discourses can help constitute reality, and if there is a disjuncture between the prevailing constellation of discourses and the structure of political reality, perhaps that reality is open to reconstitution. I have attempted to demonstrate just such a disjuncture, at least for the case of the United States. These findings are, of course, constrained by the time and place of their generation, and so no transhistorical or transnational conclusions should be drawn from them—aside from the fact that if such disjuncture exists in the home of capitalist democracy, it should probably be able to exist anywhere.

There is a sense in which each discourse represents, to greater or lesser degree, a political alternative to capitalist democracy. But this does not mean that any one of the discourses could be implemented easily; each might encounter opposition from the others. More important, each would have to face the structural state-related and international constraints detailed in Chapters 2, 3, and 4 and the world of economic rationalists described in Chapter 5 (although the very existence of discourses hostile to economic rationalism helps undermine that world). The discussion in these earlier chapters, in common with that in this chapter, has dealt with possibilities as well as constraints. What remains is to try to reach some summary judgments about the prospects for democracy that integrate the macrolevel analysis of Chapters 2, 3, and 4, the microlevel analysis of Chapter 5, and the discourse analysis of this chapter. This is the task I shall attempt in the final chapter.

7

The Outlook for Democracy

I began in the first two chapters with a recognition of the seeming power of the structure of capitalist democracy to perpetuate itself, to crush alternative political–economic models, and ultimately to erode existing democratic accomplishments. The story that unfolded in the intervening chapters both confirmed this power and exposed its limits. In this concluding chapter I will attempt to distill from this story some summary implications concerning the prospects for democracy in capitalist times.

From Economic Rationality to Discursive Democracy

Capitalist democracy remains an uneasy and perhaps unstable compromise. Democracy under capitalism is hard to sustain because of the grave-digging individuals that capitalism increasingly produces. As I argued at length in Chapter 5, the kind of instrumentally rational, egoistic persons produced by capitalism may help markets work as Adam Smith projected, but such people subvert democratic politics. Public choice theorists have demonstrated that a politics of unconstrained strategy in pursuit of individual desires is an incoherent mess in which policy outcomes are arbitarily connected to public preferences, responding instead to the narrow self-interest of politicians, bureaucrats, and concentrated interests. Thus the more that capitalism and its associated discourses, political ideologies, and public policies produce rational egoists, the more instability, arbitrariness, authoritarian drift, and loss of legitimacy that liberal democratic political systems are likely to experience.

The future of democracy in capitalist times therefore depends on the activation of alternatives to economic rationality in social and political life. The only *democratic* alternative is some kind of communicative rationality.

Communicative rationality underwrites a discursive or deliberative democracy in which preferences are not taken as given or immutable and in which individual needs and public interests alike can be discovered and debated. Democracy as discourse rather than preference aggregation is consistent with the increasingly indefinite and porous character of political boundaries, both across and within state territories. Across states, transnationalization undermines the idea of a territorially defined self-governing community, making problematical an aggregative model of democracy because it is rarely clear whose preferences are to be aggregated. Within state territories, feminist challenges to the boundaries of politics and proliferating political venues (public spheres in civil society, community politics, workplaces, etc.) again make it hard to determine whose preferences should be aggregated and when. Discursive democracy copes more easily with indefinite, porous, problematical, and contested boundaries. The political life of civil society is more easily recognized as democratic under a deliberative rather than an aggregative ideal.

Discursive democracy also contains means for coping with highly complex social problems, by providing for the effective integration of diverse perspectives on any problem without imposing an impossible burden on the center of a decision system. The volitions of disparate participants concerned with different aspects of the problem can be debated and (sometimes) brought into harmony (see Dryzek, 1990, pp. 55–76; Fischer, 1993). Observers of aggregative democracy, especially social choice theorists, fear the confusion or chaos that multiple perspectives and diverse participants can exacerbate, whereas communicative rationality presents a more benign kind of interaction.

Recognition of the importance of the discursive dimension of democratic life rules out the relevance to any democratic project of two of the four discourses of democracy existing in the United States presented in Chapter 6. Private liberalism would only increase the amount of economic rationality in society and politics, and coherent democratic politics becomes increasingly improbable with rising levels of economic rationality. Of course, private liberalism's commitment to democracy of any sort is quite thin to begin with. The same might be said of deferential conservatism, another discourse incompatible with an emphasis on the deliberative dimension of democratic life. Deferential conservatism is of comfort only to those who wish to retain the forms of democracy while attentuating the substance. This discourse certainly has little time for democratic deliberation, except perhaps by the corporate and governmental elites entrusted with political control. But even when it comes to these elites, deferential conservatives are not very enthusiastic about the liberal freedoms of expression that are the minimal conditions necessary for public debate.

Among U.S. discourses of democracy, both contented republicanism and disaffected populism are more in tune with the deliberative conception of democracy. Democratic debate and active citizenship are especially central to contented republicanism. Deliberative democracy under contented republicanism would suggest the development of institutions that emphasize decision making through discussion oriented toward consensus, as opposed to the more familiar adversarial and hierarchical institutions currently dominating most liberal democracies. It should be noted, though, that deliberative democracy could still be promoted through institutions in which (say) majority voting retains a role, provided that before the vote the opportunities for authentic debate are maximized.

Deliberative democracy is perhaps not quite so easily joined with disaffected populism. Disaffected populism seeks active citizen involvement in politics, but this involvement is most centrally a matter of mass action against established power and injustice. The conditions of this participation under disaffected populism might involve public deliberation, but they would not have to. However, despite such differences in emphasis, there is nothing to rule out an accommodation here between deliberative democracy and disaffected populism.

Democracy Now or Later?

Where and how should communicative rationality and deliberative democracy be sought? Should the end in view be postcapitalist democracy or democracy remaining in the shadow of the capitalist state? Are these two ends mutually exclusive?

The strongest argument for emphasizing postcapitalist possibilities would look forward to the demise of capitalism. The prospects for proletarian revolution having receded, ecological crisis is the most likely agent here (see Dryzek, 1992a). Capitalism is a "grow or die" system. Capitalist economies that do not grow automatically experience rising unemployment, reduced investment—and therefore economic contraction and all its associated political pathologies. Economic growth implies increasing consumption of ecological resources. And if the earth's ecosystems are ultimately finite, then capitalist development, and therefore capitalism itself, will be limited. The aggressively individualistic attitudes increasingly produced by the capitalist political economy make matters worse here because such attitudes are conducive to the "tragedy of the commons." The essence of this tragedy is that instrumentally rational, materially self-interested individual behavior leads to collectively disastrous outcomes, be it depletion of a resource, extinction of a species, or destruction of an ecosystem through pollution. The individual reaps all the benefits of his or her increased exploitation of the common property resource, whereas the costs of that increase are shared across all users. Hence it always is instrumentally rational for individuals to increase their exploitation of, and stress on, the resource. People with a conscience who restrain their use are simply suckers for the continuing exploitation by others. Such instrumentally rational, egoistic behavior is, of course, promoted under capitalism.

There are solutions to the tragedy, but all of them require major curbs on rational egoism.

In this ecological light, liberal democracy may not be much more sustainable than capitalist economics. The reason is that the currency of liberal democracy, at least in a capitalist context, consists mostly of tangible material rewards to particular interests. Such rewards are more readily available in a growing economy; without economic growth, liberal democratic politics are more divisive and bitter. In addition, states in capitalist economies (liberal democratic or otherwise) are, as I noted in Chapters 2 and 3, constrained by their fear of disinvestment and consequently obliged to pursue and promote economic growth.

The history of liberalism has involved compromises with a succession of competing doctrines and principles: notably, conservatism, democracy, and socialism. That history of compromise is one reason that liberalism as both a doctrine and a system is so slippery and elusive—as well as so successful. Ecology may constitute one set of principles with which no compromise can be sustained.

If capitalist democracy is indeed ecologically unsustainable, the implication is not that we should simply sit back and await its demise, pinning our hopes on the outcomes of the convulsions that will attend the ecological crunch. It is hard to put a time scale on the ecological demise of capitalism; empirical evidence on global environmental crisis is contested and inconclusive. So the wait might be a long one, and more important, the outcome of any such denouement is uncertain. Convulsion will not necessarily produce a more democratic political economy.

The history of revolutionary transformation noted in Chapter 3 should be sobering here. The revolutionary moment may produce opportunities for incandescent democratic politics, and the historical record shows that such politics frequently and spontaneously accompanies revolutions. But the moment is always short lived. Postrevolutionary states typically face all the constraints that led to the downfall of their predecessors. Indeed, successor states often face intensified constraints (due, for example, to an economy weakened by revolution or to the opposition of other states to the revolutionary ideology). The normal response by postrevolutionary states, irrespective of their ideology, is a centralization of authority that by definition hurts the prospects for democracy of any sort.

This generalization about the antidemocratic outcomes of successful revolutions is undermined by liberal democratic development in the wake of some of the East European revolutions of 1989. However, if anything, this experience argues against waiting for convulsive change to introduce democracy. The East European countries that negotiated postrevolutionary transformation most democratically were those that featured a flourishing oppositional and democratic public sphere under the old regime: Poland, Czechoslovakia, and Hungary. (East Germany did, too, but its immediate incorporation into the Federal Republic makes its postrevolutionary experience harder to assess.) The democratic oppositional experience enabled reasonably democratic negotiation of the political–economic transition. In short, it makes more sense to contemplate democratization in the capitalist present than in the postcapitalist future.

Democracy In, Against, and Across States

In Chapter 3 I said that contemporary possibilities for democratization may be found both in and against the capitalist state. The two U.S. discourses to which deliberative democracy might be attached nicely parallel this dichotomy of sites for democratization. Democratization of the state should interest contented republicanism, and democratization against the state should attract disaffected populism.

There are some possibilities for democratization of the capitalist state. This state is not a monolith, grinding out policies that always and effectively meet the imperatives with which it is faced. Instead, these imperatives can produce contradiction and confusion when they point in different directions. Under such complex conditions, administrative rationality fails, and legitimacy is not easily achieved. One possible consequence here is government concession to more open and participatory kinds of decision making, which, as I noted in Chapter 3, often are consistent with a deliberative conception of democracy ("discursive designs"). Such innovations often face a precarious existence, for if their operations and products threaten state imperatives, they are likely to be curbed, ignored, or abolished. Nevertheless, their presence is a real factor in the potential democratization of the state. This is the kind of democracy that would interest the discourse of contented republicanism—and within the rather severe constraints elaborated in Chapters 2 and 3, there is nothing to stop this democracy's being deliberative in character. In some cases we find that these state-associated sites for democratization have already experienced deliberative institutional innovations, related to public inquiries, impact assessment, alternative dispute resolution, mediation, regulatory negotiation, policy dialogue, and so forth.

The analysis of the economic constraints on states developed in Chapters 2 and 3 and reinforced by the international factors introduced in Chapter 4, exposes the naïveté of programs such as that of contented republicanism, which recognizes no limits to the possibilities for extended and meaningful citizen participation in state decision making. The severity of these limits means that deliberative democracy combined with contented republicanism is not a realistic program for democratic development.

In Chapter 3 I argued that there may be greater possibilities for democracy and democratization in insurgency against the state. Such insurgency can occur most notably in the form of public spheres that confront the state but do not seek a share in state power (thus they are nonrevolutionary). In industrial democracies, new social movements are currently among the most prominent and interesting public spheres. These movements, and public spheres more generally, have some affinities with the discourse of disaffected populism. However, an analysis of public spheres offers a major corrective to disaffected populism. Disaffected populism seeks to enter and capture the state, but that is a high-risk strategy, for any movement that succeeeds in its efforts here becomes subject to all the state imperatives that are so destructive to democracy. Thus disaffected populists would do well to bridle their ambitions and adopt a radicalism that involves permanent confrontation with the state. It is also worth emphasizing here that in keeping with the idea that civil society can be defined by its rejection of economic rationality, public spheres normally feature an open and discursive style of politics. Deliberative democracy is perhaps most at home here.

Democracy and democratization may be sought *across* states as well as *in* the state and *against* the state. The decentralized and anarchic character of the international system that has historically made it such a dangerous place also means that this system has no central authority analogous to the state, and so a host of impediments to democracy do not exist here. Thus when it is constructed, political authority in this system can be open to varied participants and kinds of participation, and political experimentation more generally. Deliberative styles of interaction can often be found in international political life. This kind of interaction may engage states and international organizations, but it can also involve international public spheres constituted by opposition to the authority of both states and international governmental organizations. Thus several summary judgments about democracy that apply to the domestic level also apply internationally: The deliberative dimension is vital, and democracy can be sought both within and against established authority.

With a few exceptions, democratic theorists have not caught up with the increasing transnationalization of political and economic life. And based on the evidence of Chapter 6, nor have popular discourses of democracy, at least not the ones current in the United States (whose notorious political insularity may not be reflected elsewhere in the world). Of these discourses of democracy, one suspects that disaffected populism is most easily adapted to the transnational realm, given that the essence of this discourse is popular insurgency against power unjustly constituted and exercised. The fact that this established power may be constituted internationally presents no problems for disaffected populism here. Contented republicanism fares less well in the international arena, given that it is tied to the idea of the state and a self-governing community.

An additional reason for emphasizing democratization in civil society or public spheres is that democratization of the state is unlikely without it. The choice here is not an either/or one, despite the manner in which it is sometimes framed in radical political movements. For example, the argument between the "realo" and "fundi" wings of the German Greens, paralleled in many other social movements, is obviously about such a choice, and the divisiveness of that dispute suggests that many on both sides believe it is an either/or matter. But no Green movement, or indeed any other democratic movement, should pursue participation in the state to the exclusion of confrontation with it. Participation in the state is likely to remain fruitful only as long as confrontation with the state is possible. Democracy within the liberal democratic state is, in part, a means of inducing disadvantaged groups to accept the dominant political–economic order (as Madison recognized long ago). Total commitment by such groups to action within the state means that there is less reason for the state to incorporate them. As Fisk explained, "Only if there is a continuation of politics by extraparliamentary means will democracy be able to establish limits to the power of a dominant class" (1989, pp. 178–79).

"Realo" hostility to action in the streets implies that tactical unity in the movement is essential. But compromisers with the state can in fact benefit from the existence of opponents of the state. This is especially evident in U.S. environmental politics. The most important figure in state-related environmental politics for the last several decades has been David Brower. Yet Brower has taken pains to welcome the more uncompromising activities of groups such as Earth First! on the grounds that they make people like him appear more reasonable and more likely to shift policy in an environmentally sound direction. In the United States case, such policy shifts do not automatically mean that policymaking has become any more democratic, although as I noted in Chapter 3, complexity, intractability, and the need for legitimacy in environmental policymaking have in fact led to a number of state-related democratic innovations in the last two and a half decades.

A vigorous civil society containing oppositional public spheres can, then, help maintain democracy within the state by ensuring that the state is more truly inclusive of potential troublemakers. But such inclusion has its hazards. In Chapter 3, I argued that the way in which interest representation is organized by and in the state largely determines the degree to which democracy can flourish in civil society. The pattern of interest representation most conducive to democracy in civil society is passive exclusion of the sort practiced under social democratic corporatism, which facilitates the development of a parallel polity of excluded individuals and groups.

One problem in applying this model to the United States is that the four discourses elaborated in Chapter 6 reveal little support for corporatism. (Support is more easily discerned for the actively exclusionary pattern of authoritarian liberalism, in the discourse of private liberalism.) The discourse of deferential conservatism supports passive exclusion, but it has no interest in organized labor sharing in government, let alone a politically active civil society. The United States is, of course, the least corporatist of industrial societies. More in the way of corporatist discourse should be expected in other countries.

Self-Limitation or a Policy Orientation?

What kind of politics can transpire in an oppositional polity generated by passive exclusion? Taking the principle of self-limitation in civil society to an extreme would produce talk about and a negotiation of identities, discussion of political issues, and an occasional disturbance of the political order through resistance against government actions. Some participants might regard this as a satisfactory political life. Others might be frustrated by continuing inability to find their substantive goals reflected in the content of public policy. On the other hand, self-limitation might please government officials by giving them a relatively free hand in policymaking.

The content of public policy does matter to civil society irrespective of the substantive goals of its participants, for such policy might undermine the conditions for democracy in public spheres. Clear examples are found in authoritarian liberal promotion of material inequality and associated attacks on the conditions for public association. Public spheres must somehow concern themselves with the affairs of the state. But how can they do so without succumbing to the perils of inclusion?

Democratic civil society can generate not just protest against public policies but also pressure on the content of these policies and the operations of the state. Thus orientations to consensus as well as difference, proposals as well as protests, are necessary. Let me suggest two ways of achieving such orientation without sacrificing the autonomy of civil society.

The first would be to create a public sphere around a particular social problem or policy issue. A good example of a community-based initiative challenging the policy prerogatives of government may be found in the "popular epidemiology" described by Brown and Mikkelsen (1990) and endorsed by Fischer (1993). The community of Woburn, Massachusetts, mobilized against the state government's denial of local pollution problems. With a little help from a professor at Harvard University's School of Public Health, several hundred amateur volunteers assembled by a group called FACE (For a Clean Environment) began to investigate patterns of birth defects and leukemia in the vicinity of toxic waste sites. Despite continued denial of the problem and criticism of the community effort by state and federal agencies (in part because of alleged biases introduced by nonscientific personnel and methods), the results of this exercise eventually formed the evidentiary basis for a lawsuit settled out of court by one of the companies that had dumped toxic wastes.

On a larger scale, the Global Forum, which assembled as the unofficial counterpart to the United Nations Conference on Environment and Development in Rio de Janeiro in 1992, brought together a great deal in the way of expertise and political commitment. Forum participants interacted with an array of activists who converged on Rio and with a broader global network. The Forum's concerns were oriented to the official Earth Summit intergovernmental negotiations, and the content of summit agreements was indeed responsive to this international public sphere. Among other influences, George Bush was shamed into attending and adding his signature to a number of agreements he would have preferred to ignore. This sort of international public sphere is a more permanent fixture at meetings of the International Whaling Commission. At these meetings, the main sources of information for delegates and protestors alike run through this sphere (for example, with publication of ECO as the conference journal).

A second, less obvious, way for public spheres to influence the state while retaining their autonomy draws on the idea of discourse analysis presented in Chapter 6. Discourses themselves are social constructs that can overlap civil society and the state and, for that matter, private life, the ecoonomy, and national boundaries, too. Interventions originating in civil society to change the content of discourses can affect public policy if policymakers also share in this content. This possibility does not mean that discourses are easily manipulated in strategic fashion. Michel Foucault, responsible for popularizing the idea of discourses, saw them as entities beyond anyone's control, which constituted human subjects rather than vice versa. However, I would argue against Foucault that discourses can be deliberately reconstituted at the margins and sometimes even deliberately challenged by an alternative discourse (if they could not, the whole enterprise of political theory with practical intent would make little sense, absent philosopher-kings able to engage in constitutional engineering).

The key to such reconstitution and challenge is the ancient art of rhetoric. To take a slightly insidious policy-relevant example, discourse surrounding antipollution policy has in recent years featured a relabeling of strategies once labeled (accurately and simply enough) *regulatory*. They are now known as *command and control*. This term was popularized by market-oriented opponents of regulation, but it is now used even by defenders of regulatory policies. The rhetorical import of command and control is clear: It is to associate regulatory policy with dictatorship and oppression.

Policy debates can sometimes be interpreted as struggles among different discourses. Each discourse contains particular interpretations and story lines that, if broadly accepted, can have a substantial impact on the content of government policy. It matters crucially for policy which discourse has the upper hand. Along these lines, Hajer (1993) analyzed recent acid-rain policy in Great Britain in terms of a clash between a (still-dominant) "traditional pragmatist" discourse coalition and a newer "ecological modernization" coalition. A discourse coalition is not the same as an advocacy coalition or interest alliance, for its members are united only by the "ideas, concepts, and categories" they share. Members may belong to different organizations (or to none) and may even disagree with one another on policy strategies. Particular discourse coalitions rise or fall with the rhetorical power that can be mustered on behalf of their story lines (for example, the "ecologically benign growth" story line of ecological modernization). And that power can be deployed not just in the halls of government or in interest-group bargaining but also—and perhaps most effectively—in the public sphere.

A particularly dramatic and effective use of rhetoric to reconstitute a discourse that in turn affected government policy may be found in the efforts of Martin Luther King Jr. King's rhetorical achievement was to draw on the established and dominant discourse of American liberalism and reshape it creatively and effectively to support an agenda of civil rights for African Americans. He did not step outside that discourse to advocate any suppressed alternative but, rather, paid frequent and conscious tribute to its canonical documents, such as the Declaration of Independence and the Constitution. Eventually his redefinition became broadly accepted and reflected in both legislation and judicial decisions.

Although people with the rhetorical gifts of a Martin Luther King Jr. are rare, the general lesson here is that a creative refashioning of discourses is possible, and it can have real policy effects. The appropriate image here is of a conversation to which established discourses and novel ideas and interpretations can contribute. This image drives home the point that open deliberation is central to democratic life. A discursive realm of freedom opposes a structural state-related realm of necessity. Freedom will not always prevail, but sometimes it has a fighting chance.

Idealism and Realism

Those contemplating the prospects for democracy have fallen mostly into two camps. First there are those for whom capitalist democracy *is* democracy and for whom the practical task is therefore to chart (and probably encourage) the global spread of this model. Whatever the accomplishments of this approach are in regard to the theory and practice of democracy, its imaginative deficiencies are rather glaring, and it degenerates rather easily into apology for the status quo.

A very different school of thought has little time for the status quo and is not short on imagination. This second school produces various proposals for participatory, populist, feminist, republican, global, ecological, or socialist democracy. The trouble is that these proposals are often inattentive to practical constraints and possibilities; they are idealist as opposed to realist and as such are not well placed to contribute to the real-world conversation of democratic development.

Democracy in capitalist times is better served by a combination of imagination and realism. Karl Marx had the right combination in mind when he argued that "men make their own history, but they do not make it just as they please; they do not make it under circumstances chosen by themselves, but under circumstances directly encountered, given and transmitted from the past" (1963, p. 15). When it comes to *our* circumstances, the constraints sometimes appear massive, but there is surely still democratic history to be made.

Notes

Chapter 1

1. See Hanson's (1989) history of the concept of democracy and how its meaning has changed over time.

2. Mueller provided an equally minimalist definition: "Democracy . . . takes effect when people agree not to use violence to overthrow the government and when the government leaves them free to criticize, to pressure, and to try to replace it by any other means" (1992, p. 985). Similarly, Riker (1982a) suggested that the only feasible aspiration for democracy is that elections might constitute an uncertain and imperfect way to dispose of tyrannical, corrupt, or inept leadership.

3. Cunningham observed that situation A is more democratic than situation B if "(1) proportionately more people in A have control over their common social environment than do people in B; and/or (2) people in A have control over proportionately more aspects of their social environment than do people in B; and/or (3) the aspects of their social environment over which people have control are more important from the point of view of democracy than those over which people in B have control" (1987, pp. 26–27).

Cunningham's first criterion is what I call *franchise*, and his second is what I call *scope*. I reject his third criterion because the essentially contested nature of the concept of democracy means that there is no neutral "point of view of democracy" from which to reach importance judgments. The three criteria of franchise, scope, and authenticity correspond roughly to what Cohen (1971) calls, respectively, the breadth, range, and depth of democracy.

4. A parallel can be drawn here with welfare economics. The notorious difficulty in making interpersonal comparisions of utility (that is, in deciding how to weight the relative importance of benefits and costs accruing to different individuals) leads economists to the Pareto criterion. This criterion recognizes improvements in social welfare only when at least one person is made better off without anyone's being made worse off.

5. Arendt believed that only in political interaction so defined was authentic

humanity revealed. Her analysis reveals nostalgia for the ancient Athenian *polis,* although she saw occasional glimmers of true politics in the modern world.

Chapter 2

1. Given that one of the core components of fascism is an aggressive nationalism, it is a bit odd that Fukuyama classifies it as a global competitor.

2. Fukuyama distances himself from this paradigm because of its implication that economic progress is what generates liberal democracy, in contrast to his own belief that a more universal human psychology is the motor in the drive toward liberal politics (1992, pp. 133–34).

3. In other political–economic systems, Fukuyama believes that *megalothymia* can be satisfied only through military conquest, with all its destructive results (1992, p. 316).

4. However, the marketplace in question does not have to be a capitalist one. So Sagoff's argument could also be used to justify other combinations of liberal democracy and the market.

5. Crozier, Huntington, and Watanuki (1975) also worried about social movements acting through nonliberal channels.

6. I do not mean to suggest that this slowdown was solely the result of expanding political demands. For a survey of alternative explanations, see Cherry et al., 1987.

7. Olson believes such a process can occur in any kind of society, not just liberal democratic ones.

8. Of course, the structural details can and do change with time. But some essential elements, such as the private ownership of capital and the private appropriation of profit, do not change.

Chapter 3

1. Other Greens are more hostile to the state; some are anarchists. I will discuss antistatist Green positions later.

2. As with many concepts in the study of politics, the definition of the state can be contested. My definition here is not original and, I hope, relatively uncontroversial. For discussion of the concept of the state, see Nordlinger 1981, pp. 8–12, and Krasner 1984.

3. An alternative, and much simpler, tack here would be simply to argue that the structuralists' determinism is mistaken. Taylor (1989) is one of their more incisive critics on this score. He allows that structures do indeed have the effects that Skocpol and others describe but then contends that structures themselves can be a product of choice by political elites. His examples, though, concern only rural social structure, because the peasantry figures centrally in Skocpol's (1979) celebrated theory of revolution. I have stressed the structural constraints imposed by the market economy, and later I will turn to those imposed by the international system. These structures, too, can be chosen, the former by national governments with nonmarket economic systems and the latter by any hegemonic power (or dominant group of nations) that exists. But they differ from rural social structure in that once they exist they cannot easily be changed. Markets, especially, have remarkable self-perpetuating features, which I shall describe later. And in regard to the international system, situations in which actors can change the system in the interests of their own domestic politics are very rare. In short, the structural constraints I deal with are not easily modified by intentional action.

4. The intellectual history of structural functionalism, a research approach once popular in U.S. social science, is instructive here. The basic idea was that one can explain the particular form taken by social structures through reference to the functions they perform in the society in question. Structural functionalism declined as a social science research program largely because it turned out that many different structural forms could fulfill a particular function, such as system maintenance. Thus the approach could never explain why any particular form existed (Ricci, 1984, pp. 217–18).

5. Under some dire circumstances it may be possible to reconcile growth and conservation, as clean air, clean water, and healthy people are, among other things, inputs to productive processes. Thus cleaning up a highly degraded environment may actually be good for economic growth. Particularly stark cases of this sort may be found in Eastern Europe. In less degraded environments, pleasant surroundings may help attract both employers and footloose employees whose skills are in high demand. As a result, employers may even be able to pay employees less.

6. On a more prosaic account, civil society is what Eastern Europe still lacks as a result of the Soviet-era legacy of repression of independent association: that is, interest groups standing between individuals and the state representing economic categories (notably business and labor) that would allow Western-style pluralist democracy to flourish (Ost, 1993). Civil society in this prosaic sense loses its distinctiveness, for such interest groups do seek a share in state power, and they are rooted in the economy. Thus I will discuss prosaic civil society no further.

7. In France, such developments go by the name of "autogestionnaire democracy" (Furniss, 1985).

8. Conceivably, political theorists could make a contribution here by pinpointing and interpreting the conceptual change that always attends political innovation (Farr, 1989, p. 30). The political theorist so engaged would be more than just a historian of conceptual and political change, for his or her own efforts could themselves contribute to the further re-creation of identity.

9. The absence of any such model may not be a bad thing, as I contend in Chapter 1.

10. Cohen and Rogers link their model to corporatism. I would argue that a state both active and inclusive in its interest representation is no longer corporatist.

11. On a scale whose OECD average for each year is 100, the gross domestic products per capita (adjusted for purchasing power parity) for these countries are as follows:

	1979	1992
Australia	95	91
Canada	114	107
New Zealand	86	78
United Kingdom	91	89
United States	134	126

The evidence for the corporatist countries is more mixed. For the four countries classified by Lehmbruch as strong corporatist, the figures are as follows (1984, p. 66):

	1979	*1992*
Austria	96	98
Netherlands	99	92
Norway	90	96
Sweden	101	90

The source for all GDP data is OECD, 1994, p. 66. These corporatist figures, however, do not tell the whole story, for the corporatist countries did not pursue "growth at all costs" policies to anything like the extent of the Anglo-American countries during this period.

Chapter 4

1. Unger (1987) interprets this effect in psychological terms: Political actors fear institutional innovation because it may make their state less able to confront others effectively. But more important than any such psychology is the fact that the survival constraint operates at the level of structural reality.

2. Close examination of the reality, as opposed to the rhetoric of revolution, often shows only incremental change in social structures and values (Keeler, 1989), beyond state centralization.

3. This likelihood explains why a small minority of U.S. conservatives—true Burkeans such as Samuel Francis (1989) and Thomas Fleming—fear for American distinctiveness and autonomy, knowing full well that the emerging order is unlikely to be dominated by the United States. Burkean conservatives who formerly opposed national consolidation and state building because it extinguished local tradition and autonomy today locate the tradition they wish to preserve in the very national structures they once opposed. The nation-state becomes their new locus of identity, and internationalism the foremost threat to this identity.

4. Prominent analysts of regimes (for example, Young, 1989) are apparently not interested in this possibility. Their concern is almost exclusively with the achievement of order and social welfare in the international system, not democracy.

5. The kind of authorities specified in Burnheim's (1985) model of demarchy would perform a similar kind of representative function, but of course, nothing like these authorities actually exists.

Chapter 5

1. My information on IRIS comes solely from its own propaganda material, which arrives unsolicited in my mail.

2. Curiously, Mueller's historical reference is to the essayist Sydney Smith, not Adam Smith, and so to the nineteenth rather than the eighteenth century.

3. For a review of the Rochester school, focusing on William Riker, its leading member, see Weale, 1984. For more general surveys of public choice, see McLean, 1986, and Mitchell, 1988b. The Virginia school was originally based at Virginia Polytechnic Institute and State University but later moved to George Mason University (still in Virginia).

4. Classical liberalism in public choice holds as a generalization that is confirmed by the exceptions to it. Accordingly, Brennan allows that his argument for democratic socialism is "against public choice orthodoxy" (and, he might have added, against the grain of his other writings) (1989, p. 63). And Wittman prefaces his iconoclastic thesis that political markets work well with a note that "this possibility appears to have been, for the most part, overlooked" (1989, p. 135, n. 1).

5. Formally, Arrow showed that it is impossible for any collective choice mechanism to satisfy simultaneously five seemingly innocuous criteria. These criteria are unanimity (if anyone has a preference that nobody opposes, then that preference should be included in the social choice), nondictatorship, transitivity (if society prefers A to B and B to C, then it should also prefer A to C), unrestricted domain (individuals can have any preference orderings they like across the options at hand), and independence of irrelevant alternatives (introducing an alternative C should not change society's preference between A and B).

6. However, if a trade union organization is "encompassing" in the sense that it represents all or most of a country's workers, it will lack the incentive to seek its members' good at the nation's expense, and so the nation as a whole can prosper. Thus in Olson's analysis, the economy will grow if the unions are either small and weak or *very* large, powerful, and united.

7. For Brennan, politicians should actually believe these principles and not just act as if they believed them. A similar function is performed by Downs's (1957) argument that rational parties should espouse ideologies of some stability, because otherwise, rational voters would not believe that parties will keep their election-time promises. But for Downs, it is not necessary for politicians actually to believe in their ideologies.

8. Another writer who tries to find sustenance for democracy in public-choice analysis is Przeworski, who believes that "a theory of democracy based on the assumption of self-interested strategic compliance is plausible and sufficient" (1991, p. 24). But Przeworski's is a theory only of democratic stability, under which actors will comply with collective decisions that they opposed if either (1) they think they have a reasonable chance of winning in future or (2) they fear the consequences to themselves of a breakdown in the political order.

9. The microeconomic behavioral postulate of risk-neutral maximization does not work at the level of descriptive psychology, as two decades of work in behavioral decision theory now make clear (Dawes, 1988). The implications for public choice have not been worked out. There are academic careers to be built here.

10. While recognizing the importance of ideological factors of the kind I am stressing here, Offe believes that structural economic changes are ultimately more important to explaining the rise of economic rationality and the associated loss of support for the welfare state.

11. Elsewhere (Dryzek, 1992b) I have described how public choice might profitably be interpreted as a critical theory in these terms.

12. This spectator resembles the individual behind the "veil of ignorance" in Rawls's (1971) celebrated theory of justice, and the participant in constitution making in constitutional political economy. But Smith differs from contemporary liberal moralists such as Rawls in that his impartial spectator is not a mere hypothetical figure, introduced for the purposes of constructing abstract ethical theory, but rather someone who could actually exist.

13. Another prominent practitioner of public choice analysis, Jon Elster, pro-

fesses "sympathy with the fundamental tenets" (1986a, p. 114) of Habermas's discourse ethics, which are basic to communicative rationality.

14. Critical theorists such as Habermas would also point to the influence here of education, the experience of participation in collective life, the increasing availability of information, the reduced pressure of subsistence needs, and the diffusion of democratic ideas.

15. Cultural variability in other kinds of societies may substantially limit instrumental rationality (see Almond, 1990, pp. 134–35).

16. Arguably, public choice implicitly warrants further behavioral constraints by treating particular kiinds of maximization as inevitable in particular locations. In this way, consumers maximize utility through consumption, producers maximize profits, bureaucrats maximize budgets, politicians maximize their probability of election and reelection, citizens maximize benefits to themselves by choosing among candidates for office (assuming they are irrational enough to vote), and so forth. Hindess claims that public choice is guilty of a kind of structural determinism—in which individual behavior and the shape of individual preference ordering (be it cardinal, ordinal, or lexical) is caused by one's place in established social structures—rather than freely chosen (1989, pp. 56–60). In reply to Hindess, it must be said that rational choice theorists simply point out that choice occurs within a contextually constrained feasible set, which is not the same as requiring that the individual's *method* of choice be structurally determined. Public choice also permits persons to seek to manipulate the parameters of structural situations (Riker, 1984).

17. Political order should here be taken to mean political institutions that produce collective choices in consistent, nondictatorial, and nonviolent ways, and that can lay claim to public legitimacy.

Chapter 6

1. For a survey of the various meanings of ideology, see Geuss 1981, pp. 4–44.

2. As Green said, "A usable political theory demands that we make a connection between what ordinary people ordinarily want and the kind of society (or social invention) that the theorist allegedly wills on their behalf. Only in this way does it become possible for us to avoid imputing to ordinary citizens a form of social consciousness . . . that they manifestly do not have" (1985, p. 6).

3. For details on how findings that at first seemed to undermine democracy of any sort were eventually pressed into the defense of American liberal democracy, see Dryzek 1992a.

4. Even self-styled iconoclasts such as Dye and Ziegler argue that the "irony of democracy" is that elites, rather than masses, are the guardians of democratic values (1987, pp. 14–17).

5. This idealization holds, too, for Johnson's (1991) rendition of game theory as a reconstructive science. According to him, game theory is not, contrary to the beliefs of many of its practitioners, a positive, predictive science. Rather, game theory tells us simply what strategic rationality *is* in particular contexts, which means that an empirical test is not the key to determining the theory's veracity.

6. The shift from *I* to *we* here denotes the fact that most of the remainder of this chapter is a revision of a paper written with Jeffrey Berejikian (Dryzek and Berejikian, 1993).

7. Later, Lane (1986) turned to survey research for further insight into in-

dividuals' conceptions of justice. But in so doing he lost the ability to listen closely to his subjects. Moreover, "the public" became a single, reified subject with just one point of view, as measured by the percentages of respondents agreeing with particular statements about justice.

8. Full expositions of Q methodology may be found in Brown, 1980 and 1986, and McKeown and Thomas, 1988.

9. On the related use of focus groups in political inquiry, see Conover, Crewe, and Searing, 1991.

10. As several subjects complained, one consequence here is sexist language in a few of the statements, but it is not for us to censor statements.

11. The expression *partial intelligibility* is also sometimes used in reference to the kinds of communication that can occur across the boundaries of scientific paradigms.

12. Technically, the four categories of political discourse analysis constitute one dimension of a cell structure for sampling a concourse. The other dimension of the cell structure is less crucial and more heuristic. Bearing in mind that any political discourse embodies certain claims about the world, one can follow Toulmin's (1958) classification of the sorts of claims that can be made in arguments. These types are definitive (concerning the meaning of terms), designative (concerning questions of fact), evaluative (concerning the worth of something that does or could exist), and advocative (concerning something that should or should not exist). Combining these two dimensions yields a four-by-four matrix for sampling a concourse, as shown in the following table.

A statement from cell 2 is "Community means people who interact at a personal level; have shared identity, values, and traditions; and possess the power to make decisions about their common values"; from 7, "All governments, and the elites that live off them, want to control public opinion"; from 12, "The way that democracy is manifested in our culture, some people are more equal than others. It becomes a double standard very quickly"; from 13, "Religion should be banished from politics because a democratic politics is based not on truth but on justice." After eliminating statements with no clear fit in any cell, we took 4 from each cell at random, yielding 64 statements for the Q sample.

Discourse Element

Type of Claim	Ontology	Agency	Motivations	Natural Relationships
Definitive	1	2	3	4
Designative	5	6	7	8
Evaluative	9	10	11	12
Advocative	13	14	15	16

13. The four factors were extracted in a varimax rotation of a centroid solution. We stopped at four because the extraction of additional factors produced, on interpretation, a lack of clear distinction across two or more of the factors.

14. These narratives are not constructed by simply cutting and pasting statements with extreme scores on each factor. The narratives also must take into ac-

count how statements are placed relative to one another in each discourse (apparent paradoxes may require resolution), and the comparative placement of statements in different discourses. In common with interpretive social science more generally, this exercise assumes that each discourse represents a coherent point of view. So any apparent internal inconsistencies require explanation, rather than just dismissal or criticism.

15. There is also a sense in which our methodology is *decon*structive (in the sense often used in literary criticism), in that it problematizes and picks apart seemingly consensual concepts and discourses. For an explicitly deconstructive use of Q, see Stainton Rogers and Stainton Rogers, 1988.

16. An opinion survey might show that (say) 85 percent of the population loaded heavily on one discourse and not at all on the others. But such a finding would not negate the importance of variety. The identity of the 85 percent and 15 percent is crucial. In the 1770s, 85 percent of Colonial Americans might have opposed independence. In the mid-1950s, 85 percent of Americans might have opposed the inclusive liberalism of the civil rights movement.

17. This possibility also supports conceptions of democracy emphasizing the discursive generation of reciprocal understandings across discourses (for example, Barber, 1984, pp. 173–98).

18. Putnam reported the view of a British Conservative politician: "I think the weakness in a democracy really is that you get a mass of people who really take a short-term view of what their immediate benefits are, as opposed to the person who thinks and takes a long-term view for the sake of the country" (1973, p. 166). Putnam's intent relates to our own in that he seeks in part to identify the models of democracy held by British and Italian politicians. He develops a classification of authoritarian, polyarchal, liberal, classical, and socioeconomic models of democracy. But in our terms his approach is not reconstructive, for he arrived at this classification by his own interpretation of answers to questions in an interview he structured.

19. Unlike, for example, survey research, Q methodology works best when its subjects fully understand the research questions and methodology (Dryzek, 1990, pp. 173–89; Kitzinger, 1986).

Bibliography

Alford, C. Fred. 1985. "Is Jurgen Habermas' Reconstructive Science Really Science?" *Theory and Society* 14: 321–40.

Alinsky, Saul. 1969. *Rules for Radicals.* New York: Random House.

Alker, Hayward R., Jr. and David Sylvan. 1986. "Political Discourse Analysis." Paper presented at the annual meeting of the American Political Science Association, Washington, DC.

Almond, Gabriel A. 1990. *A Discipline Divided: Schools and Sects in Political Science.* Newbury Park, CA: Sage.

Almond, Gabriel A., and Sidney Verba. 1963. *The Civic Culture: Political Attitudes and Democracy in Five Nations.* Princeton, NJ: Princeton University Press.

Amy, Douglas J. 1987. *The Politics of Environmental Mediation.* New York: Columbia University Press.

Anderson, Terry L., and Donald R. Leal. 1991. *Free Market Environmentalism.* San Francisco: Pacific Research Institute.

Arato, Andrew. 1993. "Interpreting 1989." *Social Research* 60: 609–46.

Arendt, Hannah. 1958. *The Human Condition.* Chicago: University of Chicago Press.

———. 1962. *On Revolution.* New York: Viking.

Arrow, Kenneth J. 1963. *Social Choice and Individual Values,* rev. ed. New York: Wiley.

Ash, Timothy Garton. 1990. *The Uses of Adversity: Essays on the Fate of Central Europe.* New York: Vintage Books.

Barber, Benjamin. 1984. *Strong Democracy: Participatory Politics for a New Age.* Berkeley and Los Angeles: University of California Press.

Barry, Brian, and Russell Hardin, eds. 1982. *Rational Man and Irrational Society?* Beverly Hills, CA: Sage.

Bartlett, Robert V. 1990. "Ecological Reason in Administration: Environmental Impact Assessment and Administrative Theory." In *Managing Leviathan: Environmental Politics and the Administrative State,* ed. Robert Paehlke and Douglas Torgerson, 81–96. Peterborough, Ontario: Broadview.

Bell, Daniel. 1960. *The End of Ideology.* New York: Collier Books.

Bellah, Robert, Richard Madsen, William M. Sullivan, Ann Swidler, and Steven M. Tipton. 1985. *Habits of the Heart: Individualism and Commitment in American Life.* Berkeley and Los Angeles: University of California Press.

Berger, Thomas R. 1985. *Village Journey: The Report of the Alaska Native Review Commission.* New York: Hill & Wang.

Beveridge, Sir William Henry. 1942. *Social Insurance and Allied Services.* London: HMSO.

Block, Fred. 1977. "The Ruling Class Does Not Rule: Notes on the Marxist Theory of the State." *Socialist Revolution* 33: 6–28.

———. 1992. "Capitalism Without Class Power." *Politics and Society* 20: 277–303.

Block, Fred, et al. 1987. *The Mean Season: The Attack on the Welfare State.* New York: Pantheon Books.

Bohman, James. 1989. "Participating in Enlightenment: Habermas's Cognitivist Interpretation of Democracy." In *Knowledge and Politics*, ed. Marcelo Dascal and Ora Gruengard, 264–89. Boulder, CO: Westview.

———. 1990. "Communication, Ideology, and Democratic Theory." *American Political Science Review* 84: 93–109.

Bookchin, Murray. 1982. *The Ecology of Freedom: The Emergence and Dissolution of Hierarchy.* Palo Alto, CA: Cheshire.

———. 1986. *The Limits of the City.* Montreal: Black Rose.

Bowles, Samuel, and Herbert Gintis. 1986. *Democracy and Capitalism: Property, Community, and the Contradictions of Modern Social Thought.* London: Routledge & Kegan Paul.

———. 1993. "The Democratic Firm: An Agency-Theoretical Evaluation." In *Markets and Democracy: Participation, Accountability, and Efficiency*, ed. Samuel Bowles, Herbert Gintis, and Bo Gustaffson, 13–39. Cambridge: Cambridge University Press.

Bowles, Samuel, David M. Gordon, and Thomas E. Weisskopf. 1983. *Beyond the Wasteland: A Democratic Alternative to Economic Decline.* Garden City, NY: Anchor Press/Doubleday.

Brennan, Geoffrey. 1989. "Politics *with* Romance: Towards a Theory of Democratic Socialism." In *The Good Polity: Normative Analysis of the State*, ed. Philip Pettit, 49–66. Oxford: Basil Blackwell.

Brennan, Geoffrey, and James M. Buchanan. 1985. *The Reason of Rules: Constitutional Political Economy.* Cambridge: Cambridge University Press.

Brittan, Samuel. 1975. "The Economic Contradictions of Democracy." *British Journal of Political Science* 5: 129–59.

Brown, Phil, and Edwin J. Mikkelsen. 1990. *No Safe Place: Toxic Waste, Leukemia, and Community Action.* Berkeley and Los Angeles: University of California Press.

Brown, Steven R. 1980. *Political Subjectivity: Applications of Q Methodology in Political Science.* New Haven, Conn.: Yale University Press.

———. 1986. "Q Technique and Method: Principles and Procedures." In *New Tools for Social Scientists: Advances and Applications in Research Methods*, ed. William D. Berry and Michael S. Lewis-Beck, 57–76. Beverly Hills, CA: Sage.

Brucan, Silviu. 1992. "Democracy at Odds with the Market in Post-Communist Societies." In *Trials of Transition: Economic Reform in the Former Soviet Bloc*, ed. M. Keren and G. Ofer, 19–25. Boulder, CO: Westview.

Buchanan, James M. 1986. "Then and Now, 1961–1986: From Delusion to Dystopia." Paper presented at the Institute for Humane Studies, George Mason University.

———. 1991. "Politics Without Romance: A Sketch of Positive Public Choice and Its Normative Implications." In *Contemporary Political Theory,* ed. Alan Hamlin and Philip Pettit, 216–28. New York: Macmillan.

Buchanan, James M., and Gordon Tullock. 1962. *The Calculus of Consent.* Ann Arbor: University of Michigan Press.

Bull, Hedley. 1977. *The Anarchical Society: A Study of Order in World Politics.* London: Macmillan.

Bunce, Valerie. 1992. "Two-Tiered Stalinism: A Case of Self-Destruction." In *Constructing Capitalism: The Re-Emergence of Civil Society and Liberal Economy in the Post-Communist World,* ed. K. Z. Poznanski, 25–46. Boulder, CO: Westview.

Burnheim, John. 1985. *Is Democracy Possible?* Cambridge: Polity Press.

———. 1986. "Democracy, Nation States and the World System." In *New Forms of Democracy,* ed. David Held and Christopher Pollitt, 218–39. London: Sage.

Butterfield, Herbert. 1950. *The Whig Interpretation of History.* London: G. Bell.

Cameron, David R. 1978. "The Expansion of the Public Economy: A Comparative Analysis." *American Political Science Review* 72: 1243–61.

Caney, Simon. 1992. "Liberalism and Communitarianism: A Misconceived Debate." *Political Studies* 40: 273–89.

Canovan, Margaret E. 1987. "Republicanism." In *The Blackwell Encyclopaedia of Political Thought,* ed. David Miller, 433–36. Oxford: Basil Blackwell.

Carter, April. 1989. "Industrial Democracy and the Capitalist State." In *Democracy and the Capitalist State,* ed. Graeme Duncan, 277–93. Cambridge: Cambridge University Press.

Cawson, Alan. 1986. *Corporatism and Political Theory.* Oxford: Basil Blackwell.

Cherry, Robert, Christine D'Onofrio, Cigdem Kurdas, Thomas R. Michl, Fred Moseley, and Michele I. Naples, eds. 1987. *The Imperiled Economy.* New York: Union of Radical Political Economists.

Cnudde, Charles F. 1971. *Democracy in the American South.* Chicago: Markham.

Cochrane, Allan. 1986. "Community Politics and Democracy." In *New Forms of Democracy,* ed. David Held and Christopher Pollitt, 51–77. Beverly Hills, CA: Sage.

Cohen, Carl. 1971. *Democracy.* Athens: University of Georgia Press.

Cohen, Jean. 1985. "Strategy or Identity: New Theoretical Paradigms and Contemporary Social Movements." *Social Research* 52: 663–716.

Cohen, Jean L., and Andrew Arato. 1992. *Civil Society and Political Theory.* Cambridge, MA: MIT Press.

Cohen, Joshua. 1989. "Deliberation and Democratic Legitimacy." In *The Good Polity: Normative Analysis of the State,* ed. Alan Hamlin and Philip Pettit, 17–34. Oxford: Basil Blackwell.

Cohen, Joshua, and Joel Rogers. 1983. *On Democracy.* Harmondsworth: Penguin.

———. 1992. "Secondary Associations and Democratic Governance." *Politics and Society* 20: 393–472.

Coleman, Jules, and John Ferejohn. 1986. "Democracy and Social Choice." *Ethics* 97: 6–25.

Connolly, William E. 1991. "Democracy and Territoriality." *Millennium* 20: 463–84.

Conover, Pamela Johnston, Ivor M. Crewe, and Donald D. Searing. 1991. "The Nature of Citizenship in the United States and Great Britain: Empirical Comments on Theoretical Themes." *Journal of Politics* 53: 800–32.

Crosby, Ned, Janet M. Kelly, and Paul Schaefer. 1986. "Citizen Panels: A New Approach to Citizen Participation." *Public Administration Review* 46: 170–78.

Crozier, Michel, Samuel P. Huntington, and Joji Watanuki. 1975. *The Crisis of Democracy: Report on the Governability of Democracies to the Trilateral Commission.* New York: New York University Press.

Cunningham, Frank. 1987. *Democratic Theory and Socialism.* Cambridge: Cambridge University Press.

Cutright, Phillips. 1963. "National Political Development: Measurement and Analysis." *American Sociological Review* 28: 253–64.

Dahl, Robert A. 1956. *A Preface to Democratic Theory.* Chicago: University of Chicago Press.

———. 1982. *Dilemmas of Pluralist Democracy.* New Haven, CT: Yale University Press.

———. 1985. *A Preface to Economic Democracy.* Berkeley and Los Angeles: University of California Press.

———. 1989. *Democracy and Its Critics.* New Haven, CT: Yale University Press.

———. 1993. "Why All Democratic Countries Have Mixed Economies." In *Democratic Community* (Nomos XXXV), ed. John W. Chapman and Ian Shapiro, 259–82. New York: New York University Press.

Daly, Herman E., and John B. Cobb Jr. 1989. *For the Common Good: Redirecting the Economy Toward Community, the Environment, and a Sustainable Future.* Boston: Beacon Press.

Dawes, Robyn M. 1988. *Rational Choice in an Uncertain World.* San Diego: Harcourt Brace Jovanovich.

Dawes, R., J. McTavish, and H. Shaklee. 1977. "Behavior, Communications, and Assumptions About Other Peoples' Behavior in a Commons Dilemma Situation." *Journal of Personality and Social Psychology* 35: 1–11.

Dewey, John. 1927. *The Public and Its Problems.* New York: Holt.

Di Palma, Giuseppe. 1990. *To Craft Democracies: An Essay on Democratic Transitions.* Berkeley and Los Angeles: University of California Press.

Dietz, Mary G. 1985. "Citizenship with a Feminist Face: The Problem with Maternal Thinking." *Political Theory* 13: 19–35.

———. 1987. "Context Is All: Feminism and Theories of Citizenship." *Daedalus* 116 (4): 1–24.

Downs, Anthony. 1957. *An Economic Theory of Democracy.* New York: Harper & Row.

———. 1987. "The Evolution of Democracy." *Daedalus* 116 (3): 119–48.

Dryzek, John S. 1987. *Rational Ecology: Environment and Political Economy.* Oxford: Basil Blackwell.

———. 1988. "The Mismeasure of Political Man." *Journal of Politics* 50: 705–25.

———. 1990. *Discursive Democracy: Politics, Policy, and Political Science.* Cambridge: Cambridge University Press.

———. 1992a. "Ecology and Discursive Democracy: Beyond Liberal Capitalism and the Administrative State." *Capitalism, Nature, Socialism* 3 (2): 18–42.

———. 1992b. "How Far Is It from Virginia and Rochester to Frankfurt? Public Choice as Critical Theory." *British Journal of Political Science* 22: 397–417.

————. 1992c. "Opinion Research and the Counterrevolution in American Political Science." *Political Studies* 40: 679–94.

Dryzek, John S., and Jeffrey Berejikian. 1993. "Reconstructive Democratic Theory." *American Political Science Review* 87: 48–60.

Dryzek, John S., and Robert E. Goodin. 1986. "Risk-Sharing and Social Justice: The Motivational Foundations of the Post-War Welfare State." *British Journal of Political Science* 16: 1–34.

Dryzek, John S., and David Schlosberg. 1995. "Disciplining Darwin: Biology in the History of Political Science." In *Political Science in History*, ed. James Farr, John S. Dryzek, and Stephen T. Leonard, 123–44. Cambridge: Cambridge University Press.

Dryzek, John S., and Oran R. Young. 1985. "Internal Colonialism in the Circumpolar North: The Case of Alaska." *Development and Change* 16: 123–45.

Dunn, John. 1979. *Western Political Theory in the Face of the Future*. Cambridge: Cambridge University Press.

Dye, Thomas R., and L. Harmon Ziegler. 1987. *The Irony of Democracy*, 7th ed. Monterey, CA: Brooks/Cole.

Eckersley, Robyn. 1992. *Environmentalism and Political Theory: Toward an Ecocentric Approach*. Albany: State University of New York Press.

Eckstein, Harry. 1966. *Division and Cohesion in Democracy*. Princeton, NJ: Princeton University Press.

Edelman, Murray. 1987. *Constructing the Political Spectacle*. Chicago: University of Chicago Press.

Elkin, Stephen L. 1985a. "Between Liberalism and Capitalism: An Introduction to the Democratic State." In *The Democratic State*, ed. Roger Benjamin and Stephen L. Elkin, 1–17. Lawrence: University Press of Kansas.

————. 1985b. "Pluralism in Its Place: State and Regime in Liberal Democracy." In *The Democratic State*, ed. Roger Benjamin and Stephen L. Elkin, 179–211. Lawrence: University Press of Kansas.

Elshtain, Jean Bethke. 1981. *Public Man, Private Woman: Women in Social and Political Thought*. Princeton, NJ: Princeton University Press.

Elster, Jon. 1985. *Making Sense of Marx*. Cambridge: Cambridge University Press.

————. 1986a. "The Market and the Forum." In *Foundations of Social Choice Theory*, ed. Jon Elster and Aanund Hylland, 103–32. Cambridge: Cambridge University Press.

————, ed. 1986b. *The Multiple Self*. Cambridge: Cambridge University Press.

————. 1990. "When Communism Dissolves." *London Review of Books* 12 (2): 24.

————. 1992. "Arguing and Bargaining: On Strategic Use of Communicative Behavior." Unpublished paper, University of Chicago.

Enthoven, Alan C. 1985. *Reflections on the Management of the National Health Service*. London: Nuffield Provincial Hospitals Trust.

Esping-Anderson, Gosta. 1989. "The Three Political Economies of the Welfare State." *Canadian Review of Sociology and Anthropology* 26: 10–36.

Evans, Peter, Dieter Rueschemeyer, and Theda Skocpol, eds. 1985. *Bringing the State Back In*. Cambridge: Cambridge University Press.

Evans, Sarah M., and Harry C. Boyte. 1986. *Free Spaces: The Sources of Democratic Change in America*. New York: Harper & Row.

Farr, James. 1989. "Understanding Conceptual Change Politically." In *Political*

Innovation and Conceptual Change, ed. Terence Ball, James Farr, and Russell Hanson, 24–49. Cambridge: Cambridge University Press.

Fiorina, Morris P. 1977. *Congress: Keystone of the Washington Establishment*. New Haven, CT: Yale University Press.

———. 1981. *Retrospective Voting in American National Elections*. New Haven, CT: Yale University Press.

Fischer, Frank. 1993. "Citizen Participation and the Democratization of Policy Expertise: From Theoretical Inquiry to Practical Cases." *Policy Sciences* 26: 165–87.

Fisk, Milton. 1989. *The State and Justice: An Essay in Political Theory*. Cambridge: Cambridge University Press.

Foucault, Michel. 1980. *Power/Knowledge: Selected Interviews and Other Writings, 1972–1977*. Brighton: Harvester.

Francis, Samuel. 1989. "Principalities and Powers." *Chronicles*, December, 9–10.

Freeman, Jo. 1975. *The Politics of Women's Liberation*. New York: McKay.

Freeman, John R. 1989. *Democracy and Markets: The Politics of Mixed Economies*. Ithaca, NY: Cornell University Press.

Friedman, Milton, and Rose Friedman. 1962. *Capitalism and Freedom*. Chicago: University of Chicago Press.

———. 1979. *Free to Choose*. New York: Harcourt Brace Jovanovich.

———. 1984. *Tyranny of the Status Quo*. New York: Harcourt Brace Jovanovich.

Frost, Robert. 1973. "The Figure a Poem Makes." In *Robert Frost on Writing*, ed. Elaine Barry, New Brunswick, NJ: Rutgers University Press.

Furniss, Norman. 1985. "Political Futures." In *The Democratic State*, ed. Roger Benjamin and Stephen L. Elkin, 213–36. Lawrence: University Press of Kansas.

Fukuyama, Francis. 1989. "The End of History?" *National Interest*, Summer, 3–18.

———. 1992. *The End of History and the Last Man*. New York: Free Press.

Garrett, Geoffrey, and Peter Lange. 1991. "Political Responses to Interdependence: What's 'Left' for the Left?" *International Organization* 45: 539–64.

Gaventa, John. 1990. "From the Mountains to the *Maquiladoras*: A Case Study of Capital Flight and Its Impact on Workers." In *Communities in Economic Crisis: Appalachia and the South*, ed. John Gaventa, Barbara Ellen Smith, and Alex Willingham, 85–95. Philadelphia: Temple University Press.

Gaventa, John, Barbara Ellen Smith, and Alex Willingham, eds. 1990. *Communities in Economic Crisis: Appalachia and the South*. Philadelphia: Temple University Press.

Geuss, Raymond. 1981. *The Idea of a Critical Theory: Habermas and the Frankfurt School*. Cambridge: Cambridge University Press.

Gilbert, Alan. 1992. "Must Global Politics Constrain Democracy? Realism, Regimes, and Democratic Internationalism." *Political Theory* 20: 8–37.

Gilligan, Carol. 1982. *In a Different Voice: Psychological Theory and Women's Development*. Cambridge, MA: Harvard University Press.

Goldgeier, James M., and Michael McFaul. 1992. "A Tale of Two Worlds: Core and Periphery in the Post–Cold War Era." *International Organization* 46: 467–91.

Goldstone, Jack A., ed. 1986. *Revolutions: Theoretical, Comparative, and Historical Studies*. New York: Harcourt Brace Jovanovich.

Green, Philip. 1985. *Retrieving Democracy: In Search of Civic Equality.* Totowa, NJ: Rowman & Allenheld.

Gunnell, John G. 1986. *Between Philosophy and Politics: The Alienation of Political Theory.* Amherst: University of Massachusetts Press.

Habermas, Jürgen. 1979. *Communication and the Evolution of Society.* Boston: Beacon Press.

———. 1984. *The Theory of Communicative Action I: Reason and the Rationalization of Society.* Boston: Beacon Press.

———. 1987. *The Theory of Communicative Action II: Lifeworld and System.* Boston: Beacon Press.

———. 1989. *Structural Transformation of the Public Sphere: An Inquiry into a Category of Bourgeois Society.* Cambridge, MA: MIT Press.

Hajer, Maarten. 1993. "Discourse Coalitions and the Institutionalization of Practice: Acid Rain in Britain." In *The Argumentative Turn in Policy Analysis and Planning,* ed. Frank Fischer and John Forester, 43–76. Durham, NC: Duke University Press.

Halliday, Fred. 1992. "An Encounter with Fukuyama." *New Left Review* 193: 89–95.

Hanson, Russell L. 1989. "Democracy." In *Political Innovation and Conceptual Change,* ed. Terence Ball, James Farr, and Russell L. Hanson, 68–89. Cambridge: Cambridge University Press.

Hardin, Garrett. 1968. "The Tragedy of the Commons." *Science* 162: 1242–48.

Hardin, Russell. 1988. "Constitutional Political Economy—Agreement on Rules." *British Journal of Political Science* 18: 513–30.

Harz, Louis. 1995. *The Liberal Tradition in America.* New York: Harcourt Brace.

Heilbroner, Robert. 1989. "The Triumph of Capitalism." *The New Yorker* 64 (50): 98–109.

———. 1990. "After Communism." *The New Yorker* 66 (30): 91–100.

Held, David. 1987. *Models of Democracy.* Cambridge: Polity Press.

———. 1991. Democracy, the Nation-State and the Global System. In *Political Theory Today,* ed. David Held, 197–235. Cambridge: Polity Press.

———. 1992. "Democracy: From City-States to a Cosmopolitan Order?" *Political Studies* 40 (special issue): 10–39.

Hess, Karl. 1979. *Community Technology.* New York: Harper & Row.

Hindess, Barry. 1989. *Political Choice and Social Structure.* Aldershot: Edward Elgar.

Hirschman, Albert O. 1970. *Exit, Voice, and Loyalty.* Cambridge, MA: Harvard University Press.

———. 1977. *The Passions and the Interests: Political Arguments for Capitalism Before Its Triumph.* Princeton, NJ: Princeton University Press.

Hirshleifer, J. 1977. "Economics from a Biological Viewpoint." *Journal of Law and Economics* 20: 1–52.

Hochschild, Jennifer. 1981. *What's Fair.* Cambridge, MA: Harvard University Press.

Holmes, Stephen. 1990. "The Secret History of Self-Interest." In *Beyond Self-Interest,* ed. Jane J. Mansbridge, 267–86. Chicago: University of Chicago Press.

Hont, Istvan and Michael Ignatieff. 1983. "Needs and Justice in *The Wealth of Nations.*" In *Wealth and Virtue: The Shaping of Political Economy in the Scot-*

tish Enlightenment, ed. Istvan Hont and Michael Ignatieff, 1–44. Cambridge: Cambridge University Press.

Horkheimer, Max, and Theodore Adorno. 1972. *Dialectic of Enlightenment*. New York: Herder and Herder.

Huntington, Samuel P. 1968. *Political Order in Changing Societies*. New Haven, CT: Yale University Press.

———. 1991. *The Third Wave: Democratization in the Late Twentieth Century*. Norman: University of Oklahoma Press.

Hurwitz, Roger. 1991. "What's in a Game? Behavior, Strategic Action, and Communicative Interaction in Sequential Prisoner's Dilemmas." Paper presented at the annual meeting of the American Political Science Association, Washington, DC.

Inglehart, Ronald C. 1990. "Values, Ideology, and Cognitive Mobilization in New Social Movements." In *Challenging the Political Order: New Social and Political Movements in Western Democracies*, ed. Russell J. Dalton and Manfred Kuechler, 43–66. New York: Oxford University Press.

Isaac, Jeffrey C. 1994. "Oases in the Desert: Hannah Arendt on Democratic Politics." *American Political Science Review* 88: 156–68.

Janicke, Martin. 1994. "Democracy as a Condition for Environmental Policy Success: Insights from International Comparison." Paper presented to the Workshop on Democracy and the Environment, September 9–11, Oxford.

Johansen, Robert C. 1992. "Military Policies and the State System as Impediments to Democracy." *Political Studies* 40 (special issue): 99–115.

Johnson, James. 1991. "Rational Choice as a Reconstructive Theory." In *The Economic Approach to Politics*, ed. Kristin Monroe. New York: HarperCollins.

Kavanagh, Dennis, and Anthony Seldon, eds. 1989. *The Thatcher Effect*. Oxford: Oxford University Press.

Keane, John. 1984. *Public Life and Late Capitalism*. Cambridge: Cambridge University Press.

Keeler, John T. S. 1989. "Comparing Reform Governments and Revolutions: Reflections on the Limits of State-Led Social Change." Unpublished paper, University of Washington.

Kellner, Douglas. 1992. *The Persian Gulf TV War*. Boulder, CO: Westview.

Kelman, Steven. 1981. *What Price Incentives? Economists and the Environment*. Boston: Auburn House.

———. 1987a. *Making Public Policy: A Hopeful View of American Government*. New York: Basic Books.

———. 1987b. " 'Public Choice' and Public Spirit." *The Public Interest* 87: 80–94.

Kemp, Ray. 1985. "Planning, Public Hearings, and the Politics of Discourse." In *Critical Theory and Public Life*, ed. John Forester, 177–201. Cambridge, MA: MIT Press.

Keohane, Robert O. 1983. "Theory of World Politics: Structural Realism and Beyond." In *Political Science: The State of the Discipline*, ed. Ada Finifter, 503–40. Washington, DC: American Political Science Association.

———. 1984. *After Hegemony: Cooperation and Discord in the World Political Economy*. Princeton, NJ: Princeton University Press.

———. 1990. "International Liberalism Reconsidered." In *The Economic Limits to Modern Politics*, ed. John Dunn, 164–94. Cambridge: Cambridge University Press.

Khilnani, Sunil. 1991. "Democracy and Modern Political Community: Limits and Possibilities." *Economy and Society* 20: 196–204.

Kiloh, Margaret. 1986. "Industrial Democracy." In *New Forms of Democracy*, ed. David Held and Christopher Pollitt, 14–50. Beverly Hills, CA: Sage.

Kinder, Donald R. 1983. "Diversity and Complexity in American Public Opinion." In *Political Science: The State of the Discipline*, ed. Ada W. Finifter, 389–425. Washington, DC: American Political Science Association.

Kitcher, Philip. 1985. *Vaulting Ambition: Sociobiology and the Quest for Human Nature*. Cambridge, MA: MIT Press.

Kitschelt, Herbert P. 1988. "Left-Libertarian Parties: Explaining Innovation in Competitive Party Systems." *World Politics* 40: 194–234.

Kitzinger, Celia. 1986. "Introducing and Developing Q as a Feminist Methodology." In *Feminist Social Psychology: Developing Theory and Practice*, ed. Sue Wilkinson, 151–72. Milton Keynes: Open University Press.

Knight, Jack, and James Johnson. 1992. "Aggregation and Deliberation: On the Possibility of Democratic Legitimacy." Unpublished paper, Washington University.

Krasner, Stephen D. 1983. "Structural Causes and Regime Consequences: Regimes as Intervening Variables." In *International Regimes*, ed. Stephen D. Krasner, 1–22. Ithaca, NY: Cornell University Press.

———. 1984. "Approaches to the State: Alternative Conceptions and Historical Dynamics." *Comparative Politics* 16: 223–46.

———. 1992. "Realism, Imperialism, and Democracy: A Response to Gilbert." *Political Theory* 20: 38–52.

Laclau, Ernesto, and Chantal Mouffe. 1985. *Hegemony and Socialist Strategy: Towards a Radical Democratic Politics*. London: Verso.

Lane, Robert E. 1962. *Political Ideology*. New York: Free Press.

———. 1986. "Market Justice, Political Justice." *American Political Science Review* 80: 383–402.

Lasswell, Harold D. 1948. *The Analysis of Political Behavior*. London: Kegan Paul, Trench, Tubner.

Lehmbruch, Gerhard. 1984. "Concertation and the Structure of Corporatist Networks." In *Order and Conflict in Contemporary Capitalism*, ed. John H. Goldthorpe, 60–80. Oxford: Clarendon Press.

Lienesch, Michael. 1992. "Wo(e)begon(e) Democracy." *American Journal of Political Science* 36: 1004–14.

Lindblom, Charles E. 1977. *Politics and Markets: The World's Political–Economic Systems*. New York: Basic Books.

———. 1982. "The Market as Prison." *Journal of Politics* 44: 324–36.

———. 1990. *Inquiry and Change: The Troubled Attempt to Understand and Shape Society*. New Haven, CT: Yale University Press.

Lipschutz, Ronnie D. 1992. "Reconstructing World Politics: The Emergence of Global Civil Society." *Millennium* 21: 389–420.

Lipset, Seymour Martin. 1959. "Some Social Requisites of Democracy: Economic Development and Political Legitimacy." *American Political Science Review* 53: 69–105.

———. 1960. *Political Man*. Garden City, NY: Doubleday.

Lowi, Theodore J. 1979. *The End of Liberalism*, 2nd ed. New York: Norton.

Mackie, Gerald. 1994. "Success and Failure in an American Workers' Cooperative Movement." *Politics and Society* 22: 215–36.

MacPherson, C. B. 1973. *Democratic Theory: Essays in Retrieval.* Oxford: Clarendon Press.

Manicas, Peter T. 1989. *War and Democracy.* Oxford: Basil Blackwell.

Mansbridge, Jane J. 1980. *Beyond Adversary Democracy.* Chicago: University of Chicago Press.

———. 1990. "The Rise and Fall of Self-Interest in the Explanation of Political Life." In *Beyond Self-Interest,* ed. Jane J. Mansbridge, 3–22. Chicago: University of Chicago Press.

———. 1993. "Feminism and Democratic Community." In *Democratic Community* (Nomos XXXV), ed. John W. Chapman and Ian Shapiro, 339–95. New York: New York University Press.

Marcus, George, and Russell L. Hanson, eds. 1993. *Reconsidering the Democratic Public.* University Park: Pennsylvania State University Press.

Marx, Karl. 1968 [1845]. "Theses on Feuerbach." In Karl Marx and Frederick Engels, *Selected Works,* 28–30. London: Lawrence and Wishart.

———. 1963 [1852]. *The 18th Brumaire of Louis Bonaparte.* New York: International Publishers.

Masters, Roger D. 1989. *The Nature of Politics.* New Haven, CT: Yale University Press.

McKeown, Bruce, and Dan Thomas. 1988. *Q Methodology.* Newbury Park, CA: Sage.

McLean, Iain. 1986. "Some Recent Work in Public Choice." *British Journal of Political Science* 16: 377–94.

Melucci, Alberto. 1989. *Nomads of the Present: Social Movements and Individual Needs in Contemporary Society,* ed. John Keane and Paul Mier. Philadelphia: Temple University Press.

Miller, David. 1992. "Deliberative Democracy and Social Choice." *Political Studies* 40 (special issue): 54–67.

Mitchell, William C. 1988a. *Government as It Is.* London: Institute of Economic Affairs.

———. 1988b. "Virginia, Rochester, and Bloomington: Twenty-Five Years of Public Choice and Political Science." *Public Choice* 56: 101–19.

Moore, Barrington. 1966. *The Social Origins of Dictatorship and Democracy.* Boston: Beacon Press.

Mueller, John. 1992. "Democracy and Ralph's Pretty Good Grocery: Elections, Equality, and the Minimal Human Being." *American Journal of Political Science* 36: 983–1003.

Mulgan, Richard. 1992. "The Westminster Model, Elite Capture and Popular Revolt: The New Zealand Experience." Paper presented at the Research School of Social Sciences, Australian National University.

Muravchik, Joshua. 1991. *Exporting Democracy: Fulfilling America's Destiny.* Washington, DC: AEI Press.

Nie, Norman H., Sidney J. Verba, and John R. Petrocik. 1976. *The Changing American Voter.* Cambridge, MA: Harvard University Press.

Niskanen, William A. 1971. *Bureaucracy and Representative Government.* Chicago: Aldine-Atherton.

Nordlinger, Eric A. 1981. *On the Autonomy of the Democratic State.* Cambridge, MA: Harvard University Press.

Nozick, Robert. 1974. *Anarchy, State, and Utopia.* Oxford: Basil Blackwell.

OECD. 1994. *National Accounts: Main Aggregates, 1960–92,* vol. 1. Paris: OECD.

Offe, Claus. 1984. *Contradictions of the Welfare State.* Cambridge, MA: MIT Press.
———. 1987. "Democracy Against the Welfare State." *Political Theory* 15: 501–37.
———. 1990. "Reflections on the Institutional Self-Transformation of Movement Politics: A Tentative Stage Model." In *Challenging the Political Order: New Social and Political Movements in Western Democracies,* ed. Russell J. Dalton and Manfred Kuechler, 232–50 New York: Oxford University Press.
———. 1991. "Capitalism by Democratic Design? Democratic Theory Facing the Triple Transition in East Central Europe." *Theory and Society* 22: 453–86.
Okin, Susan Moller. 1979. *Women in Western Political Thought.* Princeton, NJ: Princeton University Press.
Olson, Mancur. 1983. *The Rise and Decline of Nations: Economic Growth, Stagflation, and Social Rigidities.* New Haven, CT: Yale University Press.
Orbell, John M., Alphons J. C. van de Kragt, and Robyn M. Dawes. 1988. "Explaining Discussion-Induced Cooperation in Social Dilemmas." *Journal of Personality and Social Psychology* 54: 811–19.
Orbell, John M., Robyn M. Dawes, and Alphons J. C. van de Kragt. 1990. "The Limits of Multilateral Promising." *Ethics* 100: 616–27.
Ost, David. 1993. "The Politics of Interest in Post-Communist Eastern Europe." *Theory and Society* 22: 453–86.
Paehlke, Robert. 1988. "Democracy, Bureaucracy, and Environmentalism." *Environmental Ethics* 10: 291–308.
Pateman, Carole. 1970. *Participation and Democratic Theory.* Cambridge: Cambridge University Press.
———. 1986. "Social Choice or Democracy? A Comment on Coleman and Ferejohn." *Ethics* 97: 39–46.
———. 1988. *The Sexual Contract.* Cambridge: Polity Press.
———. 1989. *The Disorder of Women: Democracy, Feminism, and Political Theory.* Cambridge: Polity Press.
Pekkarinen, Jukka, Matti Pohjola, and Bob Rowthorn. 1992. *Social Corporatism: A Superior Economic System?* Oxford: Oxford University Press.
Phillips, Anne. 1991. *Engendering Democracy.* Cambridge: Polity Press.
———. 1992. "Must Feminists Give up on Liberal Democracy?" *Political Studies* 40 (special issue): 68–82.
———. 1993. *Democracy and Difference.* University Park: Pennsylvania State University Press.
Phillipson, Nicholas. 1983. "Adam Smith as a Civic Moralist." In *Wealth and Virtue: The Shaping of Political Economy in the Scottish Enlightenment,* ed. Istvan Hont and Michael Ignatieff, 179–202. Cambridge: Cambridge University Press.
Pickel, Andreas. 1993. "Authoritarianism or Democracy? Marketization as a Political Problem." *Policy Sciences* 26: 139–63.
Pion-Berlin, David. 1989. *The Ideology of State Terror: Economic Doctrine and Political Repression in Argentina and Peru.* Boulder, CO: Lynne Rienner.
Pogge, Thomas W. 1992. "Cosmopolitanism and Sovereignty." *Ethics* 103: 48–75.
Popper, Karl R. 1966. *The Open Society and Its Enemies.* London: Routledge & Kegan Paul.
———. 1972. *The Poverty of Historicism,* rev. ed. London: Routledge & Kegan Paul.

Poulantzas, Nicos. 1980. *State, Power, Socialism.* London: New Left Books.

Prothro, James W., and Charles M. Grigg. 1960. "Fundamental Principles of Democracy: Bases of Agreement and Disagreement." *Journal of Politics* 22: 276–94.

Przeworski, Adam. 1985. *Capitalism and Social Democracy.* Cambridge: Cambridge University Press.

———. 1991. *Democracy and the Market: Political and Economic Reforms in Eastern Europe and Latin America.* Cambridge: Cambridge University Press.

———. 1992. "The Neoliberal Fallacy." *Journal of Democracy* 3 (3): 45–59.

Pusey, Michael. 1991. *Economic Rationalism in Canberra: A Nation-Building State Changes its Mind.* Cambridge: Cambridge University Press.

Putnam, Robert. 1973. *The Beliefs of Politicians: Ideology, Conflict, and Democracy in Britain and Italy.* New Haven, CT: Yale University Press.

Quirk, Paul J. 1988. "In Defense of the Politics of Ideas." *Journal of Politics* 50: 31–41.

Rawls, John. 1971. *A Theory of Justice.* Cambridge, MA: Harvard University Press.

Reinarman, Craig. 1987. *American States of Mind: Political Beliefs and Behavior Among Private and Public Workers.* New Haven, CT: Yale University Press.

Ricci, David M. 1984. *The Tragedy of Political Science: Politics, Scholarship, and Democracy.* New Haven, CT: Yale University Press.

Riker, William H. 1982a. *Liberalism Against Populism: A Confrontation Between the Theory of Democracy and the Theory of Social Choice.* San Francisco: Freeman.

———. 1982b. "The Two-Party System and Duverger's Law: An Essay on the History of Political Science." *American Political Science Review* 76: 753–66.

Riker, William H. 1984. "The Heresthetics of Constitution-Making: The Presidency in 1787, with Comments on Determinism and Rational Choice." *American Political Science Review* 78: 1–16.

Rochon, Thomas R. 1990. "The West European Peace Movement and the Theory of New Social Movements." In *Challenging the Political Order: New Social and Political Movements in Western Democracies,* ed. Russell J. Dalton and Manfred Kuechler, 105–21. New York: Oxford University Press.

Roemer, John, ed. 1986. *Analytical Marxism.* Cambridge: Cambridge University Press.

Rorty, Richard. 1989. *Contingency, Irony, and Solidarity.* Cambridge: Cambridge University Press.

Ross, Dorothy. 1991. *The Origins of American Social Science.* Cambridge: Cambridge University Press.

Rostow, W. W. 1960. *The Stages of Economic Growth: A Non-Communist Manifesto.* Cambridge: Cambridge University Press.

Rowbotham, Sheila. 1986. "Feminism and Democracy." In *New Forms of Democracy,* ed. David Held and Christopher Pollitt, 78–109. Beverly Hills, CA: Sage.

Ruddick, Sara. 1980. "Maternal Thinking." *Feminist Studies* 6: 342–67.

Rudig, Wolfgang. 1985. "Peace and Ecology Movements in Western Europe." *West European Politics* 8: 26–39.

Rueschemeyer, Dietrich, Evelyn Huber Stephens, and John D. Stephens. 1992. *Capitalist Development and Democracy.* Chicago: University of Chicago Press.

Ryan, Alan. 1992. Introduction to *After the End of History,* ed. Gordon Marsden, 1–5. London: Collins and Brown.

Sagoff, Mark. 1988. *The Economy of the Earth.* Cambridge: Cambridge University Press.

Sartori, Giovanni. 1962. *Democratic Theory.* Detroit: Wayne State University Press.

———. 1987. *The Theory of Democracy Revisited.* Chatham, NJ: Chatham House.

———. 1991. "Rethinking Democracy: Bad Polity and Bad Politics." *International Social Science Journal* 129: 437–50.

Sawer, Marian. 1991. "Why Has the Women's Movement Had More Influence on Government in Australia Than Elsewhere?" In *Australia Compared: People, Policies and Politics,* ed. Francis G. Castles, 258–77. Sydney: Allen & Unwin.

Schweickart, David. 1993. *Against Capitalism.* Cambridge: Cambridge University Press.

Schmitter, Philippe C., and Gerhard Lehmbruch, eds. 1979. *Trends Toward Corporatist Intermediation.* Beverly Hills, CA: Sage.

Sears, David O., and Carolyn L. Funk. 1990. "Self-Interest in Americans' Political Opinions." In *Beyond Self-Interest,* ed. Jane J. Mansbridge, 147–79. Chicago: University of Chicago Press.

Seidel, Gill. 1985. "Political Discourse Analysis." In *Handbook of Discourse Analysis,* ed. Teun A. van Dijk, London: Academic.

Sewell, William H. 1992. "A Theory of Structure: Duality, Agency, and Transformation." *American Journal of Sociology* 98: 1–29.

Shapiro, Ian. 1994. "Three Ways to Be a Democrat." *Political Theory* 22: 124–51.

Shils, Edward. 1955. "The End of Ideology?" *Encounter,* November.

Sirianni, Carmen. 1993. "Learning Pluralism: Democracy and Diversity in Feminist Organizations." In *Democratic Community* (Nomos XXXV), ed. John W. Chapman and Ian Shapiro, 283–312. New York: New York University Press.

Skinner, Quentin. 1973. "The Empirical Theorists of Democracy and Their Critics: A Plague on Both Their Houses." *Political Theory* 1: 287–306.

Skocpol, Theda. 1979. *States and Social Revolutions.* Cambridge: Cambridge University Press.

———. 1985. "Cultural Idioms and Political Ideologies in Revolutionary Reconstruction of State Power: A Rejoinder to Sewell." *Journal of Modern History* 57: 86–96.

Smith, Adam. 1976a [1776]. *An Inquiry into the Nature and Causes of the Wealth of Nations.* Oxford: Clarendon Press.

———. 1976b [1759]. *The Theory of Moral Sentiments.* Oxford: Clarendon Press.

Smith, Steve. 1986. "Reasons of State." In *New Forms of Democracy,* ed. David Held and Christopher Pollitt, 192–217. London: Sage.

Soltan, Karol. 1992. "A Marriage of Gandhi and Madison." *Newsletter of the Committee on the Political Economy of the Good Society* 2 (1): 1–4.

Somit, Albert D., and Steven A. Peterson. 1991. "Democracy as an Endangered Species: Toward an Evolutionary Perspective." Paper presented at the annual meeting of the American Political Science Association, Washington, DC.

Spragens, Thomas A., Jr. 1990. *Reason and Democracy.* Durham, NC: Duke University Press.

Stainton Rogers, Rex, and Wendy Stainton Rogers. 1988. "Deconstructing 'Addiction.'" Paper presented at the annual conference of the Social Psychology Section of the British Psychological Society, Canterbury.

Steinmo, Sven. 1988. "Social Democracy vs. Socialism: Goal Adaptation in Contemporary Sweden." *Politics and Society* 16: 403–46.

Stephenson, William. 1953. *The Study of Behavior: Q Technique and Its Methodology*. Chicago: University of Chicago Press.

———. 1978. "Concourse Theory of Communication." *Communication* 3: 21–40.

Sullivan, John L., Amy Fried, Elizabeth Theiss-Morse, and Mary Dietz. 1990. "Mixing Methods: A Multi-Stage Strategy for Studying Patriotism and Citizen Participation." Unpublished paper, University of Minnesota.

Taylor, Michael. 1989. "Structure, Culture and Action in the Explanation of Social Change." *Politics and Society* 17: 115–62.

Thorndike, E. L. 1940. *Human Nature and the Social Order*. New York: Macmillan.

Thurow, Lester C. 1980. *The Zero-Sum Society: Distribution and the Possibilities for Economic Change*. New York: Basic Books.

Tilly, Charles. 1978. *From Mobilization to Revolution*. Reading, MA: Addison-Wesley.

———. 1985. "War Making and State Making as Organized Crime." In *Bringing the State Back In*, ed. Peter B. Evans, Dietrich Rueschemeyer, and Theda Skocpol, 169–91. Cambridge: Cambridge University Press.

Toulmin, Stephen. 1958. *The Uses of Argument*. Cambridge: Cambridge University Press.

Touraine, Alain, François Dubet, Michel Wievorka, and Jan Strzelecki. 1983. *Solidarity: Poland, 1980–81*. Cambridge: Cambridge University Press.

Unger, Roberto Mangabeira. 1987. *False Necessity: Anti-Necessitarian Social Theory in the Service of Radical Democracy*. Cambridge: Cambridge University Press.

van Dijk, Teun A., ed. 1985. *Handbook of Discourse Analysis*. London: Academic Press.

Vanberg, Viktor, and James M. Buchanan. 1989. "Interests and Theories in Constitutional Choice." *Journal of Theoretical Politics* 1: 49–62.

Vig, Norman J., and Michael E. Kraft. 1984. *Environmental Policy in the 1980s: Reagan's New Agenda*. Washington, DC: Congressional Quarterly Press.

Waltz, Kenneth. 1979. *Theory of International Politics*. Reading, MA: Addison-Wesley.

Weale, Albert. 1984. "Social Choice Versus Populism? An Interpretation of Riker's Political Theory." *British Journal of Political Science* 14: 369–85.

White, Stephen K. 1987. "Toward a Critical Political Science." In *Idioms of Inquiry: Critique and Renewal in Political Science*, ed. Terence Ball, 113–36. Albany: State University of New York Press.

Winch, Donald. 1983. "Adam Smith's 'Enduring Particular Result': A Political and Cosmopolitan Perspective." In *Wealth and Virtue: The Shaping of Political Economy in the Scottish Enlightenment*, ed. Istvan Hont and Michael Ignatieff, 253–69. Cambridge: Cambridge University Press.

Wittman, Donald. 1989. "Why Democracies Produce Efficient Outcomes." *Journal of Political Economy* 97: 1395–1424.

Wolin, Sheldon. 1960. *Politics and Vision*. Boston: Little, Brown.

Wright, Erik Olin, Andrew Levine, and Elliot Sober. 1992. *Reconstructing Marxism: Essays on Explanation and the Theory of History*. London: Verso.

Young, Iris Marion. 1990a. *Justice and the Politics of Difference*. Princeton, NJ: Princeton University Press.

———. 1990b. "Polity and Group Difference: A Critique of the Ideal of Universal

Citizenship." In *Feminism and Political Theory*, ed. Cass Sunstein, 117–41. Chicago: University of Chicago Press.

———. 1992. "Social Groups in Associative Democracy." *Politics and Society* 20: 529–34.

Young, Oran R. 1978. "Anarchy and Social Choice: Reflections on the International Polity." *World Politics* 30: 241–63.

———. 1989. *International Cooperation: Building Regimes for Natural Resources and the Environment.* Ithaca, NY: Cornell University Press.

Zvesper, John. 1987. "Liberalism." In *The Blackwell Encyclopaedia of Political Thought*, ed. David Miller. Oxford: Basil Blackwell.

Index